The Industrial Enterprise
in Eastern Europe

The Industrial Enterprise in Eastern Europe

EDITED BY

Ian Jeffries

PRAEGER SPECIAL STUDIES • PRAEGER SCIENTIFIC

To Kathleen

Published in 1981 by Praeger Publishers
CBS Educational and Professional Publishing
A Division of CBS, Inc.
1 St Anne's Road, Eastbourne, East Sussex BN21 3UN, UK
and 521 Fifth Avenue, New York, New York 10017, USA

Copyright © 1981 Praeger Publishers

British Library Cataloguing in Publication Data

Industrial enterprise in Eastern Europe.
1. Europe, Eastern – Industries – Congresses
I. Jeffries, Ian
338.0947   HC244

ISBN 0 03 059323 9

123456789 056 987654321

Typeset by DP Press Ltd
Printed and bound in Great Britain by
Biddles Ltd, Guildford

List of Contributors

IAN JEFFRIES, BA(Wales), PhD(Lond), Lecturer, Department of Economics, and member of the Centre of Russian and East European Studies, University College of Swansea, Singleton Park, Swansea SA2 8PP.

MICHAEL KASER, MA(Oxon), MA(Cantab), Reader in Economics and Professorial Fellow, St Antony's College, University of Oxford, Oxford OX2 6JF.

MANFRED MELZER, PhD, Deutsches Institüt für Wirtschaftsforschung, 1000 Berlin 33, Königin-Luise-Strasse 5, West Berlin.

ALEC NOVE, BSC(Econ)(Lond), DAg(hon causa), FBA, Professor, Department of International Economic Studies, Adam Smith Building, University of Glasgow, Glasgow G12 8RT.

DOMENICO MARIO NUTI, PhD(Cantab), Professor of Political Economy and Director, Centre for Russian and East European Studies, University of Birmingham, PO Box 363, Birmingham B15 2TT.

HUGO RADICE, BA(Cantab), MA(Warwick), Lecturer, School of Economic Studies, University of Leeds, Leeds LS2 9JT.

LUDĚK RYCHETNÍK, CSc(Hieher Economic School, Prague), Lecturer in Statistics, University of Reading, Whiteknights, Reading RG6 2AA.

LJUBO SIRC, Dipl iur(Ljubljana), Dr rer pol(Fribourg), Senior Lecturer in Political Economy, Department of Political Economy, Adam Smith Building, University of Glasgow, Glasgow G12 8RT.

ALAN SMITH, B Soc Sc, Lecturer, School of Slavonic and East European Studies, University of London, Senate House, Malet Street, London WC1E 7HU.

Other Participants

ANDERS ÅSLUND   (St Antony's College, Oxford)
ROBERT BIDELEUX   (Swansea)
GEORGE BLAZYCA   (Thames Polytechnic)
MARY GHULLAM   (Swansea)
ROGER PETHYBRIDGE   (Swansea)

Contents

Glossary of Commonly Used Terms

Centrală (plural **Centrale**): Central (Romania).

Comecon (CMEA): Council of Mutual Economic Assistance. (Note that the term 'Comecon countries' excludes Yugoslavia, which is not a full member.)

DSO: State Economic Organization (Bulgaria).

glavk (plural **glavki**): chief department (Soviet Union).

Gosbank: State Bank (Soviet Union).

Gosplan: State Planning Commission (Soviet Union).

khozraschyot: economic accounting.

NEM: New Economic Mechanism.

NEP: New Economic Policy (Soviet Union 1921–8).

obedineniye (plural **obedineniya**): association (Soviet Union).

tolkach (plural **tolkachi**): 'pusher'; unofficial supply agent (Soviet Union).

VEK: Nationalized Combine (GDR).

VHJ: Industrial Association (Czechoslovakia).

vstrechnye plany: counter-plans (Soviet Union).

VVB: Association of Nationalized Enterprises (GDR).

WOG: Large Economic Organization (Poland).

Preface

The papers in this volume were discussed at a symposium (held 6–9 September 1980), which had the aim clarifying important aspects of the functioning and organization of industrial enterprises in Eastern Europe, especially the question of decision-making autonomy. It seemed best to achieve this in a situation where a small group of leading authorities could meet face to face and thus continually compare and contrast these aspects.

The symposium was financed by the Centre of Russian and East European Studies in the University College of Swansea, a constituent college of the University of Wales. Professor Roger Pethybridge, the Director of the Centre, gave every assistance and encouragement. We were privileged to use 'Gregynog' for the exercise, an old and beautiful conference centre near Newtown (Powys, Wales), owned by the University of Wales and run superbly by the Warden, Dr Glyn Tegai Hughes (ably assisted by a friendly and helpful staff, especially his secretary).

The symposium took about a year to organize and involved a vast amount of administrative work, especially typing, correspondence, duplication and distribution. My thanks in this respect go to Mary Griffiths and Christine Jones of the Department of Economics, who undertook these chores with speed, efficiency and humour, chores additional to their normal duties in a large and busy department. Considerable use was made of Departmental equipment and funds and my thanks go to Professor E.T. Nevin for this.

Swansea, 1981   Ian Jeffries

1
Introduction and Summary
Ian Jeffries

This volume describes the past and present (1980) organization and functioning of the industrial 'enterprise' in Yugoslavia and the Comecon countries of Eastern Europe, especially dealing with the question of autonomy of decision-making. Current proposals offer a glimpse of possible futures, but the 1980 disturbances in Poland invite predictive caution. Nothing in the foreseeable future seems likely to disturb the essentially directive nature of most Comecon economies, but, given conducive economic and political conditions, Poland may eventually introduce a significantly decentralized economic system.

Inverted commas envelop the term 'enterprise'. With a gross oversimplification which will surely make industrial economists wince, it may be useful to think in terms of three basic categories of production unit: the plant (such as a factory or mine); the enterprise (consisting of one or more plants); and the association, an amalgamation of enterprises. The book title may seem a little misleading in the light of the Eastern European penchant for very large industrial production units, but 'enterprise' is retained because of the lack of any other common term. Readers should be aware of the sometimes differing use of terms, especially when 'enterprise' really refers to 'association' and the enterprise is relegated to the status of a 'sub-unit'! The context should clarify the situation, however.

This introduction and summary is subdivided as follows:
1. the basic features of the pre-1965 Soviet industrial enterprise, outlined partly because of its influence as a model and partly because it helps place later changes in perspective;
2. the 1960s: decade of reform;

3. the 1970s: decade of retrenchment;
4. summaries by country;
5. an overall view of the present and future.

THE PRE-1965 SOVIET INDUSTRIAL ENTERPRISE

To begin at the beginning. The typical early Soviet industrial enterprise (*pred-priyatiye*) was a State-owned plant operating on the principle of one-man responsibility and control (*edinonachalie*) by a manager (director) appointed by the State (more strictly by the Party), although influence was of course exercised by hierarchical superiors, the Party cell, the trade union branch and the State Bank (*Gosbank*). The enterprise participated vertically in the planning process, haggling with its superiors (usually the Trust, Chief Department and Ministry, in ascending order), suggesting amendments, providing information and making requests concerning the downward flowing 'control figures' (broad outline features of the central plan). The State Planning Commission (*Gosplan*) received general instructions from the Party/State apparatus together with data/requests from the lower echelons of the economic hierarchy and used the technique known as Material Balances (computations of the supply of and demand for products) to formulate the 'control figures'. To achieve workability with such a crude technique it was necessary to indulge in plan bargaining with lower-level institutions. But the essential features of the plan remained intact and, once centrally approved, the principal function of the industrial enterprise became the fulfilment, or preferably over-fulfilment, of its *tekhpromfin-plan* (technical, industrial and financial plan), broken down into annual, quarterly and monthly targets.

The enterprise plan, usually late and frequently changed, took the form of a variety of 'success indicators'. Output targets, however, were generally paramount: gross output (*val*) measured the value of finished output plus net change in the value of goods in the process of production; net output was the result of subtracting the value of inputs purchased from other enterprises; output in physical terms used various units of measurement, like weight, numbers and length; targets for more heterogeneous output were often broken down into a 'main assortment' indicator (*nomenklatura*). Other important indicators concerned labour utilization (wage fund — basic wage rates were fixed by the State, productivity, average wage and number of workers, including skill brackets), cost reduction, profit (as a percentage of costs, as opposed to capital), innovation and input use (non-labour inputs were assigned under the Materials Allocation system). Instead of a single harmonizing indicator (such as profit in the textbook market economy) the result was a mass of increasing, changing and often inconsistent indicators, although, as stated, output was generally dominant. The resulting problems are well known. For example, a weight, number or length indicator often resulted in too large, small or narrow objects respectively being produced, relative to user need; gross output encouraged the use of unnecessarily expensive non-labour inputs, while net output produced the opposite effect.

The incentive system involved both the stick (for example, loss of extensive privileges as a result of expulsion from the Party, or far worse!) and carrot. The Director's Fund (Enterprise Fund after 1955) was linked to fulfilment and especially over-fulfilment of the profit plan, although conditional on meeting important targets like output, and financed communal activities like housing and recreation and provided a (relatively minor) source of funds for personal bonuses and decentralized investment. Managerial bonuses, of far greater importance, were dependent, in a complicated fashion, on fulfilment and over-fulfilment of the more important indicators, especially output.

The Soviet industrial enterprise was a financially separate and accountable institution, with a profit and loss account. Wholesale prices were normally fixed by the State for long periods of time on the basis of branch average cost of production, plus a small profit mark-up of between 3 and 5 per cent: neither a capital nor rental charge was included in costs. (Note that the 1959 Soviet 'Standard Methodology' regulations gave formal approval to the long-standing practice of using sectorally-varying normative 'recoupment periods', effectively shadow capital charges, to help determine technology choice.) Although the marginal cost principle and demand considerations were thus ignored, these were not serious omissions in an economy where resources were mainly centrally allocated and prices were principally used for control and evaluation purposes. The enterprise account was kept in the local branch of the State Bank (*Gosbank*) and the purpose of this *khozraschyot* (economic accounting) system was to help plan fulfilment and gauge performance. Grants covered most fixed and working capital needs (*Gosbank* low-interest-bearing credits being available for above-plan working capital requests), although, for purposes of financial control, all but a small proportion of net revenue was either transferred to the State budget or retained for State-determined purposes.

The State monopoly of foreign trade provided a buffer between the domestic and international economies. Domestic and work market prices were correspondingly divorced and arbitrarily determined exchange rates gave rise to accounting profits and losses (because of overvaluation, 'losses' in the case of exports and 'profits' on imports): these accrued to foreign trade corporations, however, not to industrial enterprises, which received and paid the domestic price (of comparable home-produced products in the case of imports).

This basic model of enterprise organization played a crucial role in carrying out the principal Stalinist aim of rapid heavy industrial and military growth, but the following serious problems were engendered which led to the reforms of the 1960s: neglect of user need; a tendency to understate productive capacity; a tendency to overindent for and hoard non-labour inputs; storming; and anti-innovation bias at the micro level.

Neglect of User Need

We have already seen that output only had to be produced, not sold, and how emphasis on any particular indicator commonly led to neglect of qualitative aspects of production, especially in low-priority sectors concerned with hetero-geneous output (textiles, for example). This helps explain the paradox of in-creasing stockpiles of poor-quality products in a situation of general consumer good scarcity.

A Tendency to Understate Productive Capacity

The tendency for the director to aim for a 'slack' plan (one which calls for less than feasible output) basically revolved around the incentive system, which involved no bonuses for less than 100 per cent fulfilment and increasing bonuses for over-fulfilment (although the 'ratchet effect' — next period's plan taking this period's achievement as a starting point — ensured that over-fulfilment, if possible, would not be by too much, in the sense of endangering the prospects of success next time).

A Tendency to Overindent for and Hoard Non-labour Inputs

Several factors explain this phenomenon, especially the horrendous supply prob-lems associated with the Materials Allocation system (an administrative ration-ing system for the distribution of raw materials, component parts and capital goods) and the fact that capital was a free good to the enterprise, in the absence of a capital charge. This led to such phenomena as *tolkachi* (unofficial supply agents) and a powerful inducement to self-sufficiency in the supply of inputs, especially components. As a result parts of Soviet industry are notoriously non-specialized. (Note that labour too was hoarded, to meet unforeseen needs or changes in plan, although not generally administratively allocated in more normal times.)

Storming (Shturmovshchina)

This concerns a mad rush to fulfil plans at the end of the month (mainly due to the importance of monthly targets), which exacerbates supply problems.

Anti-innovation Bias at the Micro Level

Innovation is the application of new ideas about products and techniques to the production process. Centrally planned economies are well equipped rapidly to implement new, priority, large-scale technologies, such as those in the space or military fields, but spontaneous, micro-level innovation is hindered by the Soviet economic system: the incentive system means the jeopardizing of short-term plan fulfilment and the prospects of 'ratchet effect' deterrents; State-determined prices may mean adverse effects on value indicators, while the economic structure also causes problems, for example, the separation of research and development (traditionally taking place in specialized organizations within ministries) from production and problems with input supply (see Berliner, 1976). Innovation is crucial in more mature economies, where growth is 'intensive', that is largely accounted for by improvements in the quality of factor inputs and the efficiency with which they are used (with due allowance for embodied technological progress), as opposed to 'extensive', that is due mainly to an increase in homogeneous units of labour and capital.

Thus it seems that the interest of enterprise, user and State often conflict, but it is important to note (Nove, 1977) the impossibility of the central planners' generally knowing what is needed in precise, disaggregated detail. The price system is denied this informational role in the Soviet economy and this lies at the root of the reform problems.

THE 1960s: DECADE OF REFORM

These severe micro-economic problems helped set the scene for widespread reforms during the 1960s (although there were earlier changes, especially the 1956 Polish reform), but other events played a part: in the latter half of the 1950s growth rates in Eastern Europe generally began to fall, causing some alarm and loss of prestige; economies were becoming more complex and, therefore, more difficult to plan (mathematical planning techniques not providing a panacea); factors were becoming increasingly scarce (the vast labour reservoir in agriculture was rapidly becoming drained, for example); and increasing foreign trade, especially with the West, highlighted quality problems. Finally, relatively successful models, such as the Yugoslav version of market socialism, showed that socialist alternatives were possible.

The economies of the Comecon countries have always undergone modifications of course, but in very broad terms the 1960s saw the introduction of significant reforms, though differing in timing, form and extent. For example, the January 1st 1968 radical Hungarian move towards market socialism contrasted starkly with the piecemeal general introduction of quite modest changes in Soviet industry (after reasonably successful experiments), starting in 1965. Separate attention will be given later to Hungary and Yugoslavia (the Czech movement towards the Yugoslav system was soon halted by the 1968 Soviet invasion), but, for the rest, it is possible to generalize the main features of industrial reform.

Enterprises began or continued to be amalgamated into larger-scale units called, for example, 'associations' both in Poland (*zjednoczenia*) and the Soviet Union (*obyedineniya*) and 'centrals' in Romania (*centrale*), operating on a *khozraschyot* basis. Important reasons included the desire to reap economies of scale, encourage technological progress (by linking research and development with production) and streamline the planning system by reducing the number of production units directly controlled by central planners.

Generally the number of success indicators was reduced and there were changes in emphasis. The main desire was to improve central planning, seemingly paradoxically by reducing 'petty tutelage' over enterprises, allowing, for example, greater autonomy over output assortment details. To this end greater emphasis was placed on profit (especially profitability, expressed as a percentage of capital rather than cost) and sales, although it must be made clear that the essential elements of the *tekhpromfinplan* remained centrally determined in the traditional fashion. More specifically, as an example, the 1965 Soviet measures involved eight indicators: value of sales; profit—total profit increases and/or profitability; main assortment (key products in physical terms); wage fund; contributions to and payments from the State budget; centralized investments and the introduction of new productive capacity; basic tasks for the introduction of new techniques; material supply obligations. Three funds, the Material Incentive Fund (MIF), the Socio-cultural and Housing Fund (SCF) and the Production Development Fund (PDF) were linked to the first two, but were conditional on the others. Incentives were hopefully to be improved by the proposed application of more stable rules and normatives (overall the planning horizon was to be lengthened by fitting enterprise annual targets into the framework of five year plans). The essentials of the command economy remained, as can be seen by the de facto retention, largely intact, of the Materials Allocation system (a move towards trade in producer goods was officially declared desirable), a feature which ruled out significant decentralization of decision-making with respect to output, while a sales as opposed to output indicator was of limited significance in a 'sellers' market'.

The limited relaxation of command planning in most Comecon countries involved the greater use of 'economic levers', such as prices, interest rates, credit policy and taxes, to guide production indirectly. Generally, price changes were fairly insignificant, normally involving upward movements in wholesale prices, to eliminate the enormous subsidies, which resulted from infrequent changes, and to ensure that most enterprises covered costs and earned sufficient profit to cover the new incentive funds and obligations, such as capital charges.

Prices generally continued to be fixed on an 'average cost plus' basis, although there were improvements in cost structure (by the introduction of capital charges, interest on long-term credits and rental charges) and the profit mark-up (in percentage terms) was larger (15 per cent on average, as opposed to 3 to 5 per cent, in the Soviet Union), and on capital (as opposed to cost). In addition there were examples of proposals (as in Bulgaria) for and cases (as in Hungary) of a tiered system of prices, centrally fixed, maximum (sometimes also range) and free categories. Outside the Soviet Union attempts were made to link the prices received and paid by industrial enterprises to those prevailing in world markets, although (with the exception of Hungary and Yugoslavia) foreign trade remained essentially centrally planned in traditional fashion, old problems (such as the arbitrariness of multiple exchange rates) persisted and a blanket of restrictions and subsidies prevailed. Both the overall investment rate and the vast majority of decisions remained firmly under central control, although decentralized investment was, to varying extents, increased and there were moves towards long-term credits as opposed to grants (interest rates, however, were often low, 0.5 per cent in the case of Soviet industry).

A brief look at the Soviet industrial enterprise's post-1965 financial situation may aid clarification:

	Gross Profit (sales revenue minus a depreciation allowance and input costs)
Minus	*Payments to the State* (an average capital charge of 6 per cent of the value of fixed and working capital; interest on credit; a possible rental payment to extract the excess profit due to favourable endowment— advanced technology for example)
Equals	*Net Profit* (used for the calculation of profitability)
Minus	*Internal Funds* (MIF, SCF and PDF — note that part of the depreciation fund and revenue from sales of superfluous equipment also find their way into the PDF)
Equals	*The 'Free Remainder'* ('residual profit' or 'unused balance'). This is paid into the State budget, although retained profit for State-determined purposes is still possible. Note that part of this 'free remainder' actually goes to the Construction Bank (*Stroibank*, an institution used to dole out capital grants and loans) for repayment of long-term credits used for State-authorized investment. Thus the difference between the former system of grants and the new situation, involving a mixture of both grants and, to a limited extent, credits, is of minor significance (given that the interest rate is only 0.5 per cent per annum). Note also that penalties for contract violation are not effective, since they are paid out of profit which would go to the budget anyway, while incentives to increase profits are adversely affected by de facto alterations in plans and norms. As will be shown later, recent proposals attempt to avoid these problems.

THE 1970s: DECADE OF RETRENCHMENT

Yugoslavia and Hungary will be analysed separately, although even they were
not entirely clear of the widening net of restrictions. For the rest, certain generali-
zations are possible, although, of course, there were variations (to be discussed
below in the studies on individual countries). Generally, the limited concessions
to decentralization of decision-making were whittled away (although certain
improvements were retained, such as capital and rental charges and the increased
importance of long-term credits as opposed to budgetary grants). The number of
success indicators was increased and emphasis changed: profit was commonly
demoted to the advantage of output (more recently *net* output), quality, labour
productivity and cost reduction. Investment controls were often tightened up,
the Soviet Union, Romania and Czechoslovakia going so far as to abandon the
very idea of 'decentralized' investment (in the sense of production units' having
to obtain permission from above for all investment formerly in that category)
in order to ease severe supply problems.

External explanatory factors included rising world prices of raw materials
and fuels and the aftermath of the 1968 invasion of Czechoslovakia (especially
the fear of loss of Party control in liberalizing reforms). The main domestic
reason for retrenchment revolved around the not-surprising persistence of
traditional micro-economic problems in still highly centralized economies, where
even relatively minor changes met frequent resistance of powerful groups with
vested interests: ministries, for example, continued to meddle in areas of alleged
enterprise responsibility, frequently changing enterprise plans and the rules of
the game as if nothing had happened. Gradual changes were the rule, but piecemeal reforms brought their own difficulties in attempting to synchronize new
and old. Meaningful decentralization was not possible in the absence of efficiency
prices and in the continuing presence of administratively allocated non-labour
inputs; radical moves towards the Yugoslav or Hungarian systems were politically
out of the question. Consequently, the general mood of the 1970s was one in
which emphasis was laid on making central planning more efficient: this included
improved planning techniques (involving, for example, integrated, computerized
information and control systems to aid managerial/planning decisions: see Ellman,
1979), numerous experiments (such as that at the Soviet Shchekino Chemical
Combine) and a continuous (and continuing) series of administrative and in-
dicator/incentive changes.

SUMMARIES BY COUNTRY

The Soviet Union

The Soviet picture is clearly one of attempting to *improve* industrial command planning by means of general administration/incentive changes and experiments.

A mere decrease in the number of plan indicators does not necessarily imply greater enterprise autonomy in decision-making (since it may in fact be easier to ensure fulfilment of fewer but crucial targets than a mass of heavily conflicting ones of varying importance). The reverse is also true, of course, but, in this case, the two things go together. In 1976, for example, the very concept of decentralized investment was abandoned (because of supply problems), while after 1970 additional indicators were formally introduced, including one for quality, labour productivity (which revitalized gross output), material utilization and consumer good production in heavy industry. Informally, ministries never lost the habit of imposing additional unofficial indicators and altered plan targets and norms for individual enterprises (to meet unforeseen needs and ensure that aggregate ministerial targets were fulfilled). In fact, the decade saw a bewildering series of changes in plan indicators and incentive rules. In 1976, Schroeder (1979a) reports, ministries were able to choose, in addition to the normally compulsory enterprise fund-determining targets for labour productivity and product quality, one or two more indicators from a list that included profitability (or capital–output ratio), growth of output (in kind or in roubles), cost reduction and timely mastery of new capacities. Bonuses, of course, remained conditional on meeting other important targets, such as that for key products in physical terms. Earlier, in 1971, the concept of 'counter-plans' (*vstrechnye plany*) was introduced, with the aim of overcoming the continuing tendency for associations and enterprises to conceal productive capacity and strive for slack plans. Incentives were geared to encourage the adoption of targets higher than the compulsory ones in the five-year plan. Resistance to the idea, however, soon became apparent, due, for example, to de facto ratchet-effect deterrents and, particularly, the 1977–8 arrangements whereby counter-plans were to be submitted at the *start* of the plan bargaining process (to overcome supply problems).

In 1973 the Association (*obyedineniye*) was declared to be the basic industrial production unit (the situation, as Nove points out later, is quite complicated, although there are basically three types of associations: (1) 'production'; (2) 'science-production', involving the amalgamation of production and research units; (3) 'industrial', involving the placing of *glavki* (chief departments) on a *khozraschyot* basis). The process of amalgamation continued throughout the 1970s (Schroeder, 1979b): at the end of 1977 types (1) and (2) accounted for 44.3 per cent of sales and 45 per cent of employment in industry, the average association containing 4.5 units), although resistance, especially from ministries, hindered the process which slowed down towards the end of the decade. Problems such as the following soon arose: the hoped-for gains in research and specialization were disappointing; ministerial interference and familiar micro-economic problems persisted; many enterprises retained *khozraschyot* independence.

Familiar and persistent problems were also tackled by means of various experiments. For example, in 1967, in the Shchekino Chemical Combine, a novel attempt was made to deter the propensity for enterprises to hoard labour and overcome the disincentive effects of linking bonuses to the size of the wage fund. The scheme involved the retention of wage fund economies achieved by fulfilling or over-fulfilling plans with a given or reduced labour force. The extension of the scheme has met continual resistance ever since (almost inevitably from ministries, jealous of their powers and determined to alter rules and change plans) and largely failed to overcome the advantages of hoarding labour (to meet unforeseen needs and changes in plans, for example). The age-old difficulties of measuring indicators such as output and labour productivity have resulted in a continuing series of measures involving the use of *net output*, in this context and as part of a bonus incentive scheme linked to wage fund increases.

Several proposals were outlined in the July 1979 Decree: the role of the production unit in plan formulation should be enhanced; plans should be balanced (to avoid input shortages); plans should be stable for a five-year period (the five-year plan being divided into annual plans); norms for the following should also be stable—incentive funds, the relationship between net output and the wages fund and for profit retention (in principle this means the end of the 'free remainder of profit' and its associated problems).

Nove is highly sceptical, because of the vagueness of the proposals and past experience (plans and norms are, in practice, frequently changed). Nove argues that the new list of plan indicators, rather than implying an increase in managerial functions, amounts to a move towards *greater centralization*: there is to be less emphasis on profit and monetary aggregates, an increase in the number of compulsory indicators (such as detailed machinery nomenclature and technical improvements) and ministries are empowered to issue other obligatory targets, additional to those to be found in the general list of indicators (key products in physical terms; delivery obligations; labour productivity; sales; number of workers and employees; material and fuel utilization; profitability; cost reduction; relationship between net output and the wage bill; proportion of products of first quality; introduction of new techniques; payments into the State budget; and investment. Note that there are branch variations in indicator use and not all are used for incentive-fund determination). The materials allocation system remains highly centralized: in fact, there has been an increase in the number of centrally planned and allocated products. Much talk of 'long-term direct links' between customer and supplier signifies no real change.

As regards decision-making, Nove points out how difficult it is to make a judgement, but sees the setting up of associations as a means to streamline the control apparatus, by reducing the number of production units and enhancing concern for financial results. He assesses the net effect to be a strengthening of the powers of Gosplan, the ministries and the all-union associations (although these are still tightly controlled by ministries). There have been complaints that director-generals of production associations have no greater powers or higher salaries than enterprise directors (whose powers seem to have been reduced with the setting up of geographically and functionally nearer immediate superiors in the shape of production associations). Nove stresses that highly centralized control over prices and materials allocation rules out any meaningful de-centralization of decision-making. Thus improvements in planning and administration are striven for: one of the latest experiments involves the setting up of 'Territorial Production Complexes' to dampen the tendency towards ministerial 'departmentalism' (self-sufficiency in input supply).

Concern to reduce costs and ease the chronic material supply situation has led the Soviet Union, like other Comecon countries, to become more interested in 'net output' calculations. It is proposed that labour productivity and the wages fund be determined with reference to value added. More specifically, reference is made to 'normed value added per product'. It is not at all clear how this will work, but Nove suspects that it will lead to a clash with both existing indicators and actual net output and have adverse effects on product mix.

Poland

Significant economic reforms were implemented as early as 1956–7: enterprise decision-making powers were increased and workers' councils were formed spontaneously (and legalized). But recentralization soon began in 1958: the powers of workers' councils were curtailed and 'associations' were established which behaved essentially as administrative links between enterprise and ministry, allocating disaggregated plan tasks in traditional fashion and endowed with research, marketing and project-design functions.

The period between 1958 and 1972 was one in which a command economy was subjected to relatively insignificant administrative changes and experiments. (Blazyca, 1980a, notes, for example, the use of 'leading enterprises', involving a loose form of association; 'patron enterprises', where a technological leader benefits whole groups; and the setting up in 1969 of *kombinats*, based on the principle of vertical integration.)

In 1972, however, a surprisingly interesting blueprint appeared, which formed the basis of the significant 1973–5 experiments (see Nuti, 1977). In it pilot schemes involved the use of WOGs (Large Economic Organizations), which operated on a *khozraschyot* basis and were given enhanced powers of decision-making at the expense of both enterprise and ministry (Nuti aptly calls this 'depolarization'). These powers covered employment (less significant in practice it seems) and wage policy; price fixing (especially for new products); investment (financed by a generous Development Fund linked to profitability, and access to bank credits, available at an average interest rate of 8 per cent and after appraisal allegedly using a Western-style discounted cash flow method (in practice little applied it seems); and output assortment (note that indicators for sales, exports, in some instances the level of production in physical or value terms, investment, inputs and financial norms remained obligatory). These indicators were conditional with respect to incentives, but the basic incentive scheme involved value added and profit.

The traditional 'wage fund limit' was abandoned: instead the wage fund linked to value added (see Nuti for details), the following formula being the most commonly used:

$$DWF_n = DWF_0 \left(1 + R \cdot \frac{VA_n - VA_0}{VA_0} \right)$$

where   DWF is the disposable wage fund;
   R is a coefficient fixed by the relevant ministry, ranging from 0.3 to 0.95 (that is, less than one to ensure a falling share of wages in value added);
   n and o are given and base periods respectively.

Basic managerial salaries were tied to the growth of wage and salary scales determined by the above formula, but depended on the growth of value added being greater than employment. Managerial bonuses were related to the level of or increase in profit and were conditional both on fulfilment of the other plan indicators and on wage payments not exceeding the disposable wage fund.

A link was to be forged between domestic and international prices by means of various 'multipliers' (exchange rates effectively) and exports encouraged by WOGs being allowed a share of foreign currency earnings (very little in reality, it seems) and greater involvement in export promotion and price negotiations (the foreign trade corporation acting as an agent).

By mid 1974 approximately 100 pilot units accounted for nearly 50 per cent of socialized industry. But the latter half of the decade witnessed a re-centralization process, due to a certain extent to general world problems but mainly to domestic economic policies. From the time of the reform the Polish Government had embarked on an ambitious policy of capital investment (in the mid 1970s investment accounted for more than 35 per cent of Net Material Product), modernization and growth. Nuti stresses the inappropriateness of indulging in decentralization experiments in such circumstances, with all the accompanying supply problems. The massive State investment programme (and particular aspects of it, such as the broad spread of projects, which led to delayed contributions to domestic output and exports and the neglect of existing capital stock in need of modernization) was enhanced by considerable decentralized investment (encouraged by the lack of responsibility for failure). The central planners, in fact, seemed to loose control of macro aggregates in general, wage payments (related to value added at current prices) also increasing in uncontrolled fashion.

Recentralization after 1976 involved increasing controls on employment and (though not very effectively) wages (linked to labour productivity in 1976); the imposition of investment 'limits'; the strengthening of ministerial powers; an increase from 800 to 1200 in the number of centrally planned Material Balances; and an increase in the number of indicators imposed on enterprises (anything between 50 and 150, it seems).

The recent performance of the Polish economy has been depressing. The growth rate was negative in 1979, massive foreign trade deficits and indebtedness have built up and open inflation has increased (probably reaching double figures in 1980). In early 1980 (even before the summer strikes) a set of proposals was announced, which Nuti describes as closer to the Hungarian reform than the 1973–5 measures. The measures were to have been put into effect gradually by the beginning of 1983. A complete range of organizational types was set out (see Nuti in this volume), with varieties of relationship between centre, 'complex organization' and enterprise. Decentralization of decision-making seemed significant on paper, planning horizons to be lengthened to five years and value added demoted to the benefit of labour productivity, output and profit.

At the time of writing (October 1980) the Polish situation seems on a knife-edge. Nuti presents various scenarios of the future, but is inclined to the view that the short-term outlook is inflationary (both open and concealed), while the medium-to-long term looks more promising (with investments bearing fruit and supply problems eased). But much depends on the attitude of the newly-independent trade unions as regards wages and macro policy as a whole. Nuti traces the sorry story of the post-1958 weakening of workers' councils (the vast majority being in fact liquidated after 1975), a process which left no real outlet for workers' grievances and opinions. Independent trade unions can play a real part in a decentralized economy, but much depends on the attitude of the Soviet Union.

George Blazyca kindly sent a summary of a report in *Zycie Gospodarcze* (28 September 1980, No. 39) on the first meeting of the economic reform commission set up under the chairmanship of Premier Josef Pinkowski. The programme of action is as follows: by the end of 1980 a report on current economic management and the main direction of reform; by the end of October 1981 reform details; by the end of June 1982 details on how the reform will be introduced; and (presumably soon afterwards) implementation. Any prepared partial measures should be introduced from the beginning of 1981. So far, emphasis is to be placed on social consultation and the gaining of widespread approval for reform; creating an important role for workers' management; *clearly* defining bounds on enterprise independence and workers' management; linking independence with greater responsibility; and stability of parameters, etc.

Romania

Apart from the article by Smith in this volume, the following summary relies heavily on three other excellent sources: Granick (1975), Kaser and Spigler (1980) and Smith (1980).

The pre-1967 Romanian economy seems to have been even more highly centralized than its pre-1965 counterpart in the Soviet Union: targets were imposed on industrial enterprises with little consultation. After a series of experiments, the blueprint of industrial reform (Directives) appeared in December 1967 (under the revealing title 'Improving the Management and Planning of the National Economy'), although the first stage of implementation actually ran from 1969 to about 1972.

The basic production unit was to be the 'Central' (*Centrală*), usually the result of a country-wide horizontal integration of one large enterprise with smaller ones, with location of headquarters at the site of the former. The first central was not set up until 1969, due mainly to ministerial resistance to loss of power. Plan targets of traditional type (such as output and assortment, sales, exports, imports, cost reduction, material inputs and financial aspects) remained obligatory, but the degree of consultation was stepped up. (Note, however, Granick's classic summary: there was little real decision-making below the level of the ministry; the role of the enterprise involved little more than enhancing *technical* efficiency. For example, while ministries could reallocate individual enterprise tasks within aggregate central targets, enterprises could administer only the details of already concluded contracts. Managerial behaviour could not in any sense be explained by bonus maximization, since bonuses were easily obtained, the targets not only being slack but frequently changed. Romanian industry remained even more tightly controlled than that in the Soviet Union and German Democratic Republic.) The central was responsible for imposing disaggregated plan targets on constituent enterprises (including gross output, assortment of key products in physical terms, material supplies, labour productivity, wage fund, investment and payments to the State budget).

The Directives stressed financial discipline, showing a greater concern for cost and profit and the need to increase the role played by interest-bearing credits in the financing of State-determined investments. There were some limited concessions to decentralized investment, and credit policy in general included the use of penal interest rates if credit conditions were not met. The incentive system involved reducing the impact of bonuses by integrating most of them into basic wage and salary scales and introducing penalties for non-fulfilment of plan targets. A distinction was made between above-plan profit due to the enterprise's 'own activities' (a part of which was to finance bonuses and socio-cultural activities, with the residue going into the State budget) and that due to external circumstances, which was to be surrendered to the State budget.

A novel innovation was the replacement of 'one-man management' by 'collective management', involving a board of management at the enterprise level (called a 'workers' committee' after 1971) and an 'administrative council' at the central level (later called a 'council of the working people'). Until 1971 the de facto powers of management boards were not great and enterprise autonomy between 1971 and 1978 was negligible anyway. A fuller appraisal is to be found below, but note at this point that these committees should not be confused with Yugoslav workers' councils.

During the second stage of implementation (1973–8) the number of centrals was approximately halved, each on average constituting about 15 enterprises and 32 000 employees. The declared aim was to reduce ministerial power and move management closer to production. Consequently, centrals were to deal with intra-central material balancing and materials and labour transfer between constituent enterprises. (Note, however, that the number of centrally allocated products actually increased from 180 to 720 in 1974: Kaser and Spigler, 1980.) Centrals were to coordinate their plans with functional ministries (such as the ministries of Labour and Finance) and local authorities, while substantial numbers of engineering personnel were transferred to enterprises to concentrate on technical matters. The desirability of enhancing the importance of credits as opposed to grants was confirmed, although from 1974 State approval was needed for *all* investment.

A wholesale price revision in the period 1974–6 aimed at reducing subsidies and the considerable differences in profitability between branches. Capital and rental (land tax) charges were introduced, although the former was replaced in 1977 by a progressive tax on planned profit in excess of 15 per cent. In addition, in 1977 Romania joined Albania and Poland in eliminating personal income tax on public sector earnings, replacing it by a tax on the wage fund.

The third stage of the Romanian reform was announced in March 1978 and put into operation from the start of 1979. (Smith does not see this as an abrupt change in economic policy, but as a renewed attempt to implement the 1967 Directives, which had mainly been delayed by political factors.) In the 'New Economic–Financial Mechanism' stress is again laid on financial discipline and value criteria, with the principal aim of reducing costs in the wake of the damage caused to the Romanian economy by rising world prices of raw materials and energy. Economic and financial self-management involves ideas such as increasing the proportion of investment and socio-cultural services financed by retained profits (and by credit also in the case of the former). Cost reduction, net output and export indicators have been given enhanced importance (although a large number of other indicators, such as gross output, investment and labour productivity, still remain) in a complicated incentive scheme which divides profits between State and enterprise (thus hopefully overcoming the notorious 'residual profit' effects). Compulsory payments to the State budget (such as taxes on profit, net output and the wage fund) and repayment of bank credit have priority over the enterprise's own funds in the distribution of planned profits, but over-plan profits are divided up according to set rules. Monthly wages and salaries are affected by bonuses and penalties for over- and under-fulfilment of gross output, labour productivity, exports or material consumption targets, while funds for personal bonuses and socio-cultural activities are fed by over-plan profits caused by over-fulfilling targets such as cost reduction, physical output and exports. Bonuses from planned profits are reduced if the net production indicator and delivery contracts for physical output are not fulfilled. Despite the complexity of the scheme, bonuses account for only about 5 per cent of earnings.

'Self-management' in Romanian industry is not equivalent to its Yugoslav counterpart. While abandoning the principle of 'one-man management', self-management Romanian style, as Smith says, seems mainly to mean an obligation on the part of 'workers' committees' to use resources as efficiently as possible in implementing the State plan. 'Workers' committees' (in which workers are actually in a minority compared with managerial/technical staff and representatives from other institutions, such as the Party and trade unions: the Party Secretary replaced the enterprise director as chairman in 1973) are not equivalent to Yugoslav workers' councils, although they appear to offer a degree of real consultation in plan setting, unlike their Comecon counterparts. Smith sees them mainly as a means of providing information on 'hidden reserves' (and thus the ability to draw up tauter plans) by appealing to technical personnel and Party cadres over the heads of management. Smith also sees the possible basis of a new type of command economy, with large production units performing important social functions.

Bulgaria

In May 1963 a Decree authorized the establishment of the DSO (State Economic Organization), later to become the basic production unit, while the December 1965 Theses provided a blueprint of the new economic system. Although the Bulgarian economy remained highly centralized, Dellin describes the proposals as 'forward looking in spirit' (Dellin, 1970). The Theses mentioned only four compulsory indicators (volume of production in physical terms and 'limits', that is, ceilings, on capital investment, intermediate inputs and foreign exchange), although, in fact, others were still imposed (output assortment and quality, for example). Output details apparently were to be left to enterprise initiative, but even inter-enterprise contracts involving non-earmarked capacities were subject to confirmation from above. There was talk (only, it appears) of a tiered system of prices, including a very restricted 'free' category; profitability was to become a more important determinant of incentive funds; and there was to be a move away from investments financed by budgetary grants towards retained profits and interest-bearing credits (although investment decisions remained tightly controlled from above); a capital charge averaging 6 per cent of the value of enterprise fixed and working capital was introduced. The wage fund indicator was abandoned and replaced by a progressive income tax.

Even though pre-1968 rhetoric outstripped practice, that year still marked a clear change of course (mainly due to a fear of loss of Party control following from anything remotely approaching the Czechoslovak reforms of 1967–8). The number of plan indicators was increased (to include, for example, a wage fund limit, deliveries in volume terms and technical tasks: DSOs were also authorized to impose additional ones on enterprises); restrictions were imposed on the modest, experimental direct links between the DSOs and foreign enterprises (note that foreign trade always remained highly centralized), and even talk of tiered prices ceased.

In November 1970 the number of DSOs was reduced from 120 to 64 (35 in industry), usually horizontally integrated organizations employing an average productive workforce of about 17 000. In December 1970 enterprises were shorn of their legal autonomy, larger ones becoming 'subsidiaries' (still allowed to sign contracts and hold bank accounts) and smaller ones becoming 'subdivisions' (which were fully absorbed). The DSO dominated its constituent parts, distributing inputs, allocating plan tasks and determining investment, and relegating the subsidiary to the role of executing plan targets, especially for volume, assortment and quality of output, costs, input utilization and technical levels (Feiwel, 1979). Counter-planning was also introduced during the 1971–5 Five Year Plan, but soon gave rise to problems similar to those faced by Soviet planners.

Apart from the DSO, a number of coordinating agencies (such as the National Agro-Industrial Complex) and alternative 'economic organizations' (such as 'State economic combines') were set up after 1974. After 1973 interesting examples of vertical integration could be found in the shape of 'industro-agrarian complexes', which merged farms with industrial enterprises processing and selling agricultural products.

The term 'New Economic Mechanism' was used throughout the 1970s and still is today. But resemblance to the Hungarian system is in name only: Bulgaria always has and continues to be a command economy, which has been periodically modified by administrative/incentive changes aimed at improving plan implementation. But there are, as Kaser points out, concessions worthy of note in the 1979 proposals. The ministry may now officially impose only five broad indicators on the DSO or equivalent economic organization, instead of the previous 25, namely: 'realized production' (production in saleable form disposed of to recipients) in physical terms, subdivided into exports, cooperative deliveries and spare parts and deliveries to the domestic market; 'net output' in value terms; foreign-exchange earnings on exports and/or maximum foreign-exchange expenditure; limits on supplies of raw materials, intermediate inputs, energy and 'certain deficitary materials and equipment'; and payments to the State budget. In turn the DSO or equivalent imposes four indicators on its 'subdivisions', namely: production in physical units by type and quality; 'normed cost of production per unit of output'; tasks for the application of new techniques; and maximum number of personnel.

Note that there are no 'limits' on investment or the wage fund, but this does not mean that investment (though increasingly to be financed by interest-bearing credits and retained profits) and wages are not closely controlled: what the new practice tries to avoid is a 'residual profit' with its disincentive effects. The wage fund is now defined as a 'residual outcome magnitude', linked to productivity and allowed a share in profit increases: penalties for contract violation will thus hopefully be effective. Management staff will benefit from plan over-fulfilment, but suffer salary reductions for failure to fulfil norms.

The Bulgarian economy, as mentioned, remains tightly planned, but Kaser sees some signs of slackening in the 1979 proposals. The DSO or other economic organization is subject to fewer compulsory indicators and can sell above-plan output (in its own shops, abroad—on commission through a foreign trade corporation—or to a local government authority) once its planned production targets have been fulfilled. Economic organizations can apply for long-term (up to 10 years) credits (although investment decisions remain highly centralized) and even 'sub-divisions' have gained a little more responsibility (the number of plan indicators has been reduced for them also and they can apply for short-term credits, specifically for projects maturing in a year or less).

The German Democratic Republic (GDR)

The New Economic System (NES) in the GDR began in 1963, was amended in 1969 and essentially scrapped in the latter part of 1970 (Leptin and Melzer, 1978). The NES was an attempt to improve the efficiency of plan implementation and factor use in the context of a developed, industrial, labour-scarce, command economy facing special problems as the 'showpiece' of socialism and a major producer of high-technology capital goods. Central control over main targets was maintained, but greater use made of economic levers to steer the economy indirectly. At the micro level it appeared to have involved some small measure of increased autonomy for the VEB (nationalized enterprise) and the VVB (association of nationalized enterprises), for example, in the spheres of investment and detailed assortment choice (targets for output, main assortment, sales, major investments, science and technology, labour—principally the number of employees and wages fund; and financial aspects—mainly profit, production tax and cost reduction—all remained traditionally determined). The role of profit was increased, incentive funds being linked to net profit (profit, minus the new capital charge, made a uniform 6 per cent from 1971 onwards), but conditional on the other indicators. Profit tax rates varied by industry branch.

The precise relationships between the VEB, the VEK (nationalized combine, prominent after 1968 and dominant during the 1970s) and the VVB are not clear, although the VVB appears to have been essentially an administrative link. But it is clear that the system preserved its essentially centralized nature, with respect to output, non-labour inputs (administrative allocation remained largely intact) and prices (although the inherently conservative character of price changes does not detract from some interesting innovations: experiments with gradually declining prices for new and improved products, designed to motivate enterprises to develop new goods of a high technical standard; and 'fund-related prices', introduced over the period 1969–70 and covering a third of the value of industrial production, which involved a branch-variable profit mark-up on 'necessary' capital, thus, along with the capital charge, providing a stimulus to economize on the use of capital. A temporary price freeze was implemented at the end of 1970).

The main amendment to the NES in 1968 concerned the novel concept of 'structure-determining tasks', in which highly-detailed central planning was reserved for products, processes, investments and research projects (especially in the fields of electronics, electrical and instrument making, chemicals, engineering and vehicles) deemed paramount in an economy geared to the production of high-technology capital goods. The attempt, however, was overwhelmed by supply problems emanating from the relative neglect of the non-structure-determining sections (such as raw material extraction). The experiment was largely brought to a close in the latter part of 1970, as witnessed by the substantially increased number of success indicators (such as labour productivity) and the diminished role of net profit.

The VVBs have largely disappeared. The principal unit of production is now the combine, which has gained decision-making powers at the expense of the enterprise (the director general of the combine is not only responsible for allocating plan targets and tasks among constituent enterprises, but also has the following powers: to alter and redistribute these targets/tasks, which creates uncertainty at lower levels; to transfer machinery and financial resources between enterprises). Ministries remain powerful bodies, although the combine is responsible for carrying out the State plan and for intra-combine material balancing and has some influence on price fixing (apart from the usual duty to provide information, combines have the right to apply for surcharges on the prices of goods which meet quality specifications and can, to a certain extent, set prices for special products, following given calculation schemes).

Mergers in Comecon countries are usually the result of a horizontal integration of enterprises (that is, those producing similar products). Combines in the GDR, however, typically reveal a significant degree of vertical integration (amalgamation of enterprises standing in a user–supplier relationship): thus, a mechanical engineering combine has its own foundries and a shoe combine produces its own leather. (Examples of horizontal integration, however, can be found, such as in the furniture industry.) An important reason for this feature of East German industry is the need to ease the chronic supply problems resulting from the materials allocation system (although the administrative allocation system for non-labour inputs remains highly centralized and familiar phenomena still result, such as the 'grey men', equivalent to Soviet *tolkachi*, who indulge in 'operational adaptation'). Some foreign trade enterprises are now subordinate to combines, with the aim of increasing the quantity and quality of exports. Although some combines have been granted concessions to conduct trade in special export goods, however, foreign trade generally is still tightly controlled from above.

The combine is faced with a whole range of familiar success indicators (for example, gross output, main assortment, quality, sales, labour productivity, science and technology, investment and material supply and utilization), but in March 1980 two interesting additional indicators were introduced, namely 'net production' and 'material cost per 100 marks of commodity production'. There has been a general revival of interest in 'net output' in Comecon countries, highlighting the concern to make more efficient use of intermediate inputs, especially in a resource-poor, trade-dependent country like the GDR, facing steeply rising world prices for raw materials and energy. Indeed the need both to economize on the use of increasingly scarce labour and non-labour inputs and to encourage technological progress has been an important stimulus to efforts aimed at streamlining the economic system. An intensive pattern of growth is the only way forward for the GDR.

Czechoslovakia

The fact that Czechoslovakia was a relatively industrialized country before the Second World War in part accounts for an early attempt to modify command planning. In the late 1950s enterprises were amalgamated into associations, emphasis placed on financial planning and some small measure of decentralization of decision-making allowed. The deep-seated ills were not cured and a negative growth rate in 1962 added to the list. Recentralization, however, only seemed to make matters worse and led, in 1967, to the most radical reform measures outside Yugoslavia. (For excellent analyses see Holesovsky, 1968 and 1973; Kyn, 1970; and Staller, 1968).

The 1967 measures largely abandoned directive planning and generally allowed enterprises to determine their own output and input plans. (It is tempting to see enterprises maximizing post-tax profit in the absence of an obligatory *tekhpromfinplan*, but activity was too spontaneous, improvised and varied to make this sort of generalization. The whole process of change-over to the new system was gradual and ad hoc.) Workers' councils began to be set up in 1968.

Indirect control was exercised by the State via instruments such as a capital charge, tax on value added and payroll surcharge. The State intended to retain control of the overall share of investment and consumption in national income, but decentralized investment was to constitute as much as 40 per cent of total investment. Banks took account of commercial criteria as well as State guidelines and foreign trade considerations in allocating investment credits. A tiered system of prices, with generous 'free' category (often subject to ceilings), was introduced. The relationship between enterprise and association gave rise to difficulties (such as association influence over investment and financial transfers between enterprises), but it was intended eventually to make membership voluntary. The 1968 Warsaw Pact invasion quickly halted the whole liberalization process and by mid 1970 most of the economic reform had been abandoned. A price freeze introduced in 1970 lasted virtually for a decade.

Some 1967 elements remained, such as the stress on credits as opposed to budgetary grants in the financing of State-determined investments, but it was not until 1978 that another significant experiment was undertaken (due to increasing shortages and world prices of raw materials and fuels, which made the inefficient use of inputs less and less tolerable). This 'complex experiment' involved 12 associations, covering 150 industrial enterprises, 9 foreign trade corporations and 21 research institutes. The new system, set out in the March 1980 'Set of Measures to Improve the System of Planned Management of the National Economy after 1980', is based on this experiment and is to be made generally operational during the period 1981 to 1985.

The Industrial Associaton (VHJ) is to be the basic production unit. It usually involves a horizontal integration of enterprises, either a *koncern* (a large enterprise alone or one linked with smaller ones) or a *trust* (where enterprises of comparable size are merged), but there is also the *kombinat*, which is the result of vertical integration. The economy remains tightly controlled (familiar plan indicators, such as production, sales, technical development, fixed investment, material inputs, labour and wages and financial tasks, are still to be found), but there are several interesting features, some echoing practice and proposals in other Comecon countries. Thus it is intended to fix norms and plans for a five-year period, avoid the adverse effects of the 'residual profit' and allow an important role to be played by value added in wage bill determination (though basic wage rates are to remain centrally controlled). The 'wage bill limit' consists of two parts: a 'basic wage bill limit' linked to value added and an 'incentive component' related to profitability. Material incentives are also affected by a Rewards Fund (a share of profits dependent on meeting targets for product quality and technical level and labour economies) and the Cultural and Social Needs Funds (linked to the wage bill, profit, labour productivity, product assortment, exports, product quality and fixed asset utilization). Exports are to be encouraged by an Export Stimulation Fund. Payments to the State (such as payments out of profit, a capital charge and social security contribution) have priority over material incentive funds.

Czechoslovakia has followed the Soviet Union in abandoning decentralized investment, but budgetary grants (as opposed to retained profits and credits) are to be the exception rather than the rule. There is to be no radical change in pricing principles, though there are to be (1981–2) price increases for fuels and some raw materials (which are to be passed on in end-product prices), on top of the already announced regular increases of 2 per cent per annum in fuel prices during the period 1981 to 1985 (only partially to be passed on, however). Quality surcharges (or penalties) are allowed and attempts will be made to link domestic and world prices more effectively. There is the interesting proposal (though under conditions still to be announced) that purchasers and suppliers of capital goods may be allowed to negotiate prices.

Rychetnik concludes his article with a critical look at the Czechoslovakian proposals and a comment on the question of socialist entrepreneurship raised by Radice.

Hungary

In Hungary on 1 January 1968, a radical departure from the traditional model came in the shape of the New Economic Mechanism (NEM), which had the major aim of using the market mechanism to improve the implementation of global State targets and to determine more efficiently the disaggregated details of resource allocation. The problem was how to overcome the micro-economic defects of the Soviet-type system, while avoiding inflation, unemployment and instability at the macro level.

In essence, the typically large industrial enterprise (comprising seven plants on average even at the end of 1970) does not receive a *tekhpromfinplan*, but makes most output and input decisions (some directive elements remain, Comecon commitments for example) in the light of post-tax profit and a varying milieu of State regulators and pressures. The State still aims to control the major macro-economic aggregates, investment and consumption, both directly and indirectly. Thus new enterprises are set up (and inefficient ones may be closed down) by the State, which also controls major expansions of existing capacity (thus helping to ensure that basic product specification does not lie within the sphere of enterprise decision-making). Examples of indirect steering include taxes on wages and wage increases and varying bank credit conditions (after 1976 sectoral credit allocation was abandoned, but banks still have to take account of State guidelines, currently favouring, for example, exports and the efficient use of raw materials and energy).

The much greater use of 'economic levers' (such as prices, a complicated and changing wage and tax system, the cost and availability of credit and international trade policy) indirectly to guide the economy distinguishes the Hungarian

from the Soviet-type system. This is not to underestimate the strength of informal pressures in a highly monopolistic economy where a relatively small
number of directors (appointed and sacked by the State) can be easily con-
tacted. Concern over significant income differentials, excess demand and balance of payments problems led to more formal controls being introduced after
November 1972, such as the subjection of 50 large enterprises to special ministerial
supervision (greater information rights, for example), while the deteriorating
foreign trade situation after 1973 led to further measures, such as the introduction of 'plan juries' (inter-ministerial, functional and sectoral, advisory committees on enterprise plans) and emphasis on 'complex evaluation' of managerial
performance, involving such criteria as technological progress and other aspects
of long-term development (see Gadó, 1976).

   Although in general plan directives are absent, Radice stresses the continuing
strength of vertical relationships between large industrial enterprises and the
centre. Changes in economic policy have tended to favour direct forms of intervention rather than regulator manipulation, due to such factors as persistent
input shortages, balance of payments problems, the commitment to full employment, ambitious investment programmes and the desire to maintain Party control. Vertical bargaining continues over economic regulators, such as subsidies,
credit conditions and taxes. Horizontal links, on the other hand, have been
hindered by excess aggregate demand and the monopolistic structure of the
economy: the resulting sellers' market has led to difficulties in establishing
new sources of supply, while large State enterprises are reluctant to subcontract
to small ones or cooperatives for fear of supply unreliability and lack of the
sort of leverage typically exercised via the centre.

   Persistent labour shortages and the desire quickly to meet short-term demands
of the State give rise to labour hoarding, despite taxes on wages and wage increases. Alluring material rewards in the 'second economy' (essentially the non-
regulated sector), especially private, illegal and dubiously legal activity, have
adverse effects on the 'first economy' (although the former does help fill gaps
left by the latter).

   The 1980 round of reforms re-emphasizes the market mechanism and links
between domestic and world market prices. Regulators are to be more uniform
and stable, the prices of products involving at least 70 per cent of industrial
output are to be based on world market prices, trade subsidies reduced and the
dual system of commercial exchange rates for socialist and hard-currency trade
gradually phased out. Wholesale prices of raw materials and fuels have been
raised to improve efficiency in input use. Retail prices, too, have generally been
increased in order to reduce subsidies, but some Autumn 1980 planned increases
were put off, probably as a result of the situation in Poland. The direct trading
rights enjoyed by some large enterprises are being extended, encouragement is
given to risk-taking partnerships between enterprise and foreign trade organization (as opposed to a commission basis for contracts) and an apparently greater

role is to be played by the small enterprise: three large enterprises have been disbanded and another is destined to be, although it is uncertain how much autonomy will be exercised by each plant (see Cviic, 1980).

Radice concludes his article with a stimulating section on entrepreneurship, the problems connected with risk-taking in a socialist economy.

Yugoslavia

The 1948 rift with Stalin over the question of sovereignty quickly pushed Yugoslavia into a unique model of market socialism, based on the principle of self-management of the socially-owned industrial enterprise by the workers, via an elected workers' council. The principle of self-management arose out of a desire to stress independence (neither Soviet-type nor capitalist) as an aspect of defence policy and the nationalities problem and to avoid class distinctions between workers, managers and owners. The classical command economy, where output, inputs, prices and investment are essentially centrally determined, has been abandoned and replaced by a qualified and highly imperfect market economy, in which the State exercises mainly indirect means of control (such as tax, credit and tariff policies). Thus, taxes affect investment and banks evaluate credit requests in the light of rates of return and Government guidelines (regional or sectoral, for instance). The Yugoslav Five Year Plan is simply a statement of intent; targets are not 'addressed' to any institution. This is not to understate the influence of the Party, of course, but enterprises have no obligatory output or input plans to fulfil.

The typical Yugoslav enterprise is large (at present 200 enterprises account for about 55 per cent of output). The manager is now elected by the workers' council from a list drawn up by a nominating committee (half the members of which are politically appointed, including representatives of local government; a majority of two-thirds of all members is needed for decisions). There has been a continuing controversy, however, over the decision-taking powers of workers' council and manager: managers are nominally in charge of the 'day-to-day' running of the enterprise, within the constraints of the law and workers' council guidelines, but de facto, to a debatable and varying degree, managerial powers are greater, due to higher levels of expertise and political influence. The aims of a manager (who may also be interested in factors like growth, prestige and political favour) and a workers' council may not always coincide, but, at the risk of generalizing, the enterprise maximand seems to involve 'net income', namely wages and profits, since workers are interested in both. (Sirc argues that the maximization of 'net income' *per employee* is simply a Western theoretical abstraction: see Ward, 1967). Minimum wages are set by the State, but the distribution of 'net revenue' (determined by deducting all *non-wage* expenditure and obligations from gross revenue) between the wage and other funds (for reserves, communual activities and investment) is now determined by the workers' council, subject to, for example, prevailing 'social contracts' (between enterprises and State authorities) and 'management agreements' (between enterprises).

Since 1952 the tide has generally flowed in favour of the market as opposed to plan, interrupted, for example, especially during the inflationary decade of the 1970s, by price controls and 'social contracts' aimed at moderating the strong tendency to favour wages at the expense of plough-back profits. (These social contracts and management agreements are legally binding, but there is the threat of back-up measures, since, as Sirc argues, they are vague, difficult to enforce, given the residual accounting nature of wages, and usually too late).

Considerable post-war success, as regards rates of growth and avoidance of many of the micro-economic deficiences of the traditional command economy, has been purchased at the expense of 'capitalist' problems (persistent balance of payments deficits, inflation — retail prices are currently rising at an annual rate of over 20 per cent — and unemployment) and 'home-grown' deficiencies. Sirc's article is a critical look at the operation of the Yugoslav economy. Inflation has been aggravated by the tendency of workers to favour wages at the expense of *plough-back* profits and the strong incentive to invest using *bank credits* (because of two factors: the lack of responsibility — future losses would be cancelled by the State, which would simply 'print' money in the last resort to avoid bankruptcies, while future success would raise personal income; and substantially negative interest rates). Fixed investment is now approximately 35 per cent of Gross Domestic Product, but Sirc stresses the inefficiency with which investment resources are used, due to such factors as the lack of clear-cut investment criteria, the absence of a capital market (though inter-enterprise loans are permitted) and political interferences. Sirc discusses at length the theoretical and empirical aspects of the distribution of enterprise income and paints an uneasy picture of enterprises operating in a sort of 'vacuum', somehow neither plan nor market.

THE PRESENT AND THE FUTURE

As already stated, this volume is basically a descriptive account of the organization and operation of the production unit in Yugoslavia and the Comecon countries of Eastern Europe. While much has been written about the theory of workers' self-management (see, for example, Ward, 1967) and attempts have been made to explain managerial behaviour in command economies in terms of bonus maximization (see, for example, Granick, 1975), a theory of the socialist firm is, as George Blazyca reminded us during the symposium, essentially lacking. Radice, Nuti and Rychetník, however, offer interesting thoughts on socialist 'entrepreneurship'. Blazyca and Åslund also stressed the Eastern European neglect of the role of the 'small' enterprise (though there has been some discussion, in Poland for example: Blazyca, 1980b). The basic production unit in Eastern Europe is now 'large' by any standard: leaving aside Hungary and Yugoslavia for the moment (where 'gigantomania' is also prevalent), 'associations' of enterprises, with various names and of various sorts, dominate the industrial scene, in order to reap economies of scale, link research and development with production and streamline the planning administration by reducing the number of directly controlled lower-level institutions. It is difficult to be precise about the decision-making role of constituent enterprises, which varies between and indeed within countries, but the overall impression at the moment is one of subservience, with the association (itself tightly controlled by the ministry) sending down disaggregated plan targets. The greatest variety of association is to be found in the Soviet Union, due to its sheer size, where a distinction is made between 'production', 'science-production' and 'industrial' types and, further, between All-Union, Republican and local. Associations are typically the result of a horizontal integration of enterprises, but the GDR has made the most significant concessions to the principle of vertical integration.

The principle of 'one-man management' is still dominant and remains official policy in all countries save Yugoslavia and Romania. Yugoslav workers' councils, operating in a market environment, remain, of course, significantly different from Romanian 'workers' committees', but the latter, it must be said, seem to play a real part in plan discussion, unlike their namesakes in the other Comecon countries. Poland is now paying the price for cynical disregard of workers' views and grievances and there may be repercussions elsewhere in Eastern Europe. Bulgaria has now joined Yugoslavia, Romania, Hungary and Poland in allowing equity ventures with Western firms.

With the exception of Yugoslavia and Hungary, the socialist countries of Eastern Europe are command economies, in which decisions concerning output, inputs, prices and investment are highly centralized. Vertical relationships, as Radice points out, are still important in Hungary, but there is a difference in kind between it and its Comecon partners: enterprises in Hungary do not have to fulfil a *tekhpromfinplan*. As Nove put it in discussion, it is important to distinguish between a situation in which an enterprise has hardly any rights and one in which significant rights are interfered with.

In the command economies the enterprise plan continues to take the form of success indicators. In traditional fashion new or more serious micro-economic problems are met by increasing the number of targets and/or changing emphasis: thus, growing concern with the prices and availability of raw materials and fuels has been met by a recent general stress on net output (value added), cost reduction and material utilization norms. Net output, in particular, seems to hold the centre of the Eastern European stage at the moment, since gross output targets encourage a profligate use of non-labour inputs. 'Counter-planning', as practised in the Soviet Union and Bulgaria, for example, has been a predictable failure: enterprises simply have an extra inducement to understate capacity in the initial bargaining round.

Associations operate on an 'economic accounting' basis, but there have been proposals to move towards *'full khozraschyot'*. The former term means that each production unit has a profit and loss account, the main aim being to encourage efficiency in plan fulfilment in order at least to achieve the level of planned profit (or not to exceed planned loss). The latter term is sometimes used to describe the operation of an economic unit in a market environment, but here a less radical definition is implied. The difference between *khozraschyot* and its 'full' version in this less radical sense is not very clear, but seems to imply an even greater concern for financial stringency and efficiency of plan implementation and a desire to cover all expenditures (including investment) from sales revenue. In practical terms this has meant increasing wholesale prices, to reflect costs better and so reduce subsidies and a further shift towards retained profit and interest-bearing credits, as opposed to budgetary grants, in the financing of investment. (Note that the term 'full' or 'complete' *khozraschyot* is also sometimes used, in Czechoslovakia for example, to describe a theoretical situation in which every organization in the economic hierarchy operated on a self-financing basis.) In the wake of growing input-supply problems, investment decisions have generally been increasingly centralized in recent years, the Soviet Union, Romania and Czechoslovakia having already abandoned the concept of 'decentralized' investment. The problem of 'residual profit' in the enterprise account is now widely recognized and attempts are being made to overcome it by means of various profit distribution schemes. Efficiency prices are still lacking, although, as Robert Bideleux stressed in discussion, the importance of this is diminished in the context of command economies. Outside the Soviet Union there is still a common desire to improve the link between domestic and world prices, but practice, as ever, generally lags behind proposal.

Proposals for reform are continuously made in Eastern Europe. There are variations, mainly in rhetoric, but Poland is one of the most interesting. Even before the strikes of the summer of 1980, Polish proposals sounded more radical than most: changes of an even more radical nature may eventually be carried out under conducive economic and political circumstances.

REFERENCES

Berliner, J. S. (1976) *The Innovation Decision in Soviet Industry*. Cambridge, Mass.: MIT Press.

Blazyca, G. (1980) Industrial structure and the economic problems of industry in a centrally planned economy: the Polish case. *Journal of Industrial Economics*, March. (a) p. 317; (b) p. 319.

Cviic. C. (1980) The quiet revolution. *The Economist*, 20 September.

Dellin, L. A. D. (1970) Bulgaria's economic reform. *Problems of Communism*, September–October, p. 52.

Ellman, M. (1979) *Socialist Planning*. Cambridge: Cambridge University Press.

Feiwel, G. (1979) Economic reform in Bulgaria. *Osteuropa Wirtschaft*, 2, p. 76.

Gadó, O. (1976) *The Economic Mechanism in Hungary — How It Works in 1976.* Leyden: A. W. Sijthoff; Budapest: Akademiai Kiado.

Granick, D. (1975) *Enterprise Guidance in Eastern Europe.* Princeton: Princeton University Press.

Höhmann, H. H., Kaser, M. C. & Thalheim, K. C. (Ed.) (1975) *The New Economic Systems of Eastern Europe.* London: Hurst.

Holesovsky, V. (1968) Financial aspects of the Czechoslovak reforms. In *Money and Plan* (Ed.) Grossman, G. Berkeley: University of California Press.

Holesovsky, V. (1973) Planning and the market in the Czechoslovak reform. In *Plan and Market* (ed.) Bornstein, M. New Haven and London: Yale University Press.

Kaser, M. & Spigler, I. (1980) *Economic Reforms in Romania in the 1970s* (Paper prepared for a symposium edited by the Bundesinstitut für Ostwissenschaftliche und Internationale Studien, Cologne).

Kyn, O. (1970) The rise and fall of economic reforms in Czechoslovakia. *American Economic Review*, Papers and Proceedings.

Leptin, G. & Melzer, M. (1978) *Economic Reform in East German Industry.* London and Oxford: Oxford University Press.

Nove, A. (1977) *The Soviet Economic System.* London: Allen and Unwin.

Nuti, D. M. (1977) Large corporations and the reform of Polish industry. *Jahrbuch der Wirtschaft Osteuropas*, 7.

Schroeder, G. (1979) The Soviet economy on a treadmill of reform. In *The Soviet Economy in a Time of Change*, 1, Washington: Joint Economic Committee of the US Congress. (a) p. 326; (b) p. 316.

Sirc, L. (1979) *The Yugoslav Economy under Self-Management.* London: Macmillan.

Smith, A. (1980) Romanian economic reforms. In *Economic Reforms in Eastern Europe and Prospects for the 1980s.* London: NATO; Pergamon Press.

Spigler, I. (1973) *Economic Reform in Romanian Industry.* London and Oxford: Oxford University Press.

Staller, G. (1968) Czechoslovakia: the new model of planning and management. *American Economic Review*, 2.

Ward, B. (1967) *The Socialist Economy.* New York: Random House.

2
The Soviet Industrial Enterprise

Alec Nove

Let us begin with a glance at the 1965 reform. It will be recalled that this eliminated the regional economic councils (*sovnarkhozy*), restored the industrial ministries and sought at the same time to increase the powers and functions of directors at enterprise level. Many compulsory plan indicators were declared abolished, and the role of profits (profitability) in the computation of bonuses was enhanced. A price reform introduced in 1967 sought to eliminate loss-making sectors and did indeed substantially increase average profit margins, out of which a capital charge had to be paid into the budget. Supposedly, ministerial plan instructions were to be confined to the following indicators: value of output sold; profits and/or profit rate (*rentabel'nost'*); payments to State budget; wages fund; centralized investments.

There was a declaration about the desirability of more direct commercial links between customer and supplier, and a shift towards trade in (as distinct from administrative allocation of) the means of production. Material and technical supply functions at the centre and in the localities were to be concentrated in *Gossnab* (State Committee on Material–Technical Supplies) and its republican and local offices.

Subsequent history was one of virtually continuous retreat from the principles of 1965. The best and most detailed survey of the stages through which the reform was itself reformed is that by Gertrude Schroeder (1979). The number of compulsory indicators increased, formally and informally. Thus Aganbegyan reported (*Pravda*, 12 November 1973) that '80 per cent of directors [in a sample survey covering 1064 directors] reported that their superiors imposed compulsory indicators (such as costs of specific products, the numbers employed by category, and so on) which in accordance with the economic reform measure were not to be laid down from above'. Ninety per cent of directors considered that their powers were too small. Alongside this apparently unauthorized exercise of ministerial authority was a steady increase in the list of indicators which ministers were allowed, indeed instructed, to impose: labour productivity, material utilization norms, delivery obligations for the more important items, introduction of new techniques, quality improvements and others specific to particular sectors. Above all, output plans in physical terms (tons, square metres, etc.), with some breakdown in the nomenclature, continued to be imposed as obligatory plan targets and the fulfilment of these targets was a precondition for payments into the incentive funds. The magnitude of the payments into these funds was based on a complex and supposedly stable set of rules, related in various ways to sales (*realizatsiya*), profits and/or profitability (*rentabel'nost'*). In fact the rules governing payments of these funds were repeatedly and arbitrarily altered.

Why did the 1965 reform develop (or rather fail to develop) in this way? The following reasons suggest themselves:

1. First and foremost, prices remained based upon what Soviet reformer critics call the *zatratnyi printsip*, that is, on costs, without reflecting demand, utility, or the relative scarcity of either inputs or outputs. The 1967 price reform did indeed eliminate loss-making sectors, but profitability varied greatly, especially with the passage of time, and the variation had no connection at all with use-value or shortage. Under these circumstances profits could not be used as a rational indicator of effectiveness in any enterprise which could change its product mix;
2. There was in fact no serious move towards trade in means of production. Administrative allocation remained the rule, and so output and delivery plans were imposed in the usual way;
3. The economy continued (and continues) to operate in conditions of shortage, with all the resultant consequences. This is a 'sellers' market', and this, plus the practice of tying customers to particular suppliers through the supply plan, provides good reasons for administrative rationing of resources;
4. It is unusual for plans to be either internally consistent or to be drafted in time. Hence, frequent changes: 'in the course of one year, among only a part of the enterprises examined, there were 1554 amendments to the production plan, and this without any changes in financial indicators' (Aganbegyan, *Pravda*, 12 November 1973). Under such circumstances there could be no stable plans. Indeed, numerous published statements attest to the fact that plans were altered not only because of unforeseen needs or shortages, but also to ensure that ministries could report that plans have been fulfilled; the successful were given extra tasks, sometimes a few weeks before the end of the year, and the less successful had their plans reduced. It is impossible for

directors to have any confidence about what will be 'earned' for their incentive funds; the 'rules of the game' could be charged at any time, and the funds themselves be subject to arbitrary maxima.

It was hoped that the 1965 reform would discourage the concealing of productive potential, by increasing rewards if a plan were ambitious. This notion underlay the campaign to persuade enterprises to propose 'counter-plans' (*vstrechnye plany*): they were to be encouraged to propose a plan higher than the obligatory one, and would be rewarded even if the outcome were below the 'counter-plan', so long as they fulfilled the (lower) obligatory target. This, predictably, failed to make any impact. Plans were not only based 'on the achieved level' (see Birman, 1978), but were the subject of argument and bargaining at the stage of their formulation and liable to alteration during the period of that currency, for reasons already explained. Obviously only a foolish manager would propose a 'counter-plan', since this would (and did) lead to an upward revision of the obligatory plan.

The same fate has befallen another well-meant effort to stimulate managerial initiative and to economize on labour. It is a notorious fact that labour is hoarded, for the same reason as materials (to keep a reserve against unexpected changes of plan or future need, and so on). To encourage the shedding of surplus labour the so-called *Shchekino method* was devised: an enterprise that reduced its labour force, or operated additional productive capacity with the same labour force, was to be entitled to keep the major part of the resultant economy in wages, for distribution to the remaining employees. However, the ministries have behaved as usual, arbitrarily changing the rules and in practice preventing enterprises from reaping the benefit from the economies they have achieved.

A source of repeated criticism is the practice, which was embodied in the price reform of 1967, of removing to the State budget the whole 'free remainder of profit' (*svobodnyi ostatok prybili*), which removed the incentive to increase profits, given the arbitrary changes in the rules governing the incentive funds, while at the same time also removing the impact of penalties (e.g., for non-fulfilment of contracts), since these are generally covered by that part of profits which would in any case be transferred to the State budget.

A considerable literature exists covering the petty restrictions on the decision-making process of directors. Yashkin (in *Pravda*, 1 November 1979) complains that he has to seek permission from the ministry about how to spend money allocated to the enterprise's incentive funds, though nominally they are within his decision-making competence; he describes the procedure as 'a marathon obstacle-race'. Then he is given annually a target for reducing administrative costs, which is often impossible. A limit is set even on travel expenses, a limit so severe that lengthy correspondence must frequently be undertaken to get the necessary permission to travel on business. He also complains bitterly that enterprises are punished for failing to produce goods which could not be produced because of the absence of the necessary materials, or because of an impossible plan.

We must now turn to the important and complex theme of the creation of *obyedineniya* (associations). The process had already begun in the sixties, but a formal decision was taken in 1973 to base industry on *obyedineniya*. The process has been slow, but most of industry is now run on this basis, and the process of 'obyedeninizatiya' (to coin a phrase) should be complete by the start of the next five year plan, but this is not by any means certain. As of 1 January 1980 there were 3947 'production' *obyedineniya* in industry, containing 17 516 formerly separate enterprises, but only 147 were formed during the whole of 1979. In the Ministry of Light Industry, the 546 *obyedineniya* in existence produce 44 per cent of the total value of output of the ministry (*Ekonomicheskaya Gazeta*, 1980, 28, pp. 12–13). *Pravda* (14 September 1979) complained publicly of resistance and obstruction by those who regard the whole idea 'with scepticism'.

What difference have *obyedineniya* made to directorial power? This should be the subject of a whole research project. I can indicate only some of the complications, and the inconclusive nature of the evidence.

Obyedineniya are of many different kinds, a fact which is in itself evidence of a flexible approach, but which makes generalization difficult. Some are all-union or republican, and these may sometimes replace the former ministerial *glavki*, and differ from them only by being on *khozraschyot*, that is, to possess a profit-and-loss account. The personnel may be the same, and the relationship with the ministry and with their subordinate directors may be unaltered, though no doubt it is possible that the more direct interest in financial results may affect the kind of instructions which are issued. Thus in the Ministry of Machinery for the oil and chemical industries the *glavki* have been replaced by ten all-union *khozraschyot obyedineniya*, one of which has its headquarters in Baku. Under them are 35 'production' and five 'science-and-production' *obyedineniya*, except that some of the larger are directly under the ministry itself (*Ekonomicheskaya Gazeta*, 1980, 28, p. 12). Other ministries make different arrangements.

The production associations (*proizvodstvennye obyedineniya*), and, in those cases in which they are linked with a research centre, the science-and-production (i.e., research-linked) associations also vary immensely. Some are a merger of small factories within a relatively small area, some have their production units spread over hundreds of miles and more, within or outside a given republic. Some relate to the final product (e.g., footwear, in an area), some to a process (e.g., spinning and weaving). Some very large enterprises have in effect achieved the status of *obyedineniya*, with some smaller units subordinated to them as *filialy*: this is the case, for instance, with the ZIL works and some large machinery factories.

Another very important distinction exists: namely, between those production *obyedineniya* within which 'enterprises' retain their separate existence under that name, with their own *khozraschyot*, legal personality and bank account, and those in which formerly separate enterprises become mere branch workshops. In January 1980, of the 17 516 enterprises which were merged into *obyedineniya*, 7300 retained their separate identity (*Ekonomicheskaya Gazeta*, 1980, 28, p. 12). There are instances of both types within the same *obyedineniya*: thus the Skorokhod Footwear association, based in Leningrad and covering all north-west Russia, has treated its factories in Leningrad itself as workshops, but those outside the Leningrad area remain 'enterprises'. The press from time to time criticizes delays in creating *obyedineniya*, the small size of many of them, and the large number in certain areas and under certain ministries in which the enterprises retain their identity. In general, the very long and still incomplete nature of the reorganization is evidence of resistance, certainly within ministries and probably also in some localities: mergers which subordinate a factory in a town to an association with a headquarters in a different area cannot be in the interest of the local party's secretariat.

What has been the effect of all this on management and its role? What, furthermore, is likely to be the effect of the implementation of the 'reform' measures decreed in July 1979? It is very difficult indeed for any outsider to generalize about the internal relationships within any large organization, anywhere. Much necessarily depends on informal links and the human factor. One recalls the evidence deployed in the book by Andrle (1976) based on his Birmingham doctoral dissertation. A Hungarian economist once remarked that, in even the most apparently centralized command system, 'most commands are written by their recipients'. It is one of the main contradictions of the Soviet economic system that, while on the one hand the task of subordinates is to obey plan instructions which supposedly embody the needs of society and the best means of providing for them, everyone in fact knows that much depends on the initiative, proposals and information (or the withholding of it) by or from management. Quality, punctual deliveries, technical progress, the details of the product mix (and the satisfaction of user needs) depend in practice on management. Paradoxically, the growth in the number of obligatory instructions and compulsory indicators may not reduce managerial freedom, since these instructions are bound, in the nature of things, to be contradictory, thus giving management a wider range of choice as to which instruction to obey. Breakdown in supply arrangements, rendered inevitable by the colossal scale of the task of the supply and production plan agencies, causes management to set up its own small workshops for self-supply, and to establish with other managers informal extra-legal links which become a parallel supply system, the scale of which is the subject of a great deal of guesswork. The large number of *tolkachi* has been the subject of repeated critical comment in the Soviet press, and the cause of the phenomenon is widely discussed. Some instructions are evaded. Thus the low pay of office staff and frequent orders to reduce their number can lead to the sort of phenomenon illustrated by a *Krokodil* cartoon: an elegant lady is typing and her boss says: 'she is a fine secretary, so I have classified her as an instrument mechanic of the fifth grade'.

The conversion of a *glavk* into an all-union *obyedineniye* should make little difference to the way in which central powers can be exercised, and it is intended not as an act of decentralization but as a streamlining of the control apparatus, giving it greater concern with financial results. But quite obviously the mergers affecting thousands of enterprises must reduce the powers of their directors, whether or not they formally retain that status. Instead of having a remote ministerial 'boss', they now find themselves under a super-manager who is much closer to them in function and geographically. It is one of the purposes of the change to empower the production *obyedineniye* to sub-allocate plan tasks, to promote specialization and indeed to issue instructions on a wide range of topics in its capacity as the hierarchical superior of the production units under its authority.

The all-union *obyedineniya* appear to lack powers vis-à-vis the ministry in some important respects. Thus the *Soyuzreaktiv*, within the ministry of chemical industry, reports that it is 'not allowed to redistribute resources between production, disposals and research, it is not allowed to make agreements with outside research, experimental-construction and project-making organizations, machinery enterprises, etc.' Similar problems arise in the science-production *obyedineniya* under *Soyuzreaktiv* such as *Biokhimreaktiv*, where the production and research sides are separately financed. Even the bonus rules and pay rates of branches of management staff are different, and it is clear that it is not within the competence of the all-union body to alter them, since the paragraph ends with the words: 'to strengthen *khozraschyot* in the all-union-industrial and in the science-production *obyedineniya*, it is essential to increase the rights of their leaders' (*Planovoye Khozyaistvo*, 1980, 6, p. 30).

What, therefore, are the powers of management of the production *obyedineniye* itself, vis-à-vis its superiors? A number of complaints have been registered to the effect that the 'general directors' of *obyedineniya* have neither higher salaries nor greater powers than the common-or-garden directors (evidence cited in Nove, 1977). Indeed, one motive and effect of their creation is to reduce the number of units which the central organs administer, and this could give them more time to issue orders. Other things being equal, it seems reasonable to surmise that the net effect of the creation of *obyedineniya* is to strengthen the powers of the central organs, of *Gosplan*, the ministries and the all-union *obyedineniya*, the latter seen as ministerial subunits. This can be only a preliminary judgement, however; there is much research to be done.

A great deal depends on the organization of supply, and on certain potential effects of the July 1979 reform. I shall discuss the latter later, and deal now with the supply question. Its vital importance is obvious, from the standpoint both of the smooth functioning of the process of production and the effective powers of management. Nothing can be produced without inputs, and, if these are 'rationed' by the supply organs, nothing can be produced unless and until they authorize the necessary supplies. As already mentioned, 'trade' in the means of production remains insignificant, but much has been said and written about 'long-term direct links'. As far as can be determined, these links are under the authority of the supply agencies. In other words, they do not, as a rule, arise from the free decisions of those concerned. A is attached to B as a supplier, with the subject of negotiations being only the detailed specifications and timing. The links are long term if the planning agencies decide that they be so: that is, A is to supply B with material X for several years. In practice these links can be disrupted as and when the planning or ministerial authorities consider it necessary to do so. There seems no fundamental change here. Far more stress is laid on the fulfilment of delivery obligations, but that raises another very important question — how to enforce such obligations — which I will not go into in this paper.

Now let us turn to the reform of July 1979, and to its possible consequences (in the aspects relevant to the present paper). It is laid down that the role of the actual production units in the formulation of plans be enhanced; plans be balanced (i.e., the necessary inputs should be available); plans be stable for five years ahead (the five year plan be split into five annual plans); and various 'norms' be stable too. These 'norms' are to include those governing the rules for incentive funds, a fixed relationship between net output and the wages fund, and for retention of profits (with the residual profits no longer being automatically transferred to the State budget). These measures seem, on the face of it, to be steps in the direction of increasing managerial functions. However, apart from the large number of compulsory plan-indicators, of which more later, this part of the reform document suffers from vagueness: certainly plans should be drafted in consultation with those who carry them out, undoubtedly output is impossible without the needed inputs, and plans and norms should be stable and should not be frequently altered, but have we not heard all this before? Why should we expect any change now? Thus plans are not stable because unforeseen circumstances and emergent shortages compel a change. Indeed it would be absurd to have stable (inflexible) plans for five years ahead, unless one were to assume perfect foresight and no uncertainty. (The better mathematical planning models describe themselves explicitly as of a 'stochastic' character, and rightly so.) Of course, if inputs (and outputs too) become less scarce, if shortages become less pervasive, there would be less need for 'rationing', a better chance for stable norms actually to be stable. But here again there have been declarations of good intention before. Did not Brezhnev declare at the 24th Party congress that consumers' goods output should rise faster than incomes, so as to diminish shortages, and did not the opposite occur? He might well repeat this declaration at the 26th congress in February 1981.

The revised and consolidated list of plan indicators, contained in the July 1979 decree, must be seen as a move towards greater *centralization*. The emphasis is *less* on profits and monetary aggregates relative to the financial performance of the production unit. There appears to be an increase in the number of centrally planned and allocated products and in the number of imposed targets of various kinds. Thus, for instance, there will be an increase in detailed planned nomenclature of machinery, and 'there will be an expansion in the number of compulsory indicators for technical improvements' (*Ekonomicheskaya Gazeta*, 1979, 33, p. 3). While plan indicators will vary in different branches, and only a limited number will be used in determining payments into incentive funds, the following are mentioned in explanatory articles in the specialized press, and/or in the decree itself as subjects of obligatory targets and plans (though doubtless not all at once in every sector): physical output for principal items of output (sometimes corrected by coefficients to take quality into account); the carrying out of principal delivery obligations; labour productivity; increase in the volume of sales; numbers of workers and employees; percentage reduction in unmechanized hand labour; percentage reduction in utilization of materials and fuel; profitability; cost reduction; relationship between net output and the wages bill; proportion of goods of first quality; introduction of new techniques; payments into the State budget; various targets connected with investments.

A decision published in *Ekonomicheskaya Gazeta* (1980, 28, p. 11) recommends that no more than two or three indicators should be used in determining payments into the incentive funds, but ministries are clearly given the right to issue obligatory orders on other matters, not necessarily included in the above list. Thus, for instance, factories in the chemical industry are given a plan for increasing the range of their products (which they sometimes fulfil by literally producing a few grams of something new even if the customer wants much more than this! See *Planovoye Khozyaistvo*, 1980, 6, p. 30). All the evidence suggests that that control over enterprises will be tightened. This is true both of the *vstrechnye plany* and of decentralized investments, both of which are now to be included in the central plan. The motive is apparently to ensure the necessary material supplies and to reduce unpredictable demands on resources. Every production unit has to have a so-called 'passport', giving full details of its capacity, to facilitate the task of the central organs controlling it.

Labour productivity and the wages bill are to be calculated by reference to normed value-added, or net output. But note the word 'normed'. The calculation is vastly complex, and many articles have been devoted to explaining it. The essential point is that it is a *notional* sum made up of notional labour costs and profits, based upon sectoral averages, and not the actual costs and profits of the actual production unit. This introduces a contradiction to the basis of *khozraschyot*, which, surely, implies an emphasis on *actual* costs and profits, and some very odd relationships between the notional and the actual are bound to emerge, as for instance when producing more of product X increases 'normed' net output but in fact adds to costs and reduces profits. The price reform now being undertaken is being used to calculate net product norms for millions of products, along with their new prices.

In his comment on the reform Baibakov claimed that, as a result, differences in profitability lose their influence on the product mix (*Pravda*, 22 August, 1979). This is supposedly to be based on contractual obligations, imposed or confirmed by the supply organs, but, for familiar reasons, no plan can possible be fully disaggregated, and, under the prevailing conditions of a sellers' market, with the role of profitability diminished, it is hard to see how the new system can be made to respond adequately to user requirements. Surely, in the words of the economist Kheinman, 'there must be created the conditions which guarantee the user *freedom of choice*, thereby compelling the producer to improve and modernize his product' (Kheinman, 1980). He refers to the words of the decree of July 1979 that speak of the need for adequate reserves, and hopes that there will be no more 'planned deficits' in inputs in relation to output plans. But what meaning has 'freedom of choice' if one is attached to one supplier by the plan, and there is no provision for making it worth the producer's while to satisfy user demand? (Articles in *EKO* Nos. 5 and 6 by Kheinman, 1980, are extremely interesting and should be required reading.)

Finally, I return to the vital question of prices. Effective decentralization, which in the view of many far-sighted Soviet reformers is an indispensable precondition to efficiency, can be based only upon a price system which reflects economic reality, namely, scarcity, need, use-value etc. There is a sizeable literature on this, a good deal of which is related to mathematical programming and optimization. It is quite clear that the new prices which will be fully operative in 1982 will be based upon traditional cost-plus. The evidence is contained, inter alia, in two articles, one by Glushkov, the Chairman of the Prices Committee (Glushkov, 1980) and Yakovets (1980). There are, it is true, certain improvements. Thus prices have been raised to eliminate losses in the coal and timber industries, and certain charges have been more fully included in costs and prices, among them Social Insurance contributions, timber cutting levy, charges for the use of water, geological prospecting, etc. The idea is for costs to express social cost more fully, with some reduction in profit margins. In addition, some measures have been taken to provide for higher prices for better quality. However, it is clear that prices are intended to be fixed for at least the quinquennium. Then, the article by Yakovets appears to imply that while 'sector norms of profitability' will continue to be based on the value of basic funds, the percentage varying by sector, 'profits of specific products will be included in normed net output proportionately to cost of processing' (Yakovets, 1980a). It is not too clear to me just what this will mean, but it certainly does not mean that prices are intended to have any significant influence on choice at managerial level, choice of either output or inputs; and, of course, by being fixed for many years on end, prices will not be flexible.

This reform will hardly touch the basic ills from which the system is suffering and which are linked directly and indirectly to over-centralization. There is

38

much discussion at present on 'planning by complexes', and experiments have been undertaken in the setting up of Territorial Production Administrations. This may overcome one of the least satisfactory features of the *obyedineniya*: these are still, in the main, within ministries and so they cannot overcome the disease of 'departmentalism'. One must bear in mind that a very large number of items, especially machinery, components, and consumer durables, are made in factories under the control of numerous ministries. Thus, materials-handling equipment is made in factories under the control of more than 30 ministries, and manufacture of components, forgings and castings is almost universal. Ministerial self-sufficiency, and the resultant loss of economies of scale, is the subject of sharply critical comment in the already-cited article by Kheinman. The reform of July 1979 envisages the designation of particular ministries as principles for the production of items made by many ministries, but how can this — and the territorial complexes — be fitted into a structure in which ministries are the sources or channels of plans, finance, materials allocation, and investment funds? Furthermore, many enterprises and *obyedineniya* make a large number of different products which are also made elsewhere under other ministries. A considerable shake-up of the ministerial form of control over industry may be imminent.

REFERENCES

Andrle, V. (1976) *Managerial Power in the Soviet Union*. Farnborough: Saxon House.
Birman, I. (1978) From the Achieved Level. *Soviet Studies,* 2. pp. 153–172.
Glushkov, N. (1980) In *Planovoye Khozyaistvo,* 6.
Kheinman, S.A. (1980) In *Ekonomika i Organizatsiya Promyshlennogo Proizvodstva,* 5, p. 39.
Nove, A. (1977) *The Soviet Economic System*. pp. 82-83. London: Allen & Unwin.
Schroeder, G. (1979) The Soviet economy on a treadmill of reform. In *The Soviet Economy in a Time of Change*, 1, Washington: Joint Economic Committee of the US Congress.
Yakovets, Y. (1980) In *Voprosy Ekonomiki,* 6. (a) p. 16 and p. 18.

3
Industrial Enterprises in Poland, 1973–80: Economic Policies and Reforms

Domenico Mario Nuti

GENERAL TRENDS

The industrial enterprise that emerged in Poland in the late forties was a replica of the Soviet model: a one-man-managed administrative unit, executing within narrow margins of discretion a detailed and ambitious plan centrally determined, its formal attributes of legal personality and *rozrachunek gospodarczy* (economic accounting, identical to the Soviet *khozraschyot*) ensuring no more than a separate accounting identity. Earlier attempts at a more decentralized pattern of industrial organization gave way to a progressive centralization in 1948–9 and were abandoned with the replacement of the Central Planning Office by the Planning Commission (10 February 1949). The centralized model remained in force substantially unchanged until 1956 when, following Gomulka's rise to power and considerable public debate of the drawbacks of the system, important decentralization measures were taken. The autonomy of enterprises and their managers was considerably increased, workers' councils formed spontaneously and were legalized – reinforcing initiative at the enterprise level; land was substantially de-collectivized and markets somewhat reactivated. Already in 1958, however, a re-centralization process had begun. Workers' councils first saw their powers curtailed, then were absorbed into the broader 'conference of workers' self-management' (including also trade union and Party bodies). In 1958 the *zjednoczenia*, or associations of enterprises, operating in the same sector (and often also in the same territorial area), were set up, starting a process of industrial concentration and anticipating the Soviet transformation of industrial directorates (*zarządy*, equivalent to the Soviet *glavki*) into industrial associations (equivalent to the Soviet *obyedineniya*). The *zjednoczenie*, however, was really an extension of the State administration, and performed only a few of the functions of an enterprise: centralized research, marketing and project-designing, and distribution among enterprises of targets and means fixed by the centre, remaining basically a convenient instrument of central control.

In the period 1958–70 a large number of minor changes took place, often nominal and in any case without precise direction or sense of purpose. The pattern of change is difficult to discern, and lines of a possible periodization are blurred. Zielinski (1973) distinguishes between the following periods: 1956–8/9, the beginning of reforms, towards the 'grand design' of the 'guided market model'; 1959–64/5, an intermediate period during which the process slowed down and gradually reverted to old policies and instruments, the traditional economic system remaining substantially unscathed by the changes introduced (the 1960 price reform, the introduction of trade marks, after-season sales, etc.); 1965–8, a 'period of gradual improvements', with a new wave of reforms understood to be gradual, partial, preceded by experiments, improving success indicators and managerial incentives, overhauling the financial system, lengthening the time horizon of operational plans to two years, etc., but without a successful implementation; 1968–70, an abortive effort to reform started with the Vth Congress of the PZPR (November 1968) calling for 'a comprehensive and internally consistent system of planning and management', which produced, after numerous Central Committee meetings and a flood of legislation, 'an inconsistent, sketchy, and anti-consumer programme to be introduced from 1 January 1971 and which collapsed, together with the Gomulka leadership, after workers' protests in December 1970–April 1971' (Zielinski, 1973a). The inconclusiveness of changes, however, gives just as much justification to treating the whole period as a single stage in Polish reforms, as in Gliński (1977). Gliński regards the 1957–70 as a stage 'aiming at the synthesis of central planning with a significant area of autonomy of economic units', divided into a sub-period, 1957–63, characterized by 'the clear prevalence of changes in the direction of greater autonomy of economic units', and a second sub-period, 1964–70, 'seeking forms of organization and management leading to more intensive economizing' Gliński, 1977a). The plausibility of such different periodizations indicates the modest extent of the changes contemplated and actually implemented. The years 1958 to 1970 were 'to a greater extent wasted time' (Mujżel, 1980).

Having scrapped the reform prepared by Gomulka for implementation on 1 January 1971, Gierek set up a Party-Government Committee 'On the Modernization of the System of Functioning of the Economy and the State', with terms of reference to 'the maintenance of the principles of central planning and socialism'. Contrary to expectations (Zielinski, 1973b), major and extensive changes were proposed by the Committee. There was no mention of 'reform' in official quarters, the keynote being 'the further improvement of the process of planning, organization and management of the national economy', but the changes went further than any 'reform' previously attempted in People's Poland. The Committee reported on 12 April 1972, and the changes were partially introduced in 1973–5. In brief, the changes included a decisive role for large corporations (*Wielkie Organizacje Gospodarcze*, literally 'large economic organizations') and an accompanying rise in industrial concentration; the replacement of many directive indicators with parametric policy instruments; the use of net value added and profit as the two main indicators of economic performance; the linking of the wage fund (formerly subject to planned 'limits', in the sense of 'budgets') to the value added of enterprises; the linking of management bonuses and investment funds to enterprise profits; progressive taxation of enterprise funds to prevent excessive inter-industry and inter-firm variability of earnings (which had been reported in Hungary); a percentage turnover tax (instead of an absolute turnover tax absorbing differences between actual prices and enterprise full costs); the use of actual internal and international prices in enterprise accounting; the generalization of the principles of credit repayment and interest charges; greater self-finance and the retention by enterprises of part of the foreign currency earned; greater access to foreign currency borrowing. In sum, the changes proposed amounted to a genuine increase in the autonomy and responsibility of enterprises, especially of those large corporations turned into pilot units (*jednostki inicjujące*) under new statutes, with parameters diversified by sector of operation, and retention of the central planning of investment and macro-economic balance (see Pinkowski, 1972; *Zarys*, 1973; PTE, 1974; Nuti, 1977, and below).

From the beginning of 1973 a number of large corporations were put under the new principles of operation, on a 'voluntary' basis (though it seems to have been more a case of *lekki przymus*, or 'gentle compulsion'). By the end of 1973 there were 27 pilot units representing nearly 30 per cent of all sales of goods and services at realization prices and over 18 per cent of employment. They included the entire chemical industry, over 40 per cent of the output of the machine industry, building and building-materials industry. By mid 1974, the hundred or so pilot units whose new statutes had already been approved represented nearly 50 per cent of industrial production and over 40 per cent of employment in the whole of socialized industry.

In 1975 about 80 per cent of manufacturing was expected to operate under the new system, but the reform was not in fact extended as anticipated. The economy was suffering from the pressure of an extremely ambitious plan of investment, modernization and growth; the repercussions of the international crisis, which unfortunately coincided with a greater opening of the Polish economy to international trade and finance; the loss of central control over investment, wages and price levels. In these circumstances, central controls were restored, with the recentralization of decision powers to the level of branch ministries. The reform was effectively suspended (see below). A new design, more detailed and thought out, aimed at modifying the planning system as a whole rather than simply economic organizations, was formulated in 1980 and expected to be fully implemented by 1 January 1983 (see below). The economic crisis of 1980 and the extensive political and institutional changes of August–September 1980 have probably postponed the date by which the Polish economy can achieve the state of tranquillity necessary for the introduction of significant reforms; a new factor has arisen, under the guise of independent self-managed unions, which in spite of the Polish tradition of 'frustrated spontaneity' in workers' self-management (see below) is potentially very important in shaping macro-economic policy and therefore the environment of reforms.

The evolution of the Polish industrial enterprise illustrates, perhaps better than the experience of any other Eastern European country, including the Soviet Union, three general aspects of the socialist economy: (1) the connection between economic policy (in particular accumulation policy) and the viability of patterns of economic organizations (see also Nuti, 1979); (2) the greater proclivity of communist leaders to undertake organizational change than to revise their policy of high and accelerated accumulation, leading to a contradiction between reformed institutions and their economic environment; (3) the illusory character of apparent similarities between the 'socialist' enterprise and its counterpart in the capitalist economy.

THE 1973–5 REFORM: DEPOLARIZATION

The 'large corporations' of the 1973–5 reform were industrial associations, combines (a dozen or so vertically integrated establishments, which had been set up in the late sixties under the influence of the German experience) and multiplant enterprises, operating under new statutes that gave them economic autonomy and accountability. Most of them were already in existence at the time of the reform and simply changed their status; others were set up as a result of a process of industrial concentration, merging units formerly belonging to an industrial association into a single enterprise, or units formerly attached to local authorities with enterprises already belonging to an industrial association, or industrial associations into a single enterprise (on the concentration process, see Nuti, 1977). No clear policy emerged: concentration lagged behind in sectors (such as foundries) with obvious advantages from economies of scale, and progressed fast in sectors where little advantage could have been expected (such as furniture or confectionery). There were complaints of 'concentration fetishism' (Jakubowicz, 1973). Basically, the case for concentration rested not only on the genuine technological need for large-size units to reap economies of·scale (including organizational economies in vertical integration) but also, indeed primarily, on the sheer organizational convenience, from the viewpoint of the central planners, of having to deal with at most a few hundred units to control and steer effectively the bulk of the national economy. The essential feature of the reform was that large corporations were empowered and expected to act as *enterprises* rather than as quasi-ministerial administrative units. Yet the changes envisaged could not be described as 'decentralization', in view of the parallel concentration of output and delegation of powers from smaller producing units to the 'large corporation' encompassing them; a more appropriate description is perhaps 'depolarization', or the delegation to large corporations of powers previously belonging to higher and lower levels (see Nuti, 1977).

A major new power vested in the large corporations and the lower units belonging to them was their discretion in determining employment and wages policy, subject to a statutory connection between the growth rates of value added and the corporation's wage fund. The growth rate of the wage fund at the disposal of enterprises was to be a fraction, R (an elasticity coefficient varying in different sectors and enterprises, but *consistently lower than unity*, within the range 0.3 to 0.95), of the growth of value added (a slightly different formulation was adopted in the building industry: see Nuti, 1977). This provision amounted to a built-in mechanism for the reduction of the wage share in value added, and can be interpreted as the micro-economic counterpart of a macro-economic policy of rising accumulation and other non-consumption expenditure (as a share of national income), as well as a provision for a contingency reserve, or safety factor. Excess wage (and workers' bonus) payments over the disposable wage fund could be financed by borrowing (at a penal rate, and with managers forfeiting their own bonuses), while any surplus over actual payments could be carried over as reserves. In theory, this formula introduces the possibility of raising average wages by reducing the growth of value added and employment, but there is no evidence that corporations followed restrictive employment policies — on the contrary, their new powers led to a continued pressure on the labour market.

Value added (or rather 'production added', or *produkcja dodana*), for the purpose of determining the disposable wage fund of enterprises, differed from the familiar Western concept in that it was net of interest payments on borrowed capital (but gross of amortization); also, 'incorrect profit' (*zysk nieprawidłowy*), namely, the excess profit which is either independent of enterprise activity or due to illegal or improper activity, was deducted from value added. A substantial innovation was the use of international prices in the valuation of the enterprise's output (which had been discontinued in 1971). A double system of 'multipliers' (for the three groups of socialist, capitalist and third-world countries and for individual countries within each group) converted international prices in Polish *złotys* at what amounted to a system of floating shadow exchange rates. This, in addition to the use of current realization prices for internal sales, effectively introduced a mechanism for the transmission of inflation from prices to wages. The increased dependence of workers' earnings on actual enterprise performance was not accompanied by an increase in workers' participation in the management of enterprises (the dependence, however, was not as great as if workers' incomes had been linked to profits, rather than value added).

Managers were given material incentives from a bonus fund linked to profits in the guise of a given share in the net profits of their enterprises. The share, within the range 1.5 to 5 per cent, was fixed by ministries for a number of years and was subject to a steeply progressive tax on the growth of the fund with respect to the base position, the payment of bonuses being conditional on wage payments not exceeding the disposable wage fund.

Enterprise profits, up to a statutory maximum fixed by ministries as a percentage of the total capital employed by the enterprise (within the 3 to 9 per cent range), could be retained by the enterprise in its Development Fund, without being subject to tax, further retentions being subject to a very steep tax rate of 80 per cent rising to 90 per cent for retentions exceeding the tax-free threshold by 2 per cent of the capital employed. This was an extremely generous provision for decentralized investment, unprecedented in Eastern Europe. The share of tax-free profits that could be retained by the enterprise for decentralized investment was not determined as such, but was defined by the ratio between the tax-free retainable profits (as a percentage of capital employed) and the profit rate actually earned by the enterprise. For instance, an enterprise with a 4 per cent tax-free development fund allowance and an actual profit rate of 6 per cent was effectively allowed to retain and invest at its own discretion 2/3 of its profits; for plausible assumptions about profit rates the tax-free retentions allowed were reasonably large even by Western standards. In addition, enterprises were given greater access to bank borrowing (at a basic interest rate of 8 per cent, subsidized for particular sectors, such as mining, or uses), subject to the application of new discounted cash flow methods of Western type (see Czarnek and Glikman, 1974; *Ocena*, 1974; Nuti, 1977). The generous provisions for both reinvestment of profits and access to borrowed funds clearly contributed to an exacerbation of the accumulation propensity of the Polish economy.

Finally, one final form of managerial inducement was the retention by pilot units of a certain amount of any foreign currency they earned (over and above allocations for imports of materials, machinery and licences, assigned by ministries). The retention of export earnings was expressed as a share, D, of either the value of exports or its increase from the previous period. This was accompanied by a greater direct involvement of enterprises in export promotion and price negotiations, with specialized foreign trade corporations acting merely as their agents. In addition, enterprises were given greater access to international credit, primarily via the ministries to which they belonged, within the Gierek policy of modernization and technology transfer.

In conclusion, the blueprint for industrial organization established in a large section of Polish industry in the early seventies had a distinct Hungarian hallmark, in that it allowed enterprises (large corporations and sometimes their constituent units) a considerable latitude as to their wages and employment, price-fixing (especially for new products), investment and involvement in the international market. Research on the perception by managers of the changes introduced with the new system indicated a considerable and general increase of autonomy on wages and, on the whole, on development decisions and production and sales; while, perhaps surprisingly, some decrease in decision-making autonomy was perceived with respect to supply, industrial cooperation and employment (Poznański, 1974).

The impact of the new system of planning and management on the performance of pilot units and the entire Polish economy is clearly difficult to assess. The new system spread unevenly in different sectors; pilot units were not representative of the whole economy; the timing coincided with rapid economic changes in international trade and finance, the energy crisis and world inflation and recession. In addition, what happens during the transition from one system to another may not necessarily indicate the relative effectiveness of the two systems; a longer time horizon is needed for a conclusive assessment. The hundred or so pilot units converted to the new system by the end of 1974 exhibited a moderately above-average performance in sales, value added, labour employment and productivity, profits and exports, while significant economies of materials were registered (see Nuti, 1977, section 10, on the economic performance of the pilot units and the Polish economy). The results were encouraging, but clearly the performance of pilot units was linked to the success or failure of the Gierek model of accumulation, modernization and growth; the initial success of this policy, due to a notable improvement in Polish terms of trade in the early seventies and the ability to run substantial deficits, especially with the advanced capitalist countries, was bound to come to a halt, and affect the prospects of economic reform. (See Nuti, 1977a: 'If the constraints set by international trade make themselves felt in the near future, as it appears probable, the internal tensions created by the ambitious accumulation policy and the built-in propensity to overinvest might slow down or even reverse the current reforms, at least in the short run'.)

RECENTRALIZATION IN THE LATE SEVENTIES

The reform of large corporations introduced in 1973–4 worked roughly until 1976, though the system was not extended further to the rest of the economy. Rapidly, however, the system exhibited serious drawbacks. Under the pressure of the accumulation effort and imported inflation, open and hidden (through pseudo-novelties), price increases practised by large corporations inflated their sales and 'added production' indicators, defeating the cost-reducing purpose of the reform. Given the commitment to contain the prices of essential products, such price rises were actually consistent with the maintenance of macro-economic equilibrium, and were therefore tolerated, although this later led to social criticism of the pricing practices of large corporations. Wage payments linked to output values at current prices got out of hand; the problem was handled administratively by direct controls, thereby defeating the logic of the reform.

Almost from the beginning of the reform, a 'blockade' (*blokada*) on employment by large corporations was introduced and progressively extended, constraining employment to historical levels or even forcing a decline through natural wastage; in 1976–8 these powers to control and contain employment levels by large corporations were decentralized to ministries and provinces (voivodships), but still maintained. Naturally this encouraged labour hoarding, prevented redeployment and rationalization and reduced the efficiency in the use of labour, a very scarce resource in the Polish economy.

As early as 1975 large corporations were instructed to set aside compulsory wage reserves out of their disposable wage funds. In 1976 the link between wage fund and 'added production' was constrained by a stricter link between wages and labour productivity, according to an elasticity coefficient, O, individually set for the various large enterprises by a central committee. The income normative 'O' led to a lower wage fund because of the value of the parameter and because labour productivity growth for this purpose was calculated at *constant* instead of *current* prices. The difference between the wage fund deriving from the 'added production' formula and that deriving from the 'income normative' was set aside as reserves, under the supervision of branch ministries, which in 1977–8 acquired increasing importance, signalling a re-centralization process. Nevertheless, wage payments continued to get out of hand; as a Planning Commission officer declared in May 1980, 'If you don't pay them what they want, they won't do the work', and one way or another workers' passive reluctance to keep up the pace of work (the same kind of reluctance theorized and implemented by some Western workers' political groupings) led to mounting above-plan wage payments, which eventually led to further controls through the banking system and stiff penalties for enterprises exceeding their norms.

In spite of controls, wage payments continued to exceed norms, leading to a rapid increase in cash balances held by the population (between 1971 and 1977 these balances increased 3.3 times and attained a level roughly half the value of the annual wage bill). Official preoccupation with this phenomenon is reflected, for instance in the 10 June 1980 resolution of the Council of Ministers, stipulating bank control over wage payments by corporations and ministries, confirming the witholding of all bonuses and awards in case of wage overspending, interest on borrowing for wage payments being a prior claim on the management bonus fund, and forcing directors of enterprises with a record of overspending to present a programme aimed at eliminating excessive wage payments.

Beside wage payments the decentralized investments of large corporations, out of their development funds and access to credits, were also getting out of hand. Reinvestment provisions were too generous, interest rates too low, and the application of discounted cash flow methods remained a dead letter ('The analysis of investment effectiveness — if it took place at all — was often no more than a hobby for a few specialists': Glikman, 1980). The corporations' propensity to overinvest was reinforced by pressure from local authorities. This problem was also handled by direct controls, setting investment 'limits' (i.e., budgets) for individual large corporations. As in the case of wages, above-plan investments continued to be an endemic feature of the Polish economy in the second half of the seventies, leading to discussions of the 'excessive propensity to invest' in the economy (Kotowicz-Jawor, 1979). The provision for large enterprises to retain a share, D, of their export earnings in practice was scarcely applied (though it was reinstated for 16 corporations in early June 1980), but all the same enterprises found access to foreign currency easy, in view of the trading and borrowing policy followed by the government.

With minor formal modifications, introduced in the spring of 1977, the large enterprise regime formally survived to date. Procedures for the calculations of 'added production', initially differing between enterprises in the treatment of tax, actual or 'transaction' prices and other details, were made uniform so as to be susceptible of aggregation, and streamlined consistently with the purposes of the reform (transaction prices were extended to inputs as well as output, tax was excluded from the calculation in order to convey to enterprises the wishes of the government, new principles for the pricing of new products were based on the price of close substitutes, etc.). But in practice a substantial recentralization took place, with the strengthening of branch ministries (see Szydlak, 1977; Golinowski, 1977; Hołubicki, 1977, with an appendix listing the relevant legal documents, among which *Uchwała*, 1977, unpublished).

Besides the greater power of branch ministries there are many other symptoms of the re-centralization process: in the second half of the seventies the staff of the Central Planning Commission rose from 1100 to 1500; the number of material balances compiled by central organs rose from 800 to 1200, additional balances being also drawn to an increasing extent by large corporations (especially industry associations) for the rationing of scarce materials between its internal units; according to samples taken in 1978 by the Zespół Metodiki Planowania i Systemu Funkcjonania Gospodarki of the Polish Central Planning Commission, in 45 enterprises (internal units) belonging to 13 groupings the number of practically compulsory indices oscillated within the 50 to 150 range. In practice, 'the old system exhibited a strong tendency to reproduce itself' (Mujżel, 1980).

The re-centralization trend was the object of a sharp debate in the Polish press. The editor of *Polityka*, Mieczysław Rakowski, pointed out the practical limits of centralization and complained that 'excessive centralization can lead to the harmful limitation of initiative, and effectively free the decision-makers from real responsibility' (1977a). Ratyński (a researcher attached to the Central Committee of the Polish United Workers' Party [CC of PZPR], 1977) replied that the de-centralization option was not open to the Polish economy; it was equivalent to the extension of bourgeois management methods to the socialist economy, and therefore a 'revisionist' move, it conflicted with 'democratic centralism' and did not meet the needs of the working masses. A more conciliatory view was expressed by Chądzinski, who focused on *types* of de-centralization models (recalling the Soviet *sovnarkhozy* reform of 1957) and argued that initiative and responsibility could be strengthened within a centralized model. In a bitter reply Rakowski (1977b) rejected the 'revisionist' label as a poor substitute for a case, stressed that he had attacked *excessive* centralization (rather begging the question, *excessive* centralization being harmful by definition), accepted the *principle* of democratic centralism, but argued that not all changes of decisional competence are necessarily a threat to the socialist system, claiming the existence of a broad area for possible and desirable organizational changes. He invoked Lenin and the Party's *pogrudniowa* (i.e., 'post-December') 1970 policy and stressed the political and moral implications of de-centralization. Re-centralization, nevertheless, continued.

Re-centralization, however, did not mean that the 'Centre' had a firm control over macro-economic processes. The irreconcilable claims of different economic agents and the over-ambitious conflicting targets set for the economy led to the practical disintegration of central control. There was a proliferation of 'priorities' (exports, essential consumption goods, completion of half-finished investment projects, modernization, motorization, housing, armaments), which is a contradiction in terms: priority by definition is attributable to one objective only, and even in that case is difficult to implement in an economy characterized by complex inter-sectoral links, where the progress of the priority sector could be hindered by the neglect of sectors delivering essential *inputs* to it. In spite of re-centralization, supplies to both enterprises and consumers became increasingly disrupted.

THE NEW DESIGN FOR THE EIGHTIES

The retreat from the 1973—5 reform was primarily due to three reasons:

1. The finer details of the system introduced in 1973 had not been worked out, nor the full implications anticipated. The reformers knew this, but expected the new system to take shape and improve in the light of experience. For this to happen, another two years or so of operation would have been needed, but, as noted above, the timing was unfortunate, coinciding with the energy crisis, world inflation and depression, and the optimistic expectation of reformers, plausible as it was at the time, was disappointed.
2. The reform altered the organization of enterprises and the rules of the game, without touching the economic environment in which they operated, that is, an unchanged planning system. (Indeed the reorganized enterprises were

never really allowed to play according to the new rules and the planning
system became, gradually, even less suited to the new organizations.) This
was probably the result of a compromise between reformers and supporters
of the status quo, which denied to the proposed system the chance to prove
itself.

3. At the time of the reform the economy was about to embark on the most
ambitious programme of accumulation and growth acceleration, with record
levels of accumulation shares in national income, exceeding 35 per cent
(including inventory increases). A time of such an over-ambitious programme
of investment, modernization and growth is no time for relaxing central
controls, as experience subsequently showed. Markets are no good if buyers
or sellers are 'rationed' at the ruling prices, that is, they cannot choose
freely the volume of their transactions at those prices.

The new wave of reforms being planned early in 1980 was a serious attempt
at dealing with these drawbacks: further theoretical research and reflection on
experience had led to a clearer picture of enterprise typology and division of
competence between economic agents; the system as a whole was also being
considered; while the timing of the exercise had been scheduled for gradual
implementation, with completion by 1 January 1983, that is, at a time when
current supply problems were expected to have eased with the massive recent
accumulation effort coming to fruition at last.

The sharper definition of the new enterprise contours is exemplified in a
study on 'Organizational Structures of Complex Economic Organizations'
emanating from the Planning Institute of the Central Planning Commission
(Jakubowicz, 1980). Figure 3.1 reproduces the envisaged typology of such

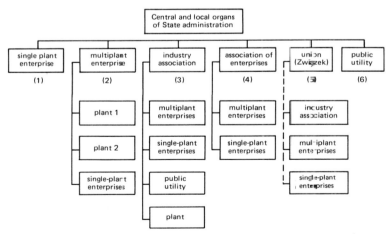

Figure 3.1 *Typology of economic organizations in Polish industry:_____ = line of subordination; – – – – = line of coordination. From Jakubowicz (1980).*

Table 3.1   Division of competence in various types of complex economic organizations

	Multiplant enterprises		*Industry associations*		*Associations of enterprises*		*Union of enterprises*	
Competences	*enterprise*	*internal units*	*association*	*internal units*	*association*	*internal units*	*union*	*internal units*
I. *Internal relations*								
1. Entitlement to take decisions about								
(a) current production[a]	+	–	+	–	–	+	–	+
(b) development[b]	+	–	+	–	+[c]	–	–	+
(c) employment and wages								
– of members of internal units management	+	–	+	–	+	–	–	+
– of other staff of internal units	–	+	–	+	–	+	–	+
(d) social welfare of internal units	–	+	–	+	–	+	–	+
(e) internal organization of internal units	–	+	–	+	–	+	–	+
2. Instruments for directing internal units								
– mostly direct	+		+				0	
– mostly indirect	–		–		+		0	
3. Contract between internal units on the functioning of the whole organization	–		–		+		+	
4. Management of the economic organization								
– designated by the centre	+		+		+		–	
– chosen by internal units	–		–		–		+	
5. Legal personality of internal units	–		+		+		+	
6. Chairman of the board of the economic organization								
– appointed by the centre	+		+		–		0	
– chosen by the internal units	–		–		+		0	
7. Financial result of internal units								
– at realization prices	–(+)		+(–)		+		+	
– at accounting (*rozliczeniowy*) prices	+(–)		–(+)		–		–	

Table 3.1 (contd)

	Types							
	Multiplant enterprises		Industry associations		Associations of enterprises		Union of enterprises	
Competences	*enterprise*	*internal units*	*association*	*internal units*	*association*	*internal units*	*union*	*internal units*
8. Financial results determine and form								
− development fund[d]	+	−	+	+	+	+	−(+)	+
− bonus fund[d]	+	−	+	+	−	+	−	+
− socio-cultural fund	−	+	−	+	−	+	−	+
9. Redistribution of means of production and capital between internal units								
− against payment	−		+		0		0	
− without payment	+		−		0		0	
II. *External legal–financial relations*								
10. Subject of relation								
− with centre	+	−	+	−	+	+	+	+
− with local authorities	−	+	−	+	−	+	−	+
11. Subject of relations with State budget	+	−	+	−	−	+	−	+
12. Subject of relations with bank system								
− investment credit	+	−	+	−	+	+	−(+)	+
− circulating capital	+	−(+)	−	+	−	+	−	+
13. Subject of relations with suppliers and buyers	+	−(+)	+(−)	+(−)	−	+	−	+
14. Responsibility vis-à-vis the centre about the results of internal units	+	−	+	−	−	+	−	+

+ = Yes; − = No; +(−) = Yes, but possibly no in determined conditions. −(+) = no, but possibly yes in determined conditions; 0 = not applicable.

a   What and how much to produce, from whom to buy and to whom to sell.
b   Level and direction of investment and R & D expenditure.
c   Associations of enterprises take decisions only about investment and research concerning the whole organization.
d   Part of the development fund is subject to centralization in both forms of association. In addition, the industry association also centralizes part of the bonus fund.

From Jakubowicz (1980).

organizations in Polish industry: the one-plant enterprise directly dependent on central or local organs, the enterprise with two or more plants (one possibly taking a leading role and itself having the basic features of the enterprise); centralized groupings of single and multiplant enterprises and, possibly, of subordinate plants, or of public utilities, having the status of an enterprise and being responsible to the centre for the results of its components ('internal units'); a looser grouping of enterprises, all partners in association, without itself having the attributes of an enterprise, but centralizing common functions especially in investment, research and international trade; even looser 'unions' of enterprises, based on contracts under civil and not administrative law; public utilities and other organizational forms not subject to principles of maximization of financial indicators. The degree of economic independence varies in the different organizational forms; this is not a simple exercise in taxonomy, but the foundation of a detailed proposal for the precise scope of responsibility and decision-making by the centre, the complex organization and its internal units. This detailed picture is summarized in Table 3.1: it is no more than a semi-official proposal, but the important point is that a very wide range of angles is covered and hardly anything is left to improvisation.

The need for a 'total' approach to economic reform is stated neatly by Mujżel (1980): 'A precondition of effectiveness of system changes is their completeness'. Not only are large corporations involved, but local arrangements, micro/macro-economic interdependencies, international contracts, sectoral decisions, and above all *supply links*. The time horizon of operational planning is shifted from the annual to the five year plan, affording greater flexibility in dealing with unexpected events. All indicators are in value terms, but instead of value added the notions of product, profit, final output take the dominant place. More initiative is envisaged for lower level, social bodies and agencies and not just enterprises, rather than taking Planning Commission directives as the starting point of economic planning. The relative scope of competence and responsibility of Planning Commission and ministries is to be defined, with a greater involvement of ministries in planning. The link between wages and productivity growth is maintained and strengthened, as a basis for incomes and prices policy. All in all, the system envisaged early in 1980 for Poland in the eighties is closer to the Hungarian reform than the 1973–5 blueprint.

The expectation that tensions and shortages would be overcome in time for an early introduction of the reform, however, was badly disappointed by the mounting economic crisis that progressively disrupted the Polish economy and society and brought the economic machine to a grinding halt in August 1980.

THE 1980 ECONOMIC CRISIS

Like all other East European countries, Poland recorded a declining growth rate of income in the second half of the seventies. An average annual growth rate of 9 per cent in 1970–75 was followed by rates of 6.8 per cent in 1976, 5 per cent in 1977, 3 per cent in 1978 (*Rocznik*, 1979), against a planned average rate of 7.3 per cent in the five year plan, and planned rates of 8.3 per cent, 5.7 per cent and 5.4 per cent in annual plans. 1979 has been the worst post-war year for Comecon countries, but among them Poland has the worst record, relative to both its own plans and to the other countries. In 1979 income produced actually fell by 1.9 per cent and income distributed fell by 1.8 per cent (IKCHZ, 1980), an unprecedented occurrence in post-war Poland. Prospects for 1980 were equally discouraging in mid year, and the modest growth of 1.6 per cent planned for 1980 was not expected to be implemented.

External disequilibrium prevailed during the 1970s. The trade deficit was 0.2 billion foreign exchange złotys in 1970, 7.5 billion in 1975 and 4.1 billion in 1979, while the Polish trade balance with capitalist countries (including underdeveloped countries with which a surplus is traditionally maintained) was 0.6 billion foreign currency złotys in 1970, -6.9 billion in 1976 and -5.2 billion in 1979. In 1979 foreign indebtedness rose from $15 to $17 billion, thus overtaking Soviet indebtedness and taking first place among Comecon countries, and rose further to $19 billion by mid 1980. This indebtedness had internal repercussions in the form of a growing 'internal export' (i.e., sales of imported and exportable goods to the public against foreign currency, including goods in scarce supply in ordinary shops) and a growing government borrowing of foreign currency from Polish citizens (with generous interest payments and provisions for the export of foreign currency to finance foreign travel); also, exportable goods were being sold abroad, because of financial stringency, in spite of being in scarce supply domestically, leading to a deterioration in supplies to consumers and firms.

Open inflation, an unfamiliar phenomenon since the mid fifties, appeared; the cost of living index rose at the following rates (*Rocznik*, 1979):

1971	1972	1973	1974	1975	1976	1977	1978
-1.2	0.0	2.6	6.8	3.0	4.7	4.9	8.7

In 1979 the index rose by 6.7 per cent (IKCHZ, 1980), but in the first half of 1980, even before the June increase in the price of meat, inflation was reported to be in the two-digit range on an annual basis. At the end of 1977 a two-tier market for meat was introduced, whereby 'commercial' state shops sold meat at a price considerably higher (up to three or four times) than did ordinary shops, where meat was cheaper but scarcer. In 1978 'commercial' meat sales were 8 per cent of total sales, rising to 18 per cent in 1979. In June 1980 the share of meat sales reserved to commercial shops was increased further. (Meat scarcity in Poland has been perhaps overplayed. Polish meat consumption is relatively high and has been rising rapidly from 43 kg per head in 1960 to 73 kg in 1979; these figures exclude poultry.) Open inflation was partly fed by world inflation and by the enterprises' ability to fix prices, especially for new products (see above), as well as the loss of control over wage payments and investments (see above).

In addition to open inflation, the occasional shortages of consumption goods, a familiar feature of central planning and tolerable at times of growing standards of living, became persistent and endemic. Shortages extended from food to many other consumption goods of daily use, against a background of unsatisfied demand for durables, from housing to furniture and motor cars. In March 1979 the Ministry of Internal trade listed 280 products for which demand was difficult to satisfy and there is no doubt that the list grew longer in the following year. Apart from popular irritation, shortages have other adverse consequences, such as the ineffectiveness of monetary incentives; the indiscriminate purchase and hoarding of anything handy consumers might be able to acquire, leading to waste and the inefficient distribution of goods, and causing shortages even of goods available in quantities normally sufficient to satisfy population needs; the rapid growth of black or 'grey' markets in which deficit goods are obtained at a higher price, or through 'connections' (*po znajomości*) or corruption, most people busily 'fixing' (*załatfiać*) each other's purchases. In these conditions the private sector thrived in the old areas of market gardening, handicraft, building and restaurants, and in new areas, such as motorcar repair. A 'second' or 'parallel' economy developed, broadly tolerated by the authorities because it actually fulfilled a social need and reduced pressure on the 'official' economy. The population resented not only the shortages, but the resulting unequal distribution of access to goods and services (as confirmed by widespread demands for meat rationing and for the abolition of 'internal exports' of deficit goods in August 1980). Some rationing was introduced in 1980; for instance, for sugar (though at the generous rate of 2 kg per worker per month), replaced in June 1980 by a price increase compensated for by wages rises, a pattern subsequently followed by the compensatory wage increases successfully obtained after the first strikes of July 1980.

Inevitably, consumption scarcities spilled over into the supply of materials and semi-finished products to enterprises, especially for imported inputs. Like consumers, firms hoard inventories of materials which are too high (they increased in 1979 by 7 per cent, that is, three times as fast as industrial production) and badly distributed (the Planning Commission last spring started a survey in 25 sectors in order to establish where in the economy inventories were being hoarded unnecessarily). At the same time, inventory levels were not sufficient to sustain continued production levels in many sectors, shortages being most apparent for paper, rolled steel, copper, plastic materials, cardboard, coal, and imported inputs. In the allocation of scarce materials the priority system was extended (see above). Shortages, of course, had a 'multiplier' effect, leading to chain losses of output and incomes. In short the whole economic system at the end of the seventies was subject to tensions and scarcities which compromised its efficiency and made nonsense of any plan for decentralization or reform.

The crisis cannot be satisfactorily explained by exogenous factors, such as natural causes, or the energy crisis and the ensuing world recession. It is true that Poland has had more than its fair share of natural disasters (frost, snow, floods) adversely affecting agriculture, building and transport, with indirect repercussions on the rest of the economy. The oil crisis has led to the importation of some inflation, and the world recession caused difficulties with exports and debt servicing (through high interest rates). But the decline of Polish growth is a long-term tendency, the agricultural crisis is chronic and due to institutional factors and economic policies, especially in investment; Poland has been and still is a net energy exporter (though net exports have fallen from 24 per cent of domestic consumption of energy in 1960 to 9 per cent in 1978, and more recently have been further eroded); Polish terms of trade have fluctuated since 1973 around a stationary trend. Nor can the slowdown of population growth, expected to continue into the next decade, explain per se the reductions in the growth rate, or actual falls, in income and consumption *per head*. Another explanation of the crisis attributes major responsibility to the incompetence or negligence of individuals; thus early in 1980 the Prime Minister and the Minister of Building were replaced and in May directors and deputy directors of 84 enterprises in the building industry were dismissed 'for gross neglect of their responsibilities'; 61 directors of State and collective enterprise were also dismissed; but when the phenomenon is so widespread clearly responsibility must be sought above the individual level.

The prime cause of the Polish crisis seems to be the over-ambitious and unchecked policies of accumulation followed under Gomułka and accelerated by Gierek, especially in his first five years, which brought up the share of accumulation in national income distributed from 25.4 per cent in 1969 to the record levels of 35.6 per cent in 1974 and 35.2 per cent in 1975. In the second half of the seventies the share of accumulation declined slightly, to 30.8 per cent of national income in 1978, but the decline was by and large decided at the time and not planned long beforehand. As a consequence the adverse pattern of the broadening of the 'investment front' with the start of a large number of projects in the early seventies, later starved of resources for completion, led to the lengthening of gestation periods of investment and the 'freezing' of resources in a form that provided neither means of consumption for the population nor exportable products, frustrating Gierek's policy of modernization and growth. Investment exceeded the absorption capacity of the system particularly in the building industry, which was later stricken by the disciplinary measures mentioned, in the construction of plants and the installation of machinery (Kotowicz-Jawor, 1979). Excessive investment demand had a negative impact on economic equilibrium, worsening the balance between the structure of demand and supply, the imbalance spilling over into the external sector; ambitious output targets led to the neglect of investment aimed at renovating existing plants in favour of new plants, lengthening the lag between investment and output. It appears that in 1971–5 the sum of investment planned by investing agencies (*rezorty*, i.e., primarily ministries) exceeded by 15.2 per cent the guidelines of the central plan; in 1976 by 25.8 per cent; investment plans in turn tended to be over-fulfilled, with enterprises stepping up their requirements once they had succeeded in 'hiking themselves onto the plan', a tendency which was stronger the lower the level at which investment decisions were taken (Kotowicz-Jawor, 1979). The absence of responsibility for unsuccessful investment decisions is often regarded as a major reason for this over-accumulation, but it is equally plausible to blame the collapse of central investment planning, traditionally regarded as a fundamental feature of the socialist economy.

Whatever its causes, the crisis explains the continued suspension of the reform; the combination of more intensive central controls, disintegration of central planning and a continued search for new organizational formulas. The eventual transformation of the economic into a political crisis was resolved with the extensive changes of August–September 1980: a change of leadership, the legalization of strikes, the formation of new, independent and self-managed unions, the extension of civil liberties, and an average increase of 10 per cent in the total wage bill. These changes, in turn, affect both the prospects of a further reform of Polish industrial enterprises and the environment in which these reformed enterprises would operate.

THE RISE, FALL AND REVIVAL OF WORKERS' SELF-MANAGEMENT

One of the factors turning the economic into a political crisis in August 1980 was the deliberate, progressive demolition, from 1975 onwards, of workers' councils, something which seems to have escaped the attention of Western observers. Workers' councils, spontaneously formed by workers early in 1956, were legalized by a law of 19 November 1956 which authorized them at the request of a majority of the workers, in order to 'realize the initiative of workers by direct participation with enterprise management, subject to respecting existing laws and the national economic plan' (*Ustawa*, 1956, art. 1). Among their tasks we find: adoption of the annual production plan, decisions on the internal organization of enterprises, quality control, labour productivity control, hygiene and work safety; work conditions, wage levels, bonuses and incentives, distribution of the enterprise fund; direct participation in the appointment and dismissal of the enterprise director. Next to the new workers' councils, there remained the old 'factory council'. Important decisions were to be taken jointly: cases of disagreement between the two councils were to be adjudicated by the workers' assembly. The law emphasized the purely internal functions of workers' councils and explicitly ruled out links between workers' councils at the national level. The Party bureaucracy, threatened by the increasing autonomy of enterprises and rising powers of both director and workers' councils in the internal life of enterprises, opposed the new organs. The IXth Plenum of the PZPR Central Committee in May 1957 put workers' councils under the direct control of the enterprise trade union. The director was instructed not to conform to workers' councils' decisions if he considered them to conflict with the law or plan, disagreements between workers' councils and directors being settled by a higher body. On 20 December 1958 a new law limited further their power and established a new organ, the KSR ('conference of workers' self-management'), composed of the factory council, the workers' council, the 'factory committee of PZPR' and the 'factory office of the union socialist youth' (*Ustawa*, 1958).

The KSR was expected to meet at least once a quarter, and its competence included general supervision and control over the running of the enterprise; participation in formulating basic development decisions; rationalization of enterprise activity; formulation of work regulations; distribution of enterprise funds among employees; approving the elected chairman or presidium of the workers' council. In practice, '. . . unfortunately, but not surprisingly, KSR played a very limited role in planning and plan implementation in the enterprise. One would be almost justified in saying none at all if not for the fact that the KSR are used by enterprise management as a "rubber stamp", especially for their more far-reaching deviations from plan targets' (Zielinski, 1973c). The KSR area of responsibility was very vaguely defined: 'It could have done much but did not have to; its partners could, but did not have to pay heed to them' (Kulpińska, 1980).

This limited role of workers' councils within the KSR was completely obliterated in 1975. Section 25 of the 12 December 1958 Law states that the Central Trade Union Council (CRZZ) determines election procedures for workers' councils, the number of council and presidium members, their terms of office, and recall procedures for elected council members; it can also dissolve councils in specific cases, for instance 'when a council's actions are against the interests of the national economy'. In 1975 the CRZZ exceeded its brief very considerably: it issued instructions on elections to trade unions and workers' councils, allowing (indeed encouraging) enterprise trade unions not to organize the election of workers' councils, for the sake of 'simplification' on the ground that workers' councils duplicated trade union councils with which they were allegedly confused. The function of the presidium was taken over by the 'directorial college'; the problem-specialized committees of the KSR were replaced by groups of administrative workers. This was no 'simplification'; it was the 'elimination of essential elements' (Kulpińska, 1980). Most enterprises took up the suggestion and already in 1976 there remained workers' councils in only one-quarter of enterprises (or rather plants, *zakłady*; see *Rocznik Statystyczny*,

1976); it is estimated that in 1980 workers' councils existed at most in 10 per cent of Polish enterprises.

Workers began to be under-represented within the KSR, so that in 1978 the Politbureau of the PZPR recommended the co-option (by trade union and Party members) of a dozen workers to the structure of each KSR in order to maintain some balance in its membership. Having thus eliminated any chance of genuine workers' participation in management, Gierek called for a national meeting of KSRs to encourage the further development of self-management under the leadership of the party.

This state of affairs, described by a Polish jurist as 'disgraceful' and 'unconstitutional', is likely to have conditioned the course of the August 1980 crisis since the only formal channel of communication for the expression of workers' views and needs, outside Party and trade union lines, was no longer there when it was most needed. The rise and fall of workers' councils from 1956 to 1980 are also bound to influence the process of legalization and evolution of the newly-born 'self-managed trade unions', which appear not only to have reinstated the powers formerly belonging to workers' councils, but to have gone very much further in their autonomy: above all there is the prospect of genuine workers' participation in the formation of basic macro-economic decisions such as the rate of accumulation, income distribution, wage and prices policy (traditionally the preserve of central planning) and creating the opportunity for politicians and workers to negotiate a 'social pact'.

CURRENT PROSPECTS FOR ENTERPRISE REFORM

The recent Baltic events and the terms of the settlement between strikers and government are bound to affect the prospects for enterprise reform, not so much directly (through possible but imponderable changes in the new leadership's attitude to reform) but indirectly, through the impact of the settlement on the level of excess demand in the economy. On the one hand, the strike losses and the wage increases (amounting to 10 per cent of the total wage bill) must have increased the level of excess demand and, in view of the leadership commitment to contain price increases, reduced the chances of early de-centralization. On the other hand, the new trade unions might exercise a restraining influence on government accumulation and growth policy, as well as pressure on wages; whatever the new trade unions' chances of effective participation and influence, the recent successful wage claims and the danger of an inflationary price—wage spiral are likely to have the same effect; this de facto restraining influence of workers on the leadership amounting to a form of 'wage-push democracy'. Additional borrowing might provide some relief from excess demand in the economy. Prospects for enterprise reform depend on the net effects of these factors (borrowing, changes in accumulation policies, changes in wage levels, price policy) and two alternatives can be imagined:

1. A bright prospect, whereby the recent money wage increases are met in real terms by higher imports (or lower exports of essential consumables) financed out of higher borrowing, and by higher productivity deriving from the newly found satisfaction of material and political needs of the working class; the newly acquired influence of workers on accumulation leading to less ambitious plans; possible necessary sacrifices being negotiated and accepted by organized labour in exchange for political concessions, in a 'social pact' package; the reduction and gradual elimination of current excess demand and generation of the kind of economic environment in which the envisaged reform would have a chance of successful implementation, in the early eighties.

2. A gloomy prospect, whereby the recent money wage increases result in either inflation (activating a spiral) or rationing, spilling over into the supply of inputs to enterprises, either because of inadequate import increases and international borrowing, or because of stagnating productivity; the restraining influence that workers might exercise on accumulation being more than compensated for by the additional pressure on consumption demand generated by organized labour; transactors in all markets continuing to be 'rationed', the economy continuing to be in the grip of a crisis and the reform either being postponed or doomed, like the 1973–5 reform.

Medium-long-run prospects for the Polish economy and for the introduction of the envisaged reform are good, because of the basic self-sufficiency in energy, fairly stable terms of trade, the high productivity of investment in the completion of half-finished projects, the eventual pay-off of sustained investment in research and development over the last decade, and access to foreign capital for both economic (good creditworthiness) and political reasons (concern for international stability). Growth prospects would not necessarily suffer from a likely reduction in investment. The most likely prospect in the short run, however, is some initial worsening of inflation and supply conditions because of the impossible arithmetic of balancing income and expenditure of the population without substantial price rises, and because the reformers have neglected the problems of *transition* to a new system of management. If the new leadership can go through this difficult period without economic problems triggering off another political crisis, Poland can look forward to a period of stability and consolidation: a credible reform of enterprises and planning organization along Hungarian lines, with strong elements of self-management (not of the Yugoslav type), could be implemented by the mid eighties.

IMPLICATIONS FOR THE DEVELOPMENT OF A THEORY OF THE SOCIALIST ENTERPRISE

Three main lessons can be drawn from the Polish experience with enterprise reform. The first is the remarkable connection between economic policy, in particular accumulation policy, and the viability of patterns of economic organization. De-centralization in Poland has always been inversely related to the intensity of the accumulation effort. Thus acceleration of investment was associated with the centralization of 1948—9; the de-centralization of 1956—7 was associated with a short burst of consumption, giving way to both an intensification of accumulation and a recentralization of planning. In the period 1958 to 1968 the sustained accumulation effort prevented any substantial organizational change, in spite of considerable experimentation. Gomulka's 'aborted reform' of 1968—70 was geared to the intensification of the accumulation effort in a fundamentally autarkic economy, and was abandoned simultaneously with that policy. The opening of the economy to international trade and borrowing allowed Gierek to undertake the 1973—5 reforms in spite of extremely ambitious accumulation policies; but the reform was suspended and held in abeyance under the pressure which occurred when investment and wage payments got out of control. The connection is there and the direction of causality is immaterial. The important point is that a de-centralization drive in industry can be successful only if:

1. Supply imbalances associated with 'taut' planning are removed beforehand (as was done in Hungary before the introduction of the New Economic Mechanism in 1968).
2. Sufficient flexibility (in the form of large stocks of consumer and producer goods characterized by high elasticity of demand with respect to income) is established in the period of transition to the new system, in order to cope with the structural changes associated with reform.
3. The traditional mechanisms generating high accumulation pressure at the micro- and macro-economic level are weakened or removed.

The second lesson to be learned from the Polish experience is that these conditions, necessary though perhaps not sufficient to the success of economic reform, are extremely difficult to satisfy. In the Soviet Union, the massive capital accumulation programme, concentrating on heavy industry, was the direct consequence of the decision to accelerate economic growth in specific Soviet circumstances (a virtually closed economy, abundant labour, availability of materials, scarcity of capital, and a poorly developed capital goods sector), but this specific policy has become a general tendency of socialist economies even where these circumstances were not (or were no longer) encountered, with Poland maintaining record accumulation rates (second only to Mongolia in recent years). Confronted with a deteriorating economic performance, communist leaders have reacted by experimenting with institutional change and industrial reorganization and reform rather than altering *economic policies*, sometimes even reinforcing rather than weakening the over-ambitious accumulation policies which were at the root of both the deterioration of performance and the ineffectiveness of reform (see Nuti, 1979). Our understanding of the macro-economic behaviour of socialist 'planners' and decision-makers is still relatively underdeveloped, while a vast literature has accumulated in the description and dissection of economic reform; yet without a deeper analysis of the accumulation bias present at all levels in the socialist economy, it appears that little progress can be expected in our understanding of the theory and practice of a more de-centralized model of the socialist enterprise and economy.

Finally, detailed analysis of the Polish experience confirms that any similarity between the 'socialist' enterprise (excepting Yugoslavia) and its capitalist counterpart is purely illusory and that the extension of results taken from the theory of the capitalist firm can be grossly misleading. Several significant specific features of the socialist enterprise are observable:

1. The birth, death and merger of enterprises are purely administrative acts, whether by the centre or by local authorities.
2. The enterprise is strictly limited to a market and a product (or broad group of related products): the enterprise is not allowed to diversify; at most there are *combines* diversifying in the limited direction of vertical integration, but there are no *conglomerates* or other forms of diversification.
3. The enterprise can borrow from banks, but cannot lend to banks and enterprises.
4. There is no stock market discipline and, therefore, there are no constraints on enterprise managers such as gearing ratios, valuation ratios, dividend payments, the danger of takeover bids, etc.

It is debatable whether these features are the necessary systematic implications of public ownership and economic planning, or simply historical accidents associated with the Soviet and East-European experience. In any case these specific features have important implications for the theory of functioning of the socialist enterprise, as they impinge on competition, pricing, self-finance, sectoral equilibrium, growth of the firm (especially of industry associations as enterprises) and the very meaning of 'entrepreneurship' in the socialist economy. Yet these features have been neglected in the literature, and the socialist enterprise, by and large, is regarded as a 'sausage-machine' transforming inputs into outputs according to given production functions (just as in the old-fashioned theory of the capitalist firm), rather than as a distinct organism living in a specific environment.

REFERENCES

Chądzyński, H. (1977) In *Życie Warszawy*, 10 September.
Czarnek, J. & Glikman, P. (1974) In *Inwestycje i Budownictwo*, 6 and 8, August and October.
Doskonalenie Procesu Planowania, Zarządzania i Kierowania Gospodarką Narodową, Materiały z Plenarnego Posiedzenia Komisji Partyjno-Rządowej dla Unowocześnienia Systemu Funkcjonowania Gospodarki i Państwa (1972) Warsaw: Kiw.
Glikman, P. (1980) *Rachunek Ekonomiczny a System Planowania Inwestycji* (Mimeo).

Gliński, B. (1977) *System Funkcjonowania Gospodarki – Logika Zmian.* Warsaw: PWE. (a) pp. 17–27.
Golinowski, K. (1977) In *Gospodarka Planowa,* 9, September.
Hołubicki, B. (1977) In *Gospodarka Planowa,* 9, September.
IKCHZ (Instytut Koniunktur i Cen Kandlu Zagranicznego) (1980) Warsaw. *Main Indicators of Polish Foreign Trade Development.*
Jakubowicz, S. (1973) *Typologia Struktur Organizacyinych* (Mimeo).
Jakubowicz, S. (1980) *Organizacyjne Struktury Złożonych Organizacji Gospodarczych,* Warsaw (Mimeo).
Kotowicz-Jawor, J. (1979) In *Gospodarka Planowa,* 3.
Kulpińska, J. (1980) *Perspektywy Rozwoju Samorządu Robotniczego* (Mimeo). p. 28.
Mujżel, J. (1980) In *Ekonomista,* 1. p. 10.
Nuti, D.M. (1977) Large corporations and the reform of Polish industry. In *Jahrbuch der Wirtschaft Osteuropas,* 7. (a) p. 400.
Nuti, D.M. (1979) The Contradictions of Socialist Economies – a Marxian Interpretation. In *Socialist Register.*
Ocena ekonomiczney efektywności inwestycji i innych zamierzeń rozwojowych – Zbiór przepisów (1974) Warsaw: PWE
Pinkowski, J. (1972) In *Gospodarka Planowa,* 8.
Poznański, K. (1974) In *Proceedings of a Symposium on Economic Calculus in the New System of Planning and Management.* Jadwisin.
PTE, *Funkcjonowanie organizacji przemisłowych w nowym systeme ekonomiczno-finansowym.* Warsaw, March 1974.
Rakowski, M. (1977a) In *Polityka,* 45, 5 September.
Rakowski, M. (1977b) In *Polityka,* 47, 19 September.
Ratyński, W. (1977) In *Życie Warszawy,* 8 September.
Rocznik Statystyczny. 1976 and 1979.
Szydlak, J. (1977) In *Gospodarka Planowa,* 9, September.
Uchwała 48/77 Rady Ministrów z dnia 18 marca 1977r. w sprawie modyfikacji systemu funkcjonowania państwowych organizacji gospodarczych w dostosowaniu do celów i warunków realizacji Narodowego Planu Społeczno-Gospo darczego na lata 1976–1980. (unpublished).
Upława, S. (1980) Kierunki doskonalenia procedur planowania centralnego (Mimeo).
Ustawa z dnia 19 listopada 1956r. o radach robotiniczych. *Dziennik Ustaw,* 53, 24 November 1956, Warsaw.
Ustawa z dnia 20 grudnia 1958r. o samorządzie robotniczym. *Dziennik Ustaw,* 77, 31 December 1958, Warsaw.
Zarys systemu funkcjonowania jednostek inicjujących, *Prace Instytutu Planowania,* 27, Warsaw 1973.
Zielinski, J.G. (1973) *Economic Reforms in Polish Industry.* London: Oxford University Press. (a) p.15; (b) pp. 22–23; (c) p. 101.

4
The Romanian Industrial Enterprise

Alan Smith

Two of the most detailed Western studies on the operation of the Romanian economy based on interviews with industrial personnel have indicated a degree of centralization of decision-making that is unusual by Comecon standards. Granick's study, based on interviews conducted in 1970, indicated that the role of 'enterprise managers has been almost exclusively centred on improving technical efficiency' (Granick, 1975a) and that 'either economic decisions are taken in ministries or higher bodies or they are not taken at all' (Granick, 1975b). Granick also argued that the Romanian leadership regarded this state of affairs as unsatisfactory and was taking steps to remedy the situation but still 'as of late 1970, had a very long way to go' (Granick, 1975b). The World Bank Report, based on work largely completed by July 1977, however, still concluded that 'industrial enterprises in Romania are organizations oriented primarily toward production with limited autonomy and decision-making responsibilities outside production' (World Bank, 1979a). Although the progress of Romanian economic reforms over the intervening seven years cannot be entirely judged by those two statements, in that a major area of the reforms was directed at increasing the powers and duties of industrial centrals (composed of associations of enterprises) rather than the enterprises themselves, they do indicate quite clearly the lack of autonomy granted to the latter. However, since the World Bank Study was completed the Romanian Government has attempted to implement a further set of economic measures described as a 'New Economic-Financial Mechanism' (*Noul Mecanism Economico-Financiar*) announced in March 1978 and put into practice from the beginning of 1979. The new mechanism places greater emphasis on financial and monetary indicators, requires enterprises to cover costs from revenues, to pay money bonuses to workers and to finance social and cultural expenditure out of planned and above-plan profits after all compulsory State levies have been met, and replaces gross output with net output as the principal enterprise indicator. A further feature of the new mechanism is to enhance the role of workers' committees in the management process and is officially described as Workers' Self-Management (*Autoconducerea Muncitoreasca*). In an earlier paper (Smith, 1980), I argued that in view of the number of compulsory indicators that enterprises have to pursue and in the absence of competitive market relations between enterprises, resulting particularly from the size and monopoly position of supplying enterprises, this mechanism should not be confused with workers' self-management on Yugoslav lines. Furthermore, I argued that the measures involved in the new economic mechanism should not be regarded as a drastic reversal of policy as the majority of the proposals had been established in the 'Directives of the Central Committee of the Romanian Communist Party on the Perfecting of Management and Planning of the National Economy', approved by the Party's National Conference in December 1967, the implementation of which had been delayed for both political and economic reasons. Although a clear economic rationale could be found for the new economic mechanism, there was still room for doubt as to how far the 1978 proposals should be viewed as a genuine attempt to implement reform proposals and how far they were the result of political manoeuvring. In particular it was difficult to reconcile statements concerning de-centralization with the evidence of continuing centralization of Romanian decision-taking and the apparent reluctance of central authorities to relinquish power.

The fact that uncertainty concerning the true nature of the economic mechanism extended as far as participants in the process was confirmed by Ceausescu in a major speech at the end of May 1980 when he argued 'I have come to the conclusion that the new economic mechanism is not understood, nor are the principles of this mechanism understood, nor is self-management (*autoconducerea*) understood, nor is self-financing (*autogestiune*) understood' (*Scinteia*, 1 July 1980).

This speech was followed by a series of major speeches in June and July 1980 in which Ceausescu appears to have launched a major initiative to implement the new mechanism which has been supported by several articles by economic authorities in Party journals explaining the principles of the reform. Furthermore, in a speech in July 1980, which effectively commemorated 15 years of his tenure of the post of Party Secretary, Ceausescu claimed that, although there had been errors in the administration of economic policy and insufficient emphasis placed on certain aspects of that policy, there had been a continuity of policy, namely the promotion of workers' democracy, self-management and self-financing, that had been basically correct.

Although it can be argued that this, not surprisingly, is a favourable interpretation of past events, it is consistent with the hypothesis that the 'New Economic Mechanism' does not represent a basic change in policy, but is an attempt to implement some of the more de-centralist proposals contained in the Directives.

Consequently, in the remainder of the paper, I will examine the roles envisaged in the Directives for the enterprise and, more importantly, the industrial central and their subsequent implementation and will finally draw some tentative conclusions on the way in which the Romanian economic system may develop if the new economic mechanism is successfully implemented.

THE INDUSTRIAL STRUCTURE PROPOSED IN THE DIRECTIVES

The Directives proposed the establishment of a three-tier system of industrial administration, similar to that adopted in several other Comecon countries, composed of the industrial ministry, the industrial central and the enterprise. The major new feature was therefore the establishment of the industrial central defined as 'an autonomous economic unit, coordinated and controlled by the relevant ministry, established by the grouping of several enterprises . . . operating on the principle of own economic administration' (Directives, a).

The industrial central was intended to be 'a body corporate' established through either the vertical or horizontal integration of enterprises and was required to operate as 'an independent profitable body' (Directives, b) with its own financial plan, financial resources and access to bank credits. Its functions were to work out (on the basis of directives received from the state plan) its own economic plan, which was to include aggregated targets of the component enterprises together with its own individual targets for external relations (material-technical supplies, foreign trade, etc.). Its major internal powers were to supervise the fulfilment of plan targets by enterprises, the fulfilment of investment programmes, to organize cooperation between component enterprises and to ensure the concentration of production and specialization of enterprises, and to bring about a closer link between research and production by establishing research and design institutes. Its major external functions were to ensure the supply of raw and auxiliary materials to enterprises on the basis of supply agreements concluded with other centrals and the Ministry of Foreign Trade. Similar agreements were to be concluded for the supply of intermediate products to other centrals, while the central was to be given increased powers for the sale of finished products on domestic and foreign markets. In addition to being responsible for the fulfilment of the State export plan for its component enterprises, the central was to be empowered directly to prospect foreign markets and conclude export contracts with foreign partners, and could establish subunits or enterprises directly involved in production for export.

The powers granted to *enterprises* in the Directives were (as subsequently observed in practice by both Granick and the World Bank) largely limited to improving their technical efficiency in accordance with detailed plan instructions; in particular the enterprise was to receive the following compulsory indicators from the industrial central, fixed in accordance with the State plan: gross output, marketable production and the assortment of key products in physical units; the volume of deliveries for the market fund and for export; deliveries of main products to other enterprises; material supplies from domestic sources and imports, and consumption norms; labour productivity; total wage fund; maximum number of wage earners; average wage; expenditure per 1000 lei of marketable product and production costs for main products; returns to be obtained on fixed and working capital; volume of payments to the State budget; and volume of investment and its specification (Directives, 1967c).

In addition, the central was empowered to determine other indicators on an ad hoc basis 'which should detail and support the achievement of obligatory indices' (Directives, d) and could establish additional output targets for enterprises in accordance with those obligations which the central had entered into on domestic and foreign markets. The central was then to be responsible for further disaggregating these indicators to formulate a detailed operational plan. A major executive power for the enterprise was that it was initially to be responsible (within the compulsory indicators established for the maximum number of wage earners, the wage fund, the average wage and labour productivity) for individual staffing decisions. Similarly it was to be responsible for the operational detail of supply contracts negotiated by the central and was to establish direct links with other enterprises for their fulfilment, and could make direct purchases of capital equipment specifically detailed in the plan. In order to stimulate a greater incentive for enterprises to reduce production costs and choose efficient production methods the enterprise was to be empowered to retain a portion of its above-plan profits for the payment of money bonuses to workers, for the provision of social and cultural activities and for undertaking certain small-scale investments.

At the top of the administrative pyramid the industrial ministry was to operate with a small staff composed of specialists employed in functional departments (economic-financial, technical, training, and operational control) and was to draw up the draft plan for its branch in accordance with the State plan and coordinate the activities of the centrals under its jurisdiction.

An apparent inconsistency in the administrative structure established in the Directives was an apparent unwillingness to give up detailed centralized control, whilst attempting to give enterprises greater autonomy in order to stimulate production efficiency, which in particular did little to overcome the 'ratchet effect'. Consequently bonuses for both enterprise and central staff were to be linked directly to the fulfilment and over-fulfilment of enterprise plan tasks, and enterprises' bonuses were to be paid not from the absolute level of profits but from above-plan profits. As a result enterprises were being instructed to mobilize internal reserves when any resulting increase in efficiency would inevitably lead to higher plan targets in subsequent periods. Furthermore, as Granick noted, central authorities tended to regard enterprise plans as having an essentially predictive rather than an economic or directive character; consequently inefficient enterprises received slacker plan instructions than efficient enterprises, and plan targets were frequently revised during the period of fulfilment to bring them closer to actual results (Granick, 1975c). More seriously, it was not initially clear how the resources to fulfil additional output instructions that enterprises might receive from centrals on the basis of domestic and foreign contracts were to be obtained unless there was to be considerable slack in the targets given to centrals in the first instance. Were centrals to be empowered to violate their centrally-determined constraints on labour, raw materials, etc., or alternatively to reduce other State-determined output targets and, if so, which criteria were they to use in making such judgements? If profitability alone were to be the criterion the problem would require the reform of the price system which was based on 1963 average branch costs and would need to be able to make accurate value comparisons between domestic and foreign prices.

The fact that these problems had not been adequately resolved was probably a major reason for the inability adequately to implement proposals contained in the Directives to de-centralize decision-making authority to industrial centrals, and accounted for the need to re-establish centralized control when areas of conflict arose. Since 1973 several of these problems have been tackled (e.g., a major price reform was launched from 1974 to 1976), but changes in the structure of material incentives launched as part of new economic-financial mechanism in 1979, which reward above-plan profits more than planned profits, do little to overcome the ratchet principle. The decision by Ceausescu in July 1980 to abolish the multi-tiered system of foreign exchange rates from January 1981 and to replace it in enterprise accounts with a single exchange rate convertible into domestic currency at 15 lei to the dollar and the rouble could, however, provided the rate is accurate, rationalize enterprise accounts and permit de-centralized decision-taking.

THE CONCEPT AND DEVELOPMENT OF INDUSTRIAL CENTRALS

Although a principal reason for the measures outlined in the Directives was to remove 'excessive centralism' and replace purely administrative measures by those with an economic character, subsequent writings have stressed that they did not envisage a 'competitive system of completely autonomous enterprises aiming at achieving maximum profits' (Rachmuth, 1972). Romanian writers frequently stress the supremacy of plan levers over market levers, and the all-embracing concept of the Unitary Plan of Socio-Economic Development and the frequent emphasis placed on the principle of democratic centralism clearly indicate the constraints within which industrial centrals and enterprises operate. This has been indicated by Murgescu (1974): 'the interests of profitability at establishment or branch level may frequently collide with one or another requirement of ensuring certain material proportions and monetary equilibria in which the national economy as a whole is interested . . . Anyone . . . may also discover differences of interest between enterprises . . . there derive in planning activities substantial differences between the conclusions reached on the microeconomic scale by the numerous economic establishments . . . on the one hand and the macroeconomic conclusion on the other; the latter can in no case be the summation of the former.'

It was, however, argued that in the pursuit of gross output targets enterprises paid insufficient attention to costs of production, resulting in operational losses and the irrational use of fixed assets and working capital. The direct financing of capital expenditure from the budget also resulted in unplanned cross-subsidization, whilst the Ministry of Finance and the Banks were considered to be too over-centralized to pay sufficient attention to problems of enterprise efficiency. The Directives should therefore be interpreted as a search for an improved system of management of the economy, and an attempt to introduce value criteria and a greater regard for costs and profitability into decision-making, rather than as a marketization of the economy. The major recipient of decentralized authority was to become the industrial central, not the enterprise.

The industrial central has clear parallels with the associations developed in the USSR and similar bodies which emerged elsewhere in Eastern Europe. To the extent that the centrals operate on the principle of self-financing (*autogestiune*) and that material incentives for central staff (who, in many cases, were former ministry personnel) are directly linked to the performance of component enterprises, they appear to be more directly analogous to the Soviet industrial associations developed since 1973. It was not, however, intended that they should be viewed purely as administrative units. Ceausescu indicated in 1971 that industrial centrals were intended to become huge production bodies, not purely administrative units (Ceausescu, 5a). Indeed, it can be argued that the concept of the industrial central was, to a considerable extent, based on that of the large Western corporation, with its own internal system of management required to cover costs from revenues overall and with component enterprises (the equivalent of the Western plant) receiving instructions from the centre and operating according to centralized rather than plant-level profit criteria. This view is strengthened by the fact that in the late 1960s studies were published in Romania commenting favourably on the role of the Western industrial corporation as generator of technical progress, together with studies of Western management techniques. Simultaneously (1967) Romania embarked on a major policy of importing Western machinery and equipment and encouraging a series of co-operation ventures with Western enterprises, including in 1971 the enactment of legislation to permit minority equity participation of Western enterprises in joint enterprises on Romanian territory (Smith, 1979).

The role of industrial centrals as generators of technical progress was stressed in an article by Olteanu (who cites a number of Western corporations in support of her arguments) in which it was proposed that centrals should play a far greater role in stimulating research and development, prospecting markets, developing new products and analysing the strong and weak points of the component enterprises, and concentrating production on the former at the expense of the latter (Olteanu, 1973).

Several distinct phases can be seen in the development of industrial centrals. The detailed operation of centrals before 1973 has been analysed by Spigler (1973a), who shows that, whilst none was established before 1969, 200 were formed in the autumn of that year. Spigler also argues that the centrals developed at that time 'had little in common with the industrial associations stipulated by the Directives of the reform', indicating that they tended to operate as 'executants of the ministries' programmes' (Spigler, 1973b) rather than as large-scale independent units. The explanation for this may well lie in political factionalism, as State officials were unwilling to relinquish power, while Ceausescu's power base largely rested in the Party apparatus. In this period Ceasescu was highly critical of the performance of centrals. In 1971 he argued: 'There are still some industrial centrals which operate like some coordinating bodies and which to a large extent do nothing but repeat with slight changes the activity of the former general managements of the ministries' (Ceausescu, 5a).

A year later, at the Party national conference, he again criticized 'excessive centralism' in the operation of centrals who 'have not taken over, even now, the full range of powers entrusted to them' (Ceausescu, 7) and further criticized the fact that not only had ministry staff been allocated to the centrals but that key engineering staff who were needed in production had also gravitated towards them.

Finally in 1973 a major reorganization of ministries, industrial centrals and enterprises was undertaken. A typical industrial central was composed of a grouping of enterprises, research and design institutes and a supply and sales base (*Viata Economica*, 19 December 1969). Prior to the 1973 reorganization centrals were largely organized on the principle of horizontal integration, being composed either of groups of enterprises producing similar outputs under the jurisdiction of the same branch ministry (viz. the Lorry-Tractor Central at Brasov subordinated to the Ministry of Machine Building) or of groups of enterprises which were again subordinate to the same industrial ministry but were connected through the use of similar technology or inputs used in production. Finally, some centrals were organized according to the principle of vertical integration, involving the collaboration of enterprises from more than one ministry, viz. the Petrochemical Central at Borzesti embraced enterprises from the petroleum and chemical industries (Dumitrescu, 1971). The stated aims of the 1973 reorganization were to reduce the power of industrial ministries, to move management closer to production and to move technical and administrative staff closer to production units, whilst simultaneously concentrating production into large-scale units (Ceausescu, 10a). According to Ceausescu the number of centrals was reduced from 207 to 102 and the number of administrative staff from 34 000 to 19 000 (Ceausescu, 10b). The World Bank (1979b), however, refers to a reduction in the number of centrals from 217 to 89 in 1973 with a subsequent increase to 112 in 1977. Despite statements by Ceausescu that the reorganized centrals were to become large-scale production units, the effect of the reorganization appears to have been that the centrals took over many of the powers of the former ministry general directorates and appeared, therefore, to reflect the simultaneous development of industrial associations that was taking place in the USSR. The majority (58) were organized on a country-wide basis and, although 83 were physically located at the site of the leading enterprises, the geographical concentration of industry in and around Bucharest meant that this did not involve any geographical dispersion. Indeed, it is probable that their link with production was still tenuous, for a year later Ceausescu was to complain that contacts between central staff and the enterprise at which they were located (let alone other subsidiary enterprises) were unsatisfactory (Ceausescu, 10c).

In the area of physical planning industrial centrals were considered to be the 'titulars' of the plan: namely, they received a large number of centrally-determined indicators, but were responsible for dividing these between component enterprises and supervising their fulfilment. Their major increase in planning autonomy consisted of greater powers to draw up their own plans in consultation with functional ministries in Bucharest and with county authorities in the areas in which component enterprises were located. Consequently industrial and functional ministries were freed of the detailed supervision of enterprises and of relations between enterprises within a central. For example, centrals took over the powers of the Ministry of Material and Technical supplies to effect material transfers between subsidiary enterprises and could reallocate labour between enterprises on a short-term or long-term basis. Aggregate employment plans had to be coordinated with the Ministry of Labour, however, and the appropriate local authorities and input and output plans involving contacts with enterprises outside the centrals had to be approved by the Ministry of Material and Technical Supplies in the form of contracts which became part of the central's annual plan.

Financially centrals had to operate under conditions of self-financing (*autogestiune*), an obligation which imposed financial discipline on centrals by requiring them to cover their costs from revenue and appears to be similar to the Soviet concept of *khozraschyot* (Rachmuth, 1972). Furthermore, centrals were to take greater responsibility for supervising and financing research and development and the provision of housing, social facilities, schools and lyceums, which implied a greater role for covering these costs directly through product prices rather than from the State budget and paved the way for the 1978 changes which linked the availability of funds for the payment of the social wage more directly to individual plant productivity.

Consequently, if the administrative rationale underlying the 1973 reorganization was to bring managers more directly into contact with the day-to-day problems of administering industry and in particular to move engineering personnel away from planning to bring them directly into contact with production problems, the economic rationale was to eliminate waste and duplication by establishing large-scale integrated units, eliminating short production runs by concentrating output in single enterprises and reducing reserve stocks held at enterprises to insure against supply failure. The process of concentration of enterprises is reviewed in the next section.

THE INDUSTRIAL ENTERPRISE

Employment and Size

For statistical purposes industrial enterprises in Romania are divided into three basic categories:

1. Republican Industry — enterprises of national importance operating under the jurisdiction of industrial ministries;
2. Local Industry — enterprises (predominantly in the field of consumer goods) responsible to the county (*judet*) authority;
3. Industrial Cooperatives — responsible to the Central Council of Cooperatives.

(1) and (2) above are designated as State industry and are the primary concern of this paper. In addition a number of small-scale artisan cooperatives operate in the industrial sector.

Prior to 1977 employment data provided by enterprises maintained a further legal distinction between those 'with a legal personality' and those 'without'. Data from the latter were stated not to be included in figures provided for 1977. However, as the data provided still cover 96 per cent of total industrial employment (as in previous years) it would appear that the latter category has been virtually eliminated. These categories probably coincide with those shown by Kaser to operate on business accounting (*intreprinderi cu gestiune economica proprie*) and those that do not (*intreprinderi cu gestiune economica interna*), and it would appear therefore that the majority of enterprises are now managed on a basis of 'business accounting' (Kaser, 1975). This impression is reinforced by the fact that Ceausescu argued that 'Even the budget-financed units should function according to the principle of self-administration and self-management and should have their own income/expenditure budget' (Ceausescu, 1980).

Tables 4.1, 4.2 and 4.3 provide data concerning enterprise size by number of

Table 4.1   Industrial employment and enterprise size

	Number of enterprises Jurisdiction				Number of all employees (thousands) (including administrative)				Number of Workers (Total)
	Total	Repub-lican	Local	Coop-erative	Total	Repub-lican	Local	Coop-erative	
1967	1575	1081	199	295	1763	1493	145	125	1526
1970	1731	1126	246	359	1997	1629	207	161	1758
1972	1896	1239	263	394	2255	1807	241	206	1988
1973	1613	1183	97	333	2388	1910	253	225	2157
1976	1752	1288	99	365	2793	2277	269	248	2549
1977	1635	1237	2	396	2899	2619	4	277	2651

Table 4.2   Average employment per enterprise

	All employees						Workers only	
	Total	State repub-lican	Local	All State	Coop-erative		Total	State industry only
1967	1119	1381	728	1280	424		969	1105
1970	1154	1447	842	1338	448		1016	1168
1972	1189	1458	916	1364	522		1048	1197
1973	1480	1614	2608	1690	675		1337	1519
1976	1595	1768	2716	1835	679		1455	1666
1977	1773	2117	1750	2114	699		1621	1931

Table 4.3   Distribution of workers by size of enterprise

	Number of enterprises			Number of workers in enterprises (thousands)			Changes 1967–72		1972–7	
	1967	1972	1977	1967	1972	1977	Wor-kers	Enter-prises	Wor-kers	Enter-prises
up to 200	209	253	149	26	32	21	+6	+44	−11	−104
201-500	478	507	323	159	175	114	+16	+29	−61	−184
501-1000	432	506	382	311	366	283	+55	+74	−83	−124
1001-2000	280	401	366	392	565	528	+173	+121	−37	−35
2001-3000	99	120	195	237	286	478	+49	+21	+192	+75
3001-5000	54	78	134	198	286	509	+88	+24	+223	+56
5000+	23	31	86	203	278	718	+75	+8	+440	+55
Total	1575	1896	1635	1526	1988	2651	+462	+321	+663	−261

All figures in Tables 4.1, 4.2 and 4.3 calculated from *Anuarul Statistic*, al RSR. Various years.
Tables 4.1, 4.2 and 4.3 first appeared in Smith, 1980, and are reproduced with the kind permission of NATO.

employees and workers and indicate a distinct change in pattern involving the concentration of enterprises following the reorganization of industrial centrals in 1973. Although it is difficult to estimate the extent to which this concentration reflects economies of scale in production (particularly where small workshops may have been amalgamated with other enterprises with little change in production processes) and the lack of information on the statistical definition of an enterprise makes international comparisons hazardous, these tables do give some impression of the administrative size of enterprises against which such concepts as workers' self-management and the degree of effective centralization may be judged. Furthermore, a more detailed analysis of the figures indicates that the concentration cannot be attributed purely to changes in statistical reporting, while the breakdown of employment by plant size in Table 4.3 indicates that changes in average figures have not been brought about purely by a reduction in the number of small plants. Two phases of enterprise concentration can be observed in the 1970s, the first in 1973 and the second in 1977, which can be interpreted as the continuation of a cyclical pattern of concentration of enterprises, followed by an increase in their number, followed by further concentration that has been continued throughout the period of socialist industrialization. Certain features of the post-1973 changes, however, appear to indicate a change in industrial patterns, a shift to 'intensive growth', as a result of which by 1977 Romania effectively had a two-scale industrial structure comprised of very large-scale State republican industry, with an average of over 2000 employees per enterprise and a smaller-scale cooperative industry.

In 1973, although the number of plants in each of the three categories was reduced and the average number of employees increased (Tables 4.1 and 4.2), the major concentration involved local industry, as a result of which local enterprises averaged 2608 employees per enterprise — a figure higher than the average for State industry and probably indicating changes in the administrative unit rather than the production unit. The concentration of 1977 resulted in the virtual abolition of local industry and a substantial reduction in the number of republican plants, while cooperative industry was virtually untouched.

The change in the pattern of industrial employment is more clearly demonstrated in Table 4.3. Between 1967 (the commencement of the reforms) and 1972 the increase in the industrial labour force of 462 000 workers was absorbed by the creation of 321 new enterprises fairly evenly distributed by plant size (250 000 workers were absorbed by enterprises employing fewer than 2000 workers). Between 1972 and 1977 the industrial workforce grew by a further 663 000 workers, while the number of enterprises actually fell by 261. The number of workers employed in enterprises employing fewer than 2000 workers fell by 192 000 (the number of enterprises by 447), whilst the entire net gain in the industrial labour force was concentrated in plants employing more than 3000 workers, the majority (440 000) in plants employing more than 5000 workers.

It is not clear if there may be some reversal of this policy in the next five year plan. In a speech in June 1980 Ceausescu attacked 'gigantism' in cooperative industry and proposed a three-fold increase in the weight of small-scale industry over the next five year plan to comprise 18 to 20 per cent of total industrial production (*Scinteia*, 21 July 1980). It would appear, however, that this would involve an expansion in the number of cooperatives and handicraft workshops rather than imply the break-up of larger-scale plants, and would indicate the continued existence of large-scale productive industry operating alongside smaller-scale cooperatives.

The Administration of the Enterprise: Workers' Self-Management

A major feature of the New Economic Mechanism announced in March 1978 was 'to bring workers' self-management to a higher level', particularly by stimulating their 'co-interest' in production through increasing the role of profit sharing. Although the official rhetoric used to describe this process is Workers' Self-Management (*Autoconducerea-Muncitoreasca*), this should not be confused with Workers' Self-Management on Yugoslav lines, principally because enterprises respond to centrally-determined plan instructions, not market signals. Secondly, it is combined with the principle of democratic centralism emphasizing order and discipline and, thirdly, the system of profit sharing follows a system of centrally-determined rules and operates only after all centrally-determined costs, including labour and compulsory budget levies, have been met.

The workers' committees give the impression principally of being transmission belts for centrally-determined objectives, but do permit some degree of discussion of plan instructions prior to their final adoption when they become binding on the workforce. In all cases workers' elected representatives are outnumbered by technical-management personnel and Party and trade union officials who sit ex-officio (currently elected representatives comprise 7 to 17 members of Councils of 15 to 35 people).

The principle of collective leadership allied to democratic centralism, as opposed to one-man management, was Ceausescu's major organizational proposal on coming to office in 1965. Statements at the time and the subsequent application of the principle appear to confirm that its purposes were in part technocratic — to stimulate enterprise efficiency partly by appealing over the heads of more conservative enterprise management to Party activists and technical personnel to reveal production reserves and draw up taut plans — in part political — to increase the role of the Party and Party-dominated organizations in economic management, and in part to reduce alienation and give workers some sense of participation in plan decisions.

At the Ninth Party Congress (1965) Ceausescu proposed: 'The elaboration of State plans, of chief economic measures, must be the fruit of collective thought and the work of leading cadres, of the most efficient activists and experts in every field of activity . . . one person, no matter how knowledgeable or how capable he may be, cannot solve the problems on his own or at best solves them with many shortcomings' (Ceausescu, 1965).

In April 1968 the collective management principle was introduced with the establishment of Boards of Management comprised of elected and ex-officio members. The initial period of operation of the Boards and their successors in 1971 — the Committees of the Working People (with roughly similar powers) — has been analysed by Spigler (1973c), who discovered that interference by ministry officials, central authorities and banks frequently prevented the Boards from exercising their judicial authority, whilst enterprise managers prevented workers' representatives from getting involved in the boards' activities. Spigler also indicates that the change of title to 'Committees of the Working People' in 1971 was not purely cosmetic, but involved changes in representation which strengthened the role of the Party on the committees. This role has been further strengthened since 1973 with the Party secretary replacing the enterprise director as chairman of the committee. Simultaneously the role of the Party in national bodies has been increased, and official rhetoric has placed greater emphasis on workers' democracy, culminating in the official rhetoric of workers' self-management to describe the March 1978 changes.

Workers' self-management currently appears to mean the obligation of workers' committees to utilize the enterprise's resources as efficiently as possible within the constraints of the single national plan. At the National Council of the Working People, which replaced the National Congress of Working People's Councils in June 1980 Ceausescu reiterated: 'Self-management and economic self-administration must not be understood as each and everyone's right to engage and spend financial and human means, to start activities as he thinks fit . . . we must understand that on developing self-management we should set out from the single development plan . . . working people's councils must *debate* both plan and budgets . . . controlling the achievement of production in the best conditions with utmost efficiency . . . working in this respect as representatives of the owners, producers and end users, of the entire people. It is *only* in this capacity . . . that the working people's councils can and must fulfil their important role' (Ceausescu, 1980).

Enterprise Success Indicators and Incentives

The major principle of the New Economic Mechanism is to introduce financial discipline and profit criteria directly into enterprise and (industrial) central decision-making. The methods of effecting this were to replace gross output as the major enterprise indicator with net output (newly-created production), which had been unsuccessfully introduced in 1974, to introduce the principle of self-financing rigorously into all fields of activity and to stimulate workers' co-interest in profitability and cost reduction by linking both material incentives and social expenditure to profitability criteria.

A major reason for the reform was to cut back on Romania's excessive consumption of energy and raw materials per unit of output (according to Ceausescu, 1980, many enterprises pursued 'high consumption of expensive materials in order to have a large gross production without having a correspond-ing net output', while other economists claimed that centrals deliberately split up production between component enterprises in order to bring about high gross outputs for enterprises which were then aggregated to form the gross output for the central as a whole) and to economize on labour, which was becoming increasingly scarce, by facilitating the transfer of underemployed labour to areas of higher productivity and to link the social wage more directly to enterprise productivity. The majority of the measures (including the use of net production as an enterprise success indicator 'to measure exactly the efforts of enterprises and their contribution to raising national income': Directives, e) were envisaged in the 1967 Directives, although they specified that only a proportion of *above*-plan profits were to be paid out in the form of bonuses to employees, social and cultural expenditure, etc., with the residue to be paid into the State budget. Planned profits, according to the Directives, were to be in part paid into the State budget and in part used to finance planned and certain small-scale unplanned investment by the industrial central (Directives, f). Linking bonuses only to above-plan profits, however, would appear to do nothing to overcome the 'ratchet effect' and would give enterprises no incen-tive to reveal productive capacity. (The fact that the proportion of above-plan profits to be paid in bonuses appears to be higher than that for planned profits indicates that this problem has still not been resolved.) The dilemma arising from equity versus efficiency arguments and the apparent unwillingness of central authorities to de-centralize too much power to enterprises, which may explain much of the reason for procrastination in implementing the reform proposals, are encapsulated in an article by Stusiac, a senior banking official (Stusiac, 1969). Reviewing the experimental use of profits as a basis for paying bonuses, Stusiac argued that profits varied considerably from enterprise to enterprise largely as result of random factors, of which the price system and the degree of plan tautness were major determinants. It was therefore necessary, he argued, to distinguish between changes in profit arising through the enterprise's own efforts and those external to the enterprise as far as bonus payments were concerned. However, in the framework of an enterprise operating according to centrally-determined output and input instructions, it can be argued that the distinction between internal and external factors is essentially false. If one hypo-thesizes a perfectly working enterprise providing perfect information to the centre, any change in profits arises from factors 'external' to the enterprise (i.e., development of new markets, transport links, etc.). Consequently the enterprise's 'own efforts' would appear to consist largely of overcoming past deficiencies or utilizing reserves 'hidden' from the central authorities.

That this dilemma affected operational practice was revealed by Granick (1975d), who argued that, because bonuses featured as a considerable proportion of workers' income prior to 1967 and failure to fulfil the plan was often deemed to be the result of external factors (or bad forecasting by planners), plans were frequently changed retrospectively in order both to ensure fulfilment and not to penalize workers for factors deemed to be beyond their control. Consequently the Directives proposed to 'raise the role of the basic wage as the determining element of total income' (Directives, g) to incorporate the current system of 'variable additions' into basic wages and to impose instead a system of penalties for the non-fulfilment of plan tasks. The Directives did not fully clarify whether the penalties were to be worker-specific or linked to some greater aggregate (the workshop or enterprise), but implied a degree of collective responsibility: 'Special attention will be paid to rigorously stating the tasks and obligations incumbent on each employee. The payment of the full basic wage is to be conditioned by the plan indicators or the work task established for the respective work place. In case these are not achieved because of the employee, the wage will be reduced by a certain proportion' (Directives, g).

However the 'judges' were still to be 'part of the system', administrative and management staff of enterprises and centrals were to receive their full monthly salary only if plan tasks for their specific area were fulfilled. In addition, annual bonuses were to be paid to workers and management out of above-plan profits as a result of the fulfilment or over-fulfilment of 'synthetic indicators which reflect most completely all the sides of activity specific to each branch' (Directives, h).

A version of this system was brought into operation between 1967 and 1979 and has been outlined by the World Bank study. Monthly bonuses were linked directly to wage rates (overcoming the problem whereby workers refused promotion because they could get higher bonuses by overfulfilling individual tasks) and were paid on the basis of a 1 per cent bonus or penalty (up to a maximum of 20 per cent) for each percentage point of over-fulfilment or under-fulfilment by the enterprise of four indicators: gross output, exports, labour productivity and material consumption. Managerial staff in enterprises, ministries and centrals were similarly penalized or rewarded for their area of responsibility, but with a 4 per cent bonus or penalty for each percentage point of over- or under-fulfilment of plan targets. Annual bonuses of up to 8 per cent of the wage fund were paid out of above-plan profits, half of which (plus an additional amount equal to 2 per cent of the wage fund) were paid proportionally to wage rates while the other half (plus a further 1 per cent component) were paid specifically to individual workers up to a maximum of three months' salary. In addition, workers who failed to fulfil personal tasks could be fined up to 10 per cent of their salary on a monthly basis (World Bank, 1979c). Despite the complexity of the scheme, either as a result of the retrospective changing of plan tasks or as a result of the cancelling out of bonuses by penalties, bonuses accounted for only about 5 per cent of earnings.

The New Economic Mechanism attempts to stimulate enterprise, industrial central and ministry interest in cost reduction by linking material incentives directly to profits and cost reduction and by defining more accurately the components of costs and ensuring that these are included in the budgets of the respective enterprises and centrals. (Details on the operation of the New Economic Mechanism have been combined from the articles by Babe, Floares, Hatos, Iuga and Spinu cited in the reference list.) Consequently, overhead costs such as investment, research and development and an increasing proportion of the social wage will be attributed directly to enterprises and will be covered from revenue from the sale of output rather than being financed directly from the State budget. State and county banks are to play a greater role in supervising the fulfilment of plan tasks and are to impose financial penalties on enterprises for the inefficient use of resources, especially capital. As a result, although all major investment decisions will still be taken centrally, the finance will to a greater extent be provided by bank loans which will be repaid out of profits with penal interest rates to be charged for commissioning plant behind schedule.

Enterprises and economic units are required to draw up revenue and expenditure plans which are intended to involve a thorough examination of costs of production, in strict connection with centrally-determined plan norms for gross output, net output, marketed output, costs of production per 1000 lei of output marketed, labour productivity, etc. Despite the price review of 1974 to 1976, norms are differentiated between different branches and different enterprises. As a result of this exercise the level of planned profits can be calculated; these are then divided between compulsory payments to the State, repayments of loans, and enterprise own funds for the payment of bonuses and socio-cultural expenditure. Above-plan profits are similarly divided according to a predetermined set of rules. The distribution of planned and unplanned profits is summarized in Table 4.4

Compulsory payments to the State and repayments to the Bank have first call on the enterprises' funds and must be made even if plan targets are unfulfilled. Should enterprises make insufficient profits to make these payments it was intended that loans would be provided by banks at penal interest rates. In 1980, however, Ceausescu revealed that certain unprofitable enterprises were still receiving grants from the budget (Ceausescu, 1980).

Any failure to meet output targets expressed in terms of net output and output in physical units results in a 1 per cent reduction in the planned fund for profit participation (Table 4.4 [A.3(e)]) for each percentage point of under-fulfilment up to a maximum of 25 per cent (as well, presumably, as affecting profits through revenue). Any other failure to meet plan norms for labour productivity, material consumption, costs per 1000 lei marketed output, etc.,

Table 4.4

A. *Planned profits*

1. Payments to the State
   (a) Payments to the Budget
   (b) Other payments established by law

2. Payments to banks
   Repayments by centrals of sums borrowed for investment

3. Enterprise own funds
   (a) Fund for Economic Development
   (b) Fund for Working Capital
   (c) Fund for Housing Construction and other Investments of a Social Character
   (d) Fund for Social Actions
   (e) Fund for the Participation of Working People in Profits

B. *Above-plan profits*

1. 10 per cent of profits resulting from exports (to be added to workers' participation in the Profit Fund [A.3 (e) above].

   Of the remainder:

2. Payments to the State
   (a) Payments to the Budget (at least 35 per cent)
   (b) Other payments established by law

3. Enterprise own funds
   (a) Fund for Economic Development [20 per cent of B.2 plus B.3]
   (b) Fund for Housing Construction and other Investment of a Social Character (5 per cent)
   (c) Fund for Participation of Working People in Profits
      (i) Maximum of 25 per cent [of B.2 plus B.3]
   + (ii) Additional bonus for over-fulfilling export plans in proportion to the degree of over-fulfilment up to 10 per cent

Source: Based on Iuga (1979).

will affect profits directly and consequently reduce the funds available for bonuses and socio-cultural expenditure. Similarly, better than anticipated performance in these areas will result in above-plan profits which are to be distributed as shown in Table 4.4. A further stimulus to achieving a high level of exports (in addition to items B.1 and B.3(c) (ii) in Table 4.4) is that 2 per cent of above-plan foreign currency receipts may be retained by the enterprise to finance collective trips overseas for workers.

There are, however, several clear indications that enterprises have not been sufficiently motivated by the new system and that planned profit levels were not reached in 1979. Iuga, for example, writing in mid 1979, argued that enterprises would retain over 37 per cent of their profits, 2.6 times more than under the old system (Iuga, 1979). In practice the Budget Law for 1979 stated that enterprises retained only 28 per cent of their profits. As the proportion of above-plan profits to be retained by enterprises was to be greater than 37 per cent, this fall would appear to indicate a failure to meet plan profit levels. Furthermore, the communiqué on plan fulfilment for 1979 referred to the failure to fulfil some plan targets as a result of 'unjustified discontinued operation of installations, delays in commissioning some productive units, failure to operate them at capacity, incomplete use of machinery and equipment . . . shortcomings in supply of technologies and materials, in production and labour organization'. In addition to confirming that some enterprises still received direct budgetary assistance Ceausescu has said (June 1980) that this procedure will stop ('starting next year') and that units that do not make profits will close; 'economic units which work without profit must be helped to improve their work and where objective conditions prevent [this] . . . they should discontinue activity and the workers should be transferred to other jobs' (Ceausescu, 1980). In 1980 it is planned that 34 per cent of profits should be retained by centrals and enterprises, and that profit-sharing funds will increase by 14 per cent and funds for economic development by 57 per cent (*Scinteia*, 15 December 1979).

CONCLUSION

It is now possible to make some assessment of the direction in which the Romanian economic system is moving. Clearly any such forecast, particularly in the case of Romania where the personality of the leader is a dominant factor in economic life, can be invalidated by political factors. However, the majority of the measures comprising the New Economic Mechanism were envisaged in the reform Directives published in 1967 and their various components have been introduced in the past either on a piecemeal basis or experimentally in individual enterprises and have been discussed in the Romanian economic press. Although the term 'Workers' Control' has been officially used to describe the new system, Romania is not moving towards a Yugoslav-type system, and the function of Workers' Councils appears to be largely to act as a transmission belt for the discussion of centrally-determined decisions. It would appear, however, that the New Economic Mechanism is not purely a cosmetic or political operation. It imposes on all economic units the need to cover costs from revenues and reduces the role of budget funding for capital investment, reduces subsidies to loss-making enterprises, etc. Similarly, other non-productive agencies in health, education, etc., are required to pay greater attention to economic efficiency and keep within individually-determined budgets. A major reason for these changes is probably the economic repercussions of increased prices (and real costs) of imported energy and raw material sources, particularly given Romania's high consumption of those per unit of output, which have made the pursuit of gross output targets untenable and have necessitated the shift to net output. Enterprises still possess little economic autonomy and the system still remains highly centralized, particularly in the following respects:

1. Industrial investment is still largely centrally determined. Figures indicating changes in the source of finance (i.e., de-centralizing from the budget to the bank) should not be confused with de-centralized authority to invest. Ceausescu's 1980 statements would appear to indicate more, rather than less, centralization of investment decisions.
2. Industrial centrals and enterprises still receive detailed plan instructions.
3. Industry remains highly concentrated and monopolistic.
4. Enterprise authority to draw up long-term economic contracts is constrained by the fact that they must be based on (centrally-determined) annual plan targets. They appear, therefore, to be more concerned with the detailed specification of output, timing of deliveries, etc., rather than wtih the introduction of competitive factors.

The major recipients of economic power in the period since 1967 are the industrial centrals, which have taken over some of the powers of both ministries and enterprises. This development appears to have clear parallels with the VVBs in the GDR, the WOGs in Poland, and the DSOs in Bulgaria. Although Ceausescu has frequently stressed that these are intended to be productive organizations, the three-tier system of administration and the apparent trend to horizontal integration since 1973 appear to have very close parallels with industrial associations in the USSR. The industrial centrals appear to have been quite effective in rationalizing production between constituent enterprises, improving resource transfers between those enterprises and reducing stocks at enterprise level, and can reallocate labour between enterprises on a long- or short-run basis (the latter presumably applying more often to technical personnel). Analogies between Western corporations and industrial centrals may not be inappropriate. Although it would appear highly unlikely that market relations will be introduced *between* centrals, the requirement that both centrals and component enterprises cover their costs will necessitate the use of more rational allocation procedures within centrals, which could clearly involve the use of computers and could even involve calculating internal shadow prices. The major planning control over centrals is provided by coordination with the appropriate functional ministries − viz., employment with the Ministry of Labour, and similarly with foreign trade, finance, construction, etc. − whilst regional balance is ensured by coordination with the 40 county (*judet*) authorities. In theory it is possible to envisage the system operating without industrial ministries.

Three clear trends are apparent in the development of the industrial enterprise. The first is the concentration of enterprises and the emphasis since 1973 on large-scale production. Consequently, Romania has effectively a two-scale industrial system with large industrial enterprises operating alongside smaller-scale cooperatives and handicraft cooperatives, particularly providing industrial services. Secondly, enterprise autonomy still appears to lie largely in questions of production efficiency. Changes in planning methods since 1967, and especially since 1973, increase the powers of industrial centrals to draw up their own plans in consultation with the centre, and the New Economic Mechanism is intended to make enterprises more interested in the efficient use of inputs by linking material incentives to profits; these activities, however, are largely directed at the efficient use of inputs to meet centrally-determined objectives. Moreover, there seems little intention of designing systems to overcome the ratchet effect, particularly as it appears that bonuses derived from above-plan profits are greater than those derived from plan profits. The appeal to draw up taut plans appears to be principally directed at Party activists on workers' committees. Finally, an increasing role is being played by the workplace in social and cultural life. This appears to be in part a result of both economic and ideological factors. This policy was first developed by Ceausescu in 1971 when he proposed that housing for sale as well as for rent should be distributed through workers' councils, not municipal authorities (Ceausescu, 5b). This clearly ties the worker more firmly to the workplace, particularly as repayment of housing loans to the enterprise is to be a prerequisite for a change of job. The policy was clarified by Ceausescu later that year. He proposed the allotting of funds to enterprises in order to finance social provisions with a view to 'ensuring a closer connection between employees and the respective enterprise' (Ceausescu, 5c), while in a number of speeches between 1971 and 1973 he proposed a series of measures designed to link education more directly to production, including enterprises sponsoring lyceums and students in further and secondary education who were participating in production (see, for example, Ceausescu, 6a and 6b).

Since 1973 further attempts have been made to link housing, clubs, canteens, hostels, health facilities and education more closely to the workplace. Furthermore, the role of the enterprise as the tax-gathering unit is now almost total and taxes are linked to enterprise, not individual income, whilst entitlements to participants in large sections of the social welfare system (including sickness benefits and pensions) are largely confined to State employees.

Clearly the financial basis for these measures has been enhanced by the provision for social and cultural expenditure through enterprise own funds paid out of profits. Although this has a macro-economic rationale in keeping the social wage in line with the growth of enterprise profitability it may also have an ideological role. The growing size of the enterprise combined with its increased social role may lead one to ask whether this will produce a form of economy that could be described as Socialist Corporatism.

REFERENCES

Babe, A. (1980) In *Era Socialista*, 11.
Ceausescu, N. (1965) *Report to the Ninth Congress of the Romanian Communist Party*. Bucharest: Meridiane.

Ceausescu, N. (1965–1978) *Romania on the Way of Building up the Multilaterally Developed Socialist Society: Reports, Interviews, Speeches, Articles, 1965–78.* Bucharest: Meridiane. 5 (a) p. 540; (b) pp. 494–495; (c) pp. 556–557; 6 (a) p. 222; (b) p. 812; 7 p. 467; 10 (a) pp. 404–426; (b) pp. 407–408; (c) p. 409.

Ceausescu, N. (1980) Speech. 13 June 1980. Bucharest: Agerpress.

Directives (1967) *Directives of the Central Committee of the Romanian Communist Party on the Perfecting of Management and Planning of the National Economy.* Bucharest: Agerpress. (a) p. 20; (b) p. 21; (c) p. 83; (d) p. 84; (e) p. 32; (f) p. 110; (g) p. 123; (h) p. 125.

Dumitrescu, M. (1971) In *Probleme al Perfectionarii Conducere Interprinderilor Industriale.* Bucharest: Editura Academie: Republicii Socialiste Romania. pp. 67–68.

Floares, A. (1980) In *Era Socialista*, 12.

Granick, D. (1975) *Enterprise Guidance in Eastern Europe.* Princeton: Princeton University Press. (a) p. 127; (b) p. 128; (c) p. 97; (d) pp.101–102.

Hatos, E. (1979) In *Era Socialista*, 8.

Iuga, C. (1979) In *Era Socialista*, 14.

Kaser, M. (1975) In *The New Economic Systems of Eastern Europe* (ed.) Höhmann, H, Kaser, M. & Thalheim, K. London: Hurst. pp. 183–184.

Murgescu, C. (1974) *Romania's Socialist Economy.* Bucharest: Meridiane. p. 90.

Olteanu, I. (1973) In *Revue Romaine des Sciences Sociales*, 2.

Rachmuth, I. (1972) In *Revue Romaine des Sciences Sociales,* 1, p. 81.

Smith, A. (1979) Romanian economic relations with the EEC. In *Jahrbuch der Wirtschaft Osteuropas*, 8.

Smith, A. (1980) Romanian economic reforms. In *Economic Reforms in Eastern Europe and Prospects for the 1980s.* London: NATO; Pergamon Press.

Spigler, I. (1973) *Economic Reform in Rumanian Industry.* London: Oxford University Press. (a) pp. 60–70; (b) pp. 60–61; (c) pp. 81–86.

Spinu, N. (1980) In *Era Socialista*, 13.

Stusiac, O. (1969) In *Probleme Economice*, 12.

World Bank (1979) *Romania* (Ed.) Tsantis, & Pepper. Washington: World Bank. (a) p. 413; (b) p. 409; (c) pp. 66–68.

5
The Industrial Enterprise in Bulgaria
Michael Kaser

EXPERIENCE BEFORE 1979

In running State industry and cooperative agriculture Bulgaria has tried everything except the market. Of the present Comecon states in Europe Bulgaria was foremost in the installation of the Soviet-type model: it was the first with complete nationalization of industry (1947), the collectivization of agriculture (1958) and, with Czechoslovakia, a five year plan (1949). The particular conditions favouring an early start range from pre-war experience of cooperative farms – 29 were established between 1925 and 1944 – to priority in the wave of Stalinist purge-trials (for a detailed and balanced account, see Tomaszewski, 1980). The hierarchical command economy has never been modified, for the 'New Economic Mechanism' introduced in 1979/80 maintains for the enterprise the structure of imposed 'success-indicators' and compliance therewith. The Party and Government have, on the other hand, been eclectic in their choice of micro-economic organization. In 1958–9 the Chinese commune seems to have begun to emerge as the desired form of agricultural unit: the Secretariat of the Economic Commission for Europe, in a special survey of Bulgaria, *Economic Survey of Europe in 1960*, ch. VI, p. 19, pointed out that in 1959 Bulgarian farms were 'the largest in Europe': the 972 cooperatives held an average area of 4186 ha and the 58 State farms one of 3376 ha in 1963. Then 'production committees' (later 'economic committees'), with half the membership elected by the staff of the enterprise, implied a trend towards the Yugoslav model until their management-advisory functions were withdrawn in 1971.

Between 1965 and 1979 the focus of decision-making in industry (and from 1970 in agriculture) was on large-scale management entities, in a system entitled by Wiedemann, the leading Western expert on Bulgarian economic organization, the 'streamlined centralized system with decomposition' (SCSD). (The term first appears, and is defined in Wiedemann, 'Economic reform in Bulgaria: coping with the kj problem', Wiener Institut für Internationale Wirtschaftsvergleiche, *Forschungsberichte*, 62, July 1980.) His definition of that system covers three other East European mechanisms; 'a centre' (the central planners), a set of 'second-level large economic organizations — in the planning practice of Eastern Europe these could be the DSO in Bulgaria, WOG in Poland, centrala in Romania or VVB in the GDR — and finally a third level of enterprises subordinate to the associations'. (Later in the article it is argued that it is really a 'two-level' system.) 'In our understanding of the SCSD system the enterprises play a very secondary role, particularly when they give up their legal and economic independence to the associations' (Wiedemann, 1980, p. 6). The objective of the system 'was to generate increased planning efficiency by reducing the number and changing the nature of the control figures (success indicators) to make them more internally consistent and generally reduce the amount of detail handled at the centre. At the same time, administrative control was to be increased by reducing by several fold the number of economic units which had to be centrally controlled. The control mechanism is therefore made efficient using the principles of decomposition'. Such is the solution of what Wiedemann terms 'the kj problem — the problem of too many central controls (the k's) and too many production units (the j's) to control' (Wiedemann, 1980, pp. 5-6 and 2 respectively).

In the following brief description of the evolution of Bulgarian practice between 1965 and the introduction of the present system, reference must be made to agriculture because its vertical integration with food-processing has been a major objective since 1970 and because of the transfer to it of large-scale management techniques tested first in the industrial sphere.

A decree authorizing the establishment of the 'state economic association' (*Durzhavenski Stopanski Obedineniya*, DSO) was promulgated in May 1963 (*Rabotnichesko Delo*, 17 May 1963); more and more were set up between then and November 1968, when they became universal under a further decree, entitled 'On the Gradual Application and Further Development of the New System of Economic Guidance' (*Rabotnichesko Delo*, 25 July 1968, quoted the Party Central Committee resolution requiring the enactment and the Decree — No. 50 of the Council of Ministers — was promulgated on 6 November). The authority of industrial ministries to give a DSO operational instructions was withdrawn and it became, in the words of the Party leader, Todor Zhivkov, to the November 1968 Plenum of the Central Committee, 'the basic entity for the management of enterprises in the individual branches and sub-branches of the national economy' (Vogel, 1975a).

The general introduction of the DSO coincided with a new-found reliance on central coordination within a framework of cybernetics rather than of negotiation. The concept of the 'New System' sketched by the Plenum of the Central Committee in December 1965 had been 'improved coordination, guidance and management by central planning' (*Rabotnichesko Delo*, 4 December 1965); the system of success indicators had been maintained but the number operative for the enterprise had been reduced to four: quantities of specified products in physical terms, a maximum for investment outlay, volume of raw materials and intermediate inputs and, where appropriate, import or export targets. As an ensuing Plenum confirmed (April 1966), freedom for enterprises to conclude contracts among themselves was limited to deliveries from non-earmarked capacities, and that was subject to superior confirmation. The 'New System' also introduced the construct of 'funds' into which enterprise profit was to be distributed (Vogel, 1975b). Similar to the Soviet appropriation procedure, it was to be significantly developed in the 'New Mechanism' of 1979–80.

The 1968 re-centralization involved an increase in the number of success indicators for enterprises of which three additional ones (specific volumes under contractual delivery, maximum wage-bill and installation of technology) notably limited the freedom of the enterprise with respect to the situation in 1966–8 and an authorization to the DSO concerned to impose further indicators. The 'fund' allocation system for the enterprise was differentiated by branch, and the DSO (from this date the key decision-maker) was endowed with a complex fund allocation system of its own (Vogel, 1975c). Another sign of recentralization was the abandonment of a modest area of wholesale-price de-control initiated in 1965.

The final phase in the application to the non-farm sector of the SCSD came in November 1970 (Decree published in *Durzhaven Vestnik*, 10 January 1971; the decision in principle had been taken at a Plenum of the Central Committee in September 1969; *Rabotnichesko Delo*, 25 September 1969) when the number of DSOs was halved by merger from 120 to 64 (of which 35 were in industry), and the enterprises under them were deprived of their juridical autonomy (with effect from 31 December 1970). The enterprise thus disappeared from the planning and management hierarchy, although for accounting purposes enterprises compiled their own balance sheets, held bank accounts and could sign contracts. The practice was given the name the New Economic Mechanism (for a symposium on the system see Shopov et al, 1972), familiar from the then-recent Hungarian example, but patently unlike the latter's enterprise autonomy: the name was to recur as that for the changes of 1979–80. There was an average of five DSOs for each branch ministry and 27 sub-branches under each DSO (the productive workforce of each of which was around 17 000) (Allen, 1979).

In this monopoly form, the DSO lasted only until 1974, when a range of coordinatory or alternative agencies was introduced. The agencies of coordination were termed an 'economic complex', the first to be set up being a National Transport Complex on 1 January 1974, followed by a National Construction

Complex on 1 April and a National Agro-Industrial Complex on 5 August. With another established in January 1977 (the National Trade Tourism and Consumer Services Complex), they were described as 'the basic structural units of the national economy' (to be distinguished from the central coordination agency established in 1973, NAPK). Forms alternative to the DSO were also authorized ('State economic combines' and 'united economic enterprises'), such that the term 'economic organization' (*stopanska organizatsia*) became standard for all entities in the hierarchy, including the branch ministries, which were perceived as having a function both as an organ of the State and an economic (self-financing) organization.

The term also covered the entities introduced into agriculture after a Plenum of the Central Committee in April 1970. The first was the 'agro-industrial complex' (*Agrarno-Promishlen Komplex*, APK), an experiment which had been initiated in 1968 with the merger into one of five State farms; 12 had been created by the end of 1969, and, after their encouragement by the Plenum, there were already 138 by January 1971. Eventually, the 744 cooperative farms (TKZSs) and the 56 state farms (DZSs) were amalgamated into 161 APKs – some of TKZSs, others of DZSs and others mixed – by the end of 1971 (Wiedemann, 1980). Since this chapter is concerned with industry alone, mention need only be made of the 'unified' APK (the majority), in which 'the form of management changes from territorial to branch (i.e., section managers become concerned with spheres of specialization rather than separate territorial units). Each previously independent farm becomes a branch or sub-farm of the APK with its own production specialization (e.g., grain growing, livestock breeding, fodder production, fruit production, etc.) (Jacobs, 1977a; see also Wiedemann, 1980, and Clayton, 1981).

The link with industrial organization emerged in 1973 when seven 'industro-agrarian (or industro-agricultural) complexes' (PAKs) were formed, within the Industro-Agrarian Organization (PAO), vertically integrated with industrial enterprises processing and selling agricultural produce. The PAO became the administrative supervisor for the PAKs and, formed in September 1976, a National Agro-Industrial Complex (*Natsionalen Agrarno-Promishlen Kompleks*, NAPK), which oversaw the APKs (Jacobs, 1977b). When even this degree of centralization was judged inadequate both were subordinated in 1979 to the National Agro-Industrial Union (*Natsionalen Agrarno-Promishlen Suyuz*, NAPS: on its forecasting – and effectively, planning – functions see Atanasova, 1979), which replaced the Ministry of Agriculture and the Food Industry to become the repository of central authority for agriculture, food processing, agricultural engineering and agricultural research (*Rabotnichesko Delo*, 30 March 1979; see Wiedemann, 1980, pp. 16–17).

THE NEW ECONOMIC MECHANISM OF 1979

There are modest signs in the newly-introduced practice to return a little responsibility down the administrative line, but to the brigade within the enterprise rather than to the enterprise itself. The broad issues were posed by the
Party leadership to a National Party Conference in 1978 and new regulations
were applied to agricultural organizations from 1 January 1979, to foreign-trade
organizations from 1 July, to industry from 30 July (Subev et al, 1979a) to
transport (Vulkov, 1979) and in domestic trade and consumer services from
1 January 1980 (Rangelov, 1980); dates for construction and for research and
technical organizations appear to have been respectively in mid 1979 and mid
1980 (Angelov, 1979, and Ilnev, 1980).

In authoritatively presenting the new industrial regulations, three authors from
the State Planning Committee set out the following objects of the New Economic
Mechanism: to establish a better balance between de-centralization and centralization; to widen the scope for initiative and independence for economic organizations (particularly in technical and managerial decision-making); to promote the
conformity of output to market conditions while corresponding to socialist
commodity production; to ensure self-financing in productive-economic operations by means of cost accounting; to introduce new finance relations between
the State and economic organizations and between and within such organizations;
and to apply incentives to the personnel and technical directorate which conform
to the improvement of the organization's economic performance (Subev et al,
1979b).

The economic organization (i.e., DSO or entity at that level) may in future
receive from its supervising ministry only five plan indicators. The first is 'realized
production' (i.e., production in saleable form disposed of to recipients) in
physical measures, divided into three categories: exports (with destination);
cooperative deliveries and spare parts; deliveries to the domestic market. The
second 'success-indicator' is volume of net product (in value) and a third, where
appropriate, is foreign-exchange earnings on exports and/or maximum foreign-
exchange expenditure (*valutni limit za vnosa*), also by destination. The two other
indicators are maxima (*limiti*) on supplies of raw materials, intermediate inputs,
energy and 'certain deficitary machines and equipment', and payments to the
State budget. In turn the economic organization imposes four indicators on its
'subdivisions' (*podeleniya*; the term 'enterprise' is not used). The first and last
correspond to those at the higher level and each may thus be characterized in
the Soviet sense as a *skvoznoy pokazatel* (through indicator). The first (using
the order shown) is production in physical units by type and quality (and with
statement of its user); the second is 'normed cost of production per unit of
output (by product, product-group or by type of work)'; the third is tasks for
the application of technological change; and the last is a maximum for number
of personnel (Subev et al, 1979c). (At both 'organization' and 'subdivision'

level, a 'normed quota' can be substituted for a maximum with respect to the number of personnel. At the 'subdivision' level 'other specific indicators', *drugi spetsifichni pokazateli*, may be substituted for the first and second indicators in the case of repair work and service contracts.)

Decree No. 36 of the Council of Ministers of 1978 required the abandonment of capital-investment 'limits' on economic organizations, and Decree No. 29 of the same year devolved the establishment of an economic organization's investment plan to its contracts with the Bulgarian National Bank (which has its own rules for assuring funds in accordance with the type of project or end-use of funds), with the construction organization and with the agency supplying equipment. No central targets are established for labour productivity, profits or shift-coefficients (though they may be utilized within the economic organization on its own initiative but not as obligatory 'indicators'), but a central set of material balances is maintained, built upon the supply limits imposed on user-organizations. The formulation of the material balances is described as a combination of contractual agreement and of central planning (Subev et al, 1979d).

Self-finance is the watch-word for the economic organization. It must operate on 'cost accounting', concluding contracts with suppliers and customers to ensure a cash balance and borrowing from the banking system when required. With respect to wages, three novel relationships are introduced. The 'Wage Fund' (RZ) for an economic organization is defined as the 'residual outcome magnitude' (*rezultativno-ostatuchna velichina*) after other deductions from gross income (*brutni dokhod*): these deductions are considered below. The second is that the Wage Fund must be related to productivity with a maximum relationship of a 0.5 per cent rise in remuneration to a 1 per cent rise in 'social productivity'. The third is the inclusion of sanctions for management staff (*rukovodni kadri*), up to 20 per cent deduction from pay in case of failure to fulfil 'normatives', which cumulate to the incentives long established for over-fulfilment. It is specified that these sanctions apply to both economic organizations, subdivisions and productive units (Subev et al, 1979e).

The revenue of a production unit is divided between itself and the economic organization and, after settlement of suppliers' accounts, is divided into three categories (Ivanov, 1979a). The first comprises bank interest, social insurance premia, and payments to the economic organization (in the case of the latter to the ministry). The second (for all branches) is to the various Funds which finance both investment and remuneration: the Wage Fund (RZ), the Funds for Social, Living-conditions and Cultural Measures (SBKM), Assimilation of New Production (UNP), Foreign Exchange (V), Service Operations (SD), Innovation and Rationalization (IR) and Reserve (R), the last-named being supplied by a 2 per cent levy on revenue (Ivanov, 1979c). In a number of branches (including industry and agriculture) there is a further Fund, for Expansion and Technological Improvement (RTU), into which a 'productive subdivision' is also authorized to add 80 per cent of depreciation allowances scheduled for capital repair and 20 per cent of depreciation allowances scheduled for replacement of assets (Subev et al, 1979f). The RTU at both economic-organization and productive-subdivision level must be allocated a minimum of 4 per cent of sales income (or more in the case of economic organizations and where authorized by the Council of Ministers) (Ivanov, 1979b). A share of profits is added into the Wage Fund. At the lowest level of subdivision, brigade cost accounting is actively encouraged under the New Economic Mechanism. The examples so far cited are either in agriculture or in agriculture-related industries (for example, a large piggery, 12 000 pigs and pig-meat producer [Petrov, 1979], or a refrigeration plant [Chushev, 1980]; the only *Ikonomicheski Zhivot* supplement on the topic, of 5 July 1980, discusses agriculture), but there are references to the general advisability of carrying 'plan-accounting' (*plan-smetka*) below the hitherto conventional level of the enterprise.

Finally, an important provision is that it is now the 'client purchaser' which accepts the goods or services according to the terms of the contract negotiated with the supplier and no longer the latter which fulfils its plan by the act of production and sound delivery. Once an economic organization has completed its planned production, however, it can freely sell all above-plan output and output outside the plan: such output can be sold 'on the free market', in its own shops, abroad (on commission through a foreign-trade organization) or to the local government authority in whose territory it is located for sale at retail or for its own use (Mishev, 1980).

The new elements of flexibility at the enterprise level, namely the productive subdivision of the economic organization, lie in freedom to invest without restriction from its RTU Fund provided that the period from investment to completion (*realizatsiya*) does not exceed 12 months (Ivanov, 1979c), the reduction in the number of success indicators (the figure at the economic organization level is from 25 to 4, or 5 in the case of industry; Mishev, 1980, p. 39) and in the disposal of its various remuneration funds. Although it has not regained its autonomy it is distinctly more responsible for its own current operations, gaining a tangible return from profits earned. It remains more limited in its access to longer-term capital funds (i.e. more than it can self-finance for projects maturing in less than a year). It may borrow from the banking system for capital projects in its own name, but must obtain permission to do so from its economic organization, which also is required to furnish a guarantee to the bank (Grozdanov, 1979a). The economic organization, on the other hand, can borrow for up to 10 years from a bank, subject to being able to put up from its own resources a minimum contribution (e.g., 20 000 leva for a loan of 450 000 but 10 per cent for large sums) (Grozdanov, 1979b). Either an economic organization or a productive subdivision can borrow working capital from the banking system within specified norms concerning the purpose for which the credit is required; most working capital should, however, be built up from the RTU Fund (Grozdanov, 1979c).

Wholesale-price Reform

It is a significant characteristic of the New Economic Mechanism that the
end-user of an import and the supplier of an export have a direct financial
interest in the purchases or sales of a foreign-trade corporation, which in general
is to be employed not as a compulsory middleman but as commissionaire: the
monopoly—monopsony of the corporation is preserved but the initiative and the
decisions are those of the economic organization. This change urgently posed the
problem of the conversion rate from domestic wholesale prices to the prices paid
or received on the foreign market. On 1 January 1980, in the words of President
Zhivkov, 'domestic wholesale prices were made to conform to prices on the
international market, from which they had considerably diverged' (speech to
the National Council of the Fatherland Front, of 11 February 1980).

The new price-lists replace those of 1 January 1971 and were issued in
pursuance of a Resolution of the Party Central Committee and the Council of
Ministers of 10 November 1979; for wholesale prices to have been constant for
nine years is not, of course, unusual among Comecon members (the Soviet
wholesale price-lists were changed in 1955 and 1967 and will next be changed in
1981—2) and compares with 15 years for the lists superseded in 1979 (which had
entered into force on 1 April 1971). Relative world-price changes between 1971
and 1979 are said to have resulted in 80 per cent of domestic wholesale price
relativities not conforming to world relativities, causing 'deformities in the
cost of production for finished goods and the irrational use of raw materials and
fuel'; nor did domestic prices stimulate the productive use of imports or accelerate the introduction of technical progress (Pekhlivanov, 1979).

Under the new prices many 'branches and products will be temporarily
unprofitable' (Nikolov, 1980a) until they can eventually adjust, and 'temporary
subsidies' have been authorized to economic organizations making losses because
their input prices have been raised further than their output prices. Such subsidies may be made either as a direct grant or as reductions in taxation, such as
deductions from profits or the turnover tax (Nikolov, 1980b).

The Role of the Contract

Some 200 000 contracts annually are signed among economic organizations and
subdivisions. Although the present law on contracts dates from 1950, what is
known as 'the contractual system' was experimentally introduced from 1964,
and in 1968 was confirmed as the appropriate direction for the execution of
plans and normatives. Only under legislation of 1979 for domestic transactions
and of 1980 for exports and imports did the system, under new regulations,
become general (Panchev, 1980a). While contracts must conform to plans
and 'state tasks embodied in control figures', they serve to construct relations

'from the bottom up' (*otdoly nagore*), rather than as under the previous practice 'from the top down' (*otgore nadolu*) (Panchev, 1980b), and particularly serve adaptability to the international market (Panchev, 1980c). Under the New Economic Mechanism the contract system was strengthened, penalties being increased for non-fulfilment.

The Penetration of Foreign Enterprises

Laws extending the practice of industrial cooperation to include the right of western firms to establish joint equity ventures in Eastern Europe have been on the books for some time in Hungary, Poland, Romania and Yugoslavia, and in March 1980 Bulgaria adopted a new policy on foreign equity investment, a move that can be directly related to its attempts to pursue a policy alternative to that of the last decade, and reduce the hard currency burden of Western imports, and to serve to as a supplement to the policies on export stimulation introduced in recent years.

The Bulgarian law permits foreign firms (though not individuals) to take an equity stake in Bulgarian State-owned enterprises (Decree of 25 March 1980) and adds a new dimension to the position of the enterprise in Bulgaria. Either a minority or a majority holding may be purchased, depending on the nature of the specific project, and the buyer can take part in the management of the enterprise, in the sense that he can control activities such as quality control and market research, though the managing director of such an enterprise must be a Bulgarian citizen (*Durzhaven Vestnik*, 28 March 1980). The Decree authorizes the Ministers of Finance and of Foreign Trade to levy tax at null or reduced rates for the initial three years. The enterprise is subject to Bulgarian law and may be operative for between three and 15 years, at the end of which period the government can either wind the enterprise up or extend the period of its operation.

The industrial cooperation agreements that have been created so far have been in machine-building, in the electronics industry and in agriculture, but the new joint ventures are to be concentrated in areas concerned with the extraction of Bulgarian raw materials, their processing and their export to third countries. Among the products for which the Bulgarian authorities see the potential for possible joint-equity ventures are hard coal, manganese, tungsten and copper, the deposits of which have in many cases proved inaccessible in the past with the technology readily available to the Bulgarians.

For sales of a joint-venture production in third countries the foreign firm will receive its share of the profits in hard currency. It is also forseen that the production of the joint venture enterprise may be sold for convertible currency in Bulgaria, in which case the profit share would also be paid in such currency. The First Deputy Minister for Foreign Trade, Atanas Ginev, has also stated that Bulgaria would be prepared to sell the production of the joint venture to other

Comecon countries, but again only against convertible currency (*Sofia News*, 9 April 1980).

ACKNOWLEDGEMENT

Comments made after the symposium by Dr Paul Wiedemann are warmly acknowledged for the final version of this chapter.

REFERENCES

Allen, M. (1977) The Bulgarian economy in the 1970s In *East European Economies Post-Helsinki*. Washington: Joint Economic Committee of the US Congress. p. 668.

Angelov, L. (1979) In *Ikonomicheski Zhivot*, supplement, 178.

Atanasova, M. (1979) In *Planovo Stopanstvo*, 5.

Chushev, K. (1980) In *Planovo Stopanstvo*, 2. pp. 74–75.

Clayton, E. (1981) Bulgaria and Romania: prospects for 1980. In *Economic Reforms in Eastern Europe and Prospects for the 1980s*. To be published by the NATO Economics Directorate.

Dellin, L.A. (1970) Bulgarian economic reform – advance and retreat. In *Problems of Communism*, September–October. pp. 52ff.

Feiwel, G.R. (1977) *Growth and Reforms in Centrally-Planned Economies: the Lessons of the Bulgarian Experience*. New York: Praeger.

Feiwel, G.R. (1979) Economic reform in Bulgaria. In *Osteuropa Wirtshaft*, June. pp. 71–91.

Grozdanov, G.S. (1979) In *Ikonomicheski Zhivot*, supplement. 177. (a) p. 6; (b) p. 3; (c) p. 8.

Ilnev, N. (1980) In *Ikonomicheski Zhivot*, supplement, 14 May.

Ivanov, K. (1979) In *Ikonomicheski Zhivot*, supplement, 175. (a) whole article; (b) p. 14; (c) p. 15.

Jacobs, E.M. (1977) Recent developments in organisation and management of agriculture in Eastern Europe. In *East European Economies Post-Helsinki*. Washington: Joint Economic Committee of the US Congress. (a) p. 343; (b) p. 344.

Mishev, V. (1980) In *Planovo Stopanstvo*, 3. p. 39.

Nikolov, I. (1980) In *Ikonomicheski Zhivot*, supplement, 182. (a) p. 5; (b) p. 9.

Panchev, B. (1980) In *Planovo Stopanstvo*, 5. (a) pp. 16–19; (b) p. 19 (he puts the phrases within inverted commas); (c) p. 20.

Pekhlivanov, V. (1979) In *Ikonomicheski Zhivot*; supplement, 177. p. 14.

Petrov, I. (1979) In *Planovo Stopanstvo*, 3. pp. 72–75.

Rangelov, N. (1980) In *Planovo Stopanstvo*, 2.

Shopov, D. et al (1972) *Noviyat Ikonomicheski Mekhanisum*, Sofia. 496 pp.

Subev, I. et al (1979) In *Planovo Stopanstvo*, 9. (a) whole article; (b) pp. 3–4; (c) p. 5; (d) pp. 6–7; (e) p. 10; (f) p. 9.

Tomaszewski, J. (1980) *Rozwoj Bulgarii w latach 1944–1956*, Warsaw (esp. pp. 68–79 and 101–124).

Vogel, H. (1975) Bulgaria. In *The New Economic Systems of Eastern Europe*. (Ed.) Höhmann, H.H., Kaser, M. & Thalheim, K.C. London: Hurst; Berkeley, CA: University of California Press. (a) p. 209; (b) p. 205; (c) pp. 210–211.

Vulkov, V. (1979) In *Planovo Stopanstvo*, 10.

Wiedemann, P. (1980) The origins and development of agro-industrial development in Bulgaria. In *Agriculture Policies in the USSR and Eastern Europe* (Ed.) Francisco, R.A., Laird, B.A. & Laird, R.D. Boulder, Colorado: Westview Press. pp. 100–102.

ANNEX

Relevant texts appearing in Planovo Stopanstvo *in 1979 and 1980*

Author	*Title*	*Issue*
M. Atanasova	Forecasting in the National Agrarian–Industrial Complex	5, 1979, pp. 32–44
I. Subev, S. Kalinov & S. Videnov (State Planning Committee)	Improving the management of economic organizations in industry	9, 1979, pp. 3–10
V. Vulkov (Deputy Minister of Transport)	The new economic method in transport management	10, 1979, pp. 3–14
Kh. Kirov	The economic autonomy of economic organizations and productive enterprises	10, 1979, pp. 15–22
N. Rangelov	The economic method in the activity of domestic trade and consumer services	2, 1980, pp. 37–44
V. Mishev	The New Economic Mechanism in the national economy	3, 1980, pp. 38–49
I. Kalcheva	The economic method in the management of agriculture and the raising of efficiency of its production	5, 1980, pp. 3–15
B. Panchev	The role of contracts between economic organizations under the New Economic Mechanism	5, 1980, pp. 16–24

Relevant 'supplements' to Ikonomichesky Zhivot *in the series* 'Help in Mastering the New Economic System' *in 1979 and 1980*

Number	*Title*	*Issue*
175	Financial Operation of an Economic Organization	7 September 1979
177	Credit for Economic Organizations and Productive Units in Industry; the Reform of Wholesale Prices	5 December 1979
178	The Economic Mechanism for the Management of Building-Assembly Organizations	12 December 1979
181	The Basic Statute of the New Economic Mechanism for . . . Domestic Trade, Local Industry and Services	27 February 1980
182	Temporary Subsidies to Wholesale Prices	3 March 1980
183	Basic Principles of the New Economic Mechanism in Transport, Building and Domestic Trade	19 March 1980
184	The Economic Approach to Material-Technical Supply	26 March 1980
185	Economic Accounting under the New Economic Mechanism	9 April 1980
187	The Economic Approach to the Management of Scientific Research and of Experimental-Development Engineering	14 April 1980
188	The Business Contract in Conditions of the New Economic Mechanism	11 June 1980
189	Basic Trends in the Further Improvement of Brigade Organization in Agriculture	9 July 1980

6
Combine Formation and the Role of the Enterprise in East German Industry

Manfred Melzer

PROBLEMS AND WEAKNESSES IN THE ECONOMIC SYSTEM

During the second half of the 1970s there were unsuccessful attempts to remedy the deficiencies associated with the 1970–71 re-centralization by means of improvements in planning methods (*Gesetzblatt der DDR*, 775a and 780, 1974 and 1975). Standardization of procedures, to counteract over-regulation, was striven for but, where introduced, was met with new, more exact and more extensive plan control (Leptin and Melzer, 1978). Thus bureaucracy, already excessive, was increased even further.

The utilization of factors of production has remained inefficient: manpower is wasted in insufficiently-mechanized processes; raw materials and machinery are not employed efficiently; obsolete plant is replaced only very slowly; there has been an increase in the number of unplanned investment projects, projects which officially should not even exist (thus Günter Mittag [1978, 5] came to the conclusion that 'Acute economic disturbances will be created if, for example, in this year alone, unplanned investments worth billions are carried out'. He explained this phenomenon by the fact that small investments are initially applied for and then, when the project is in progress, increasingly large investments are requested); and price increases are becoming more and more apparent (East German economists Kurt Matterne and Siegfried Tannhäuser have pointed out that '. . . up to 50 per cent of the actual price demanded has been excessive to regulations' [Matterne and Tannhäuser, 1978]). Furthermore, investments are often inadequately prepared and, therefore, their realization takes far too long.

Technological progress is very poor. The lack of interest in innovation at the enterprise level is, to a large extent, responsible for these problems, but it should be stressed that the regulations relating to profit utilization do not provide any incentive to be innovative or to take risks. Planning methods for increasing efficiency have also proved to be inadequate (Mätzig and Neumann, 1975; Ritzschke and Steeger, 1975): the extreme distortion of prices makes meaningful measurement impossible, despite the use of efficiency indicators, such as cost reduction and labour productivity.

In the past few years, a relatively new problem has come to light, namely weakness in management. East German experts have mentioned the following as indicative of this weakness (collective authors, 1976): the increasing failure to fulfil production plan indicators; discontinuous productivity; the declining rate of growth; inability to meet demand; the increasing amount of work stoppage, due to such factors as input shortages; increasing overtime; the large increase in special shifts; the stagnation in innovations; growing discontent among employees, as well as the increased number of complaints from the lower ranks. These are caused by functional weaknesses in the system: an information system which concentrates more on the needs of the central authorities, thus neglecting other management levels; the overlapping decision-making authority of the central authorities; the lack of feedback in plan-drafting; insufficient coordination in inter-branch relations; lack of willingness to make decisions on the part of higher authorities; and insufficient flexibility when break-downs occur.

In addition to these intrinsic problems there is also the main economic problem in the GDR, namely the increasing burden of foreign trade. Since the mid 1970s, the GDR, which has very few natural resources of its own, has been confronted by rapidly rising world prices for raw materials and energy, leading to a deterioration in the commodity terms of trade, a situation which is expected to deteriorate further (Honecker, 1979, 12). Faced with the prospect of a continuing decline in the growth of national income, exports must increase, even at the expense of domestic development.

DESIRED IMPROVEMENTS

East German leaders have suggested certain improvements, in part still being discussed (Melzer and Scherzinger, 1978), but especially concentrated on increased combine formation, in order at least to succeed in achieving greater productivity by means of careful and partially increased decision-making competence for their management committees. The merger of enterprises aims '. . . to unify those capacities which are components of a particular production complex and belong together naturally in the national economy' (Gerisch and Hofmann, 1979). 'The combines are therefore more than just a sum of their parts. The possible division of labour and rational cooperation between enterprises increases their performance' (Hartmann, 1978). There seems to be a greater chance of success for rationalization, in other words increasing productivity through the modernization of existing machinery and for economizing on raw materials and manpower, because they can be better planned by the combine management than the central planners. Also it is hoped that combines will be able to work better in all ways, both with the ministries above them and with the enterprises within them, and that a harmonizing of central with selective enterprise aims will result. Shorter and more efficient channels of information will be created and more meaningful intersectoral coordination will be possible.

Director generals of combines have a dual role: on the one hand to help fulfil the five year plan by improving plan coordination and harmonizing State-defined performance expectations and actual production possibilities of the enterprises comprising the combine (Scholl, 1978); on the other hand to streamline the management structure of combines and improve internal organization, for example, by means of a more intensive concentration of processes concerned with production preparation, execution and sale (Hofmann, 1979). Thus the director general is both the 'minister's delegate' and an 'enterpreneur' at one and the same time, an extremely difficult position to be in, especially since management is a much more complicated task now than it was ten years ago (conference report in Wirtschaftswissenschaft, 6, 1980, p. 749).

Combine formation is, in the words of Honecker, '. . . at the present time, the most important step towards perfect management and planning' (Honecker, 1978). The reason for this is that '. . . within the combine the most important phases of the process of reproduction are coordinated, beginning with research and development, followed by the projecting and self-sufficient production of rationalization means, leading to production itself, including high quality products and sales to both the domestic and foreign markets' (Mittag, 1978, 8). In particular, it is hoped that combines will produce the following benefits: advantages resulting from size, especially in production and distribution; coordination of the capacities of the various enterprises within the combine; improved supply conditions, both as a result of combining appropriate enterprises and the more rational use of materials; lasting rationalization improvements, especially as a result of the discarding of obsolete machinery and the more efficient use of modern machinery; the better preparation and realization of investment projects; the production of goods which are of better quality and satisfy user demand; an increase in exports by means of the development of products which are competitive on the world market; greater scientific and technological progress as a result of increased research at the combine level. Expectations are illustrated by the following statement made by the Director-General of the Carl-Zeiss Jena Combine: 'If all the 129 directly subordinate combines in industry and construction succeed in achieving better economic results at the necessary pace, then we will have several billion more marks of distributable finished products. That is what we are concerned with' (Huber, 1980). Thus the combines committed themselves to a level of productivity two billion marks above that in the 1980 plan (*Neues Deutschland*, 24 March 1980, pp. 1 and 3). However, with the exception of a few 'ideal combines', progress has not been very significant (*Neues Deutschland*, 22/23 March 1980, p. 3).

THE RESTRUCTURING OF ECONOMIC ADMINISTRATION

With only a few exceptions, the VVBs (associations of nationalized enterprises) have been replaced by combines, of various types and endowed with enhanced decision-making rights. The GDR is attempting to build up a more efficient information system and therefore improved planning model, by reducing the number of different levels in the general economic administration system from three (ministry − VVB − enterprise/combine) to two (ministry − combine). The VVB, acting as an intermediate link between ministry and enterprise, worked primarily as an administrative authority, responsible for the planning and management of the enterprises under their control and, therefore, not concerned with branch-external relations and coordination processes. This led to planning and supply problems, since responsibility for material balancing and groups of products (product group work involves the cooperation or division of work between enterprises making similar products or employing the same technology) was split up between different authorities (Burian, 1978).

Combines, directly subordinate to the relevant ministry, have been formed by the amalgamation of enterprises formerly belonging to one VVB (under a particular ministry) with those constituting important branch-external suppliers, formerly belonging to another VVB (and under a different ministry). The reasons for this include the following: to reduce inter-branch and inter-sectoral coordination problems, to overcome the dispersal of branch management tasks over several authorities; to shorten information flows; speedier decisions; more flexible planning processes; and the creation of a more clear-cut and less awkward overall economic and management system. The central planners thus hope to improve planning and management by better coordination and by giving combines responsibilities for the distribution of plan targets and tasks and material balancing.

This is illustrated in Figure 6.1 in which 45 hypothetical enterprises are distributed among three ministries. Consider, for example, enterprises 12 and 19. Formerly it was necessary for enterprise 12 to provide information to VVB (b) and Ministry I and enterprise 19 to VVB (D) and Ministry II, so that, finally, in the case of important groups of products, Ministries I and II were able to coordinate decisions. However, the more extensive the branch-overlapping production flow became, the more prohibitive and time-consuming the coordination proved to be because it involved several authorities. Combine formation allows a considerable rationalization of the management system. So, for example, enterprises 32 and 35 in Ministry III, which were responsible for supplying enterprises in the former

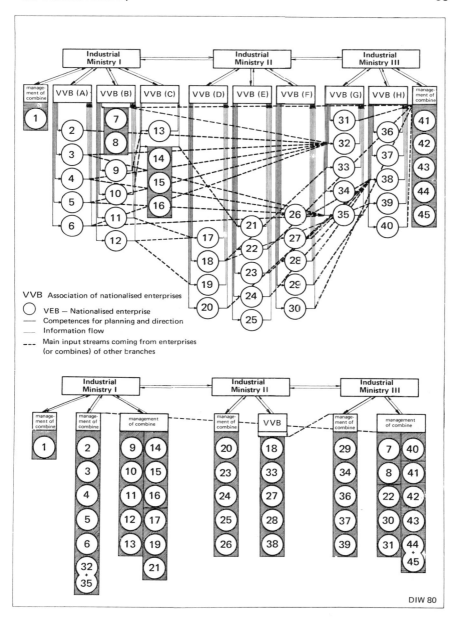

Figure 6.1 *Improvements in GDR's administration structure achieved by the introduction of combines (via a change from inter-sectoral to intra-sectoral relations); schematic diagram.*

VVB (A) in Ministry I, have been incorporated into a combine in Ministry I. This combine comprises the enterprises of the former VVB (A), together with enterprises 32 and 35.

Different types of combines are possible. For example, an existing combine, consisting of enterprises 14, 15 and 16, incorporates enterprises from different VVBs in the same ministry (9, 10, 11, 12, 13), as well as from VVBs in another ministry (17, 19, 21). Another type involves the transfer of an existing combine (comprising enterprises 7 and 8) from Ministry I to Ministry III; it is then merged with another combine in Ministry III (enterprises 41, 42, 43, 44 and 45) and with other enterprises which are both branch-related (31, 40) and branch-external (22, 30). It is also possible initially to take branch-related (18, 27, 28) and branch-external enterprises (33, 38) and unite them temporarily into a combine still controlled by a VVB, at a later date to form a combine directly subordinate to Ministry II.

At present it is possible to identify five main types of combines (Melzer, Scherzinger and Schwartau, 1979), all presented in Figure 6.1:

1. A traditional combine with one single enterprise (for example, Leuna-Werke).
2. A VVB made into a combine, with or without the incorporation of other enterprises (for example, Takraf, the heavy machinery combine and the Wool and Silk Combine).
3. An existing combine incorporates other enterprises (for example, Zeulenroda-Triebes, the furniture combine, and Esda, the hosiery combine).
4. Two or more combines form a larger combine, with or without the incorporation of other enterprises (for example, Robotron from the former combines Robotron, Zentronik and AHB Office Machines Export, AHB standing for nationalized foreign trade enterprise).
5. An existing combine is used as the basis of a new combine, subordinate to a different ministry (for example, Ruhla, the timepiece manufacturing combine, which was previously directly managed by the Ministry for Machine Tools and Processing Machine Manufacture, moved into the field of electronics and took over management responsibility for the new Micro-electronics Combine).

In virtually every type of combine, the incorporation or setting-up of new, branch-external suppliers, ranging from producers of raw materials to manufacturers of highly specialized finished goods, played a very important role (so, for example, mechanical engineering combines have their own foundries, the shoe industry produces its own leather, the metallurgy industry has its own power stations, the electronics industry produces its own glass, and nautical electronics has become part of the ship-building industry). At the beginning of 1980 there were 129 industrial and construction combines, directly subordinate to ministries, accounting for 91 per cent of employees in centrally-managed industry and construction (Mittag, 1979). Approximately 110 industrial combines, directed by 11 industrial ministries, were responsible for 90 per cent of production. There were only 37 industrial combines in 1973, 43 in 1977 (accounting for 30 per cent of output) and 89 at the beginning of 1979, accounting for 72 per cent of industrial production (Arnold, 1980). Several problems have arisen however: combines tend to favour the incorporation and try to avoid the loss of enterprises; thus non-optimal amalgamations may occur (for example, chemical plant construction takes place both in the Chemical Ministry, as part of the Leipzig–Grimma Combine for Chemical Plant Construction, and in the Ministry for Heavy Machinery and Plant Construction, as part of the Ernst Thälmann Combine for Heavy Machinery Construction in Magdeburg); suppliers changing branches are confronted with new coordination problems with new branch-external buyers. The creation of larger combines causes both temporary friction and numerous intra-sectoral management problems.

Despite the highly centralized nature of production and supply planning, the restructuring has had a positive effect on combine decision-making rights: the transference of decision-making powers from VVB to combine (transference effect); these former decision-making powers have been enlarged because of the expansion and incorporation of branch-external suppliers (size and lateral extension effect); increased decision-making powers at the expense of individual enterprises, for example in machinery transfer (intensification effect); and increased influence with ministries with respect to coordination processes (co-determination effect). The new combine regulations (*Gesetzblatt der DDR*, 38, 1979) state that the Council of Ministers decides on the foundation of directly subordinate combines, while the basic structure and alterations, restructuring and the combine statute are in each case determined by the relevant minister. An important point is that the director-general has the right to alter the functions/tasks of enterprises, and indeed to transfer them between enterprises; he may create new enterprise sections and transfer machinery and production tasks to other enterprises. In addition, the director-general determines which tasks (concerned with, for example, research, investment, distribution, market research, accounting and professional qualifications) are to be centralized and which are to be the concern of individual enterprises. He is totally responsible for justifying the draft of the plan to the minister, apportions planning functions among enterprises and supervises their implementation. The following functions, up to now in the hands of central organs, are also carried out by the director-general: intra-combine material balancing; special goods pricing; standardization; and socialist economic integration (with respect to Comecon countries the combines now have the following responsibilities: to present, together with foreign trade enterprises, suggestions and alternative solutions for economic, scientific and technological cooperation; to guarantee the scheduled fulfilment of commitments ensuing from international trade contracts; to coordinate the development of research and productivity with the relevant Comecon member countries and to organize the exchange of experience; to form trade contracts concerning specialization and production cooperation with Comecon partners together with the relevant foreign trade enterprises; Klinger, 1980). Apart from this, ministers can delegate responsibility to combine management, as well as consulting about important politico-economic matters. The director-general is personally responsible for combine development and the implementation of planning functions, and appoints the enterprise manager, who can be involved in discussion relating to important matters. Thus authority of the combine director has been increased both quantitatively and qualitatively, especially in relation to internal organization (Hochbaum and Siefarth, 1978).

Nevertheless, the position with regard to combine decision-making rights is not clear. Honecker's comment (1979, 2), that ministries should concentrate on 'main issues', is open to various interpretations. This is also admitted in the literature on economics in the GDR (Kühnau, 1979). Thus it must be assumed that ministries will continue to have far-reaching rights, which allow them to intervene, even as far as enterprises themselves, in important matters. For example, while some combines determine product mix, others have production programmes wholly laid down by the relevant minister (Gabler and Wichler, 1979). Finally, it is also evident on the basis of virtually total agreement about the spheres of action of ministries (as stated in East German economic literature [Collective authors, 1979a] and combines (as stated in combine regulations, Erdmann, 1979).

It is possible to distinguish four basic types of combine with respect to internal management organization (Collective authors, 1979b), in which the management of a combine comprising (see Figures 6.2 and 6.3):

1. one enterprise is carried out by a *central combine management* (for example Leuna-Werke);
2. more than one enterprise is carried out by an *independent management body* (for example, VEB Combine Carl Zeiss Jena);
3. several enterprises is carried out by the *parent enterprise* (for example Mansfeld Combine, Bitterfeld Chemicals Combine and IFA Passenger Vehicles Combine);
4. several enterprises is carried out by the *leading enterprises* in the various product groups (for example, the Microelectronics, Deko and Radio and Television Combines).

Individual enterprises within the combines in Categories 2, 3 and 4 remain independent legal and economic entities (Penig et al, 1978).

The problems associated with types 1 and 2 are as follows: lengthy internal planning and decision-making procedures, delayed responses in the case of coordination processes and, consequently, the possibility of unrealistic decisions being taken. The combines could be organized so that, similar to holding companies, they have a controlling and supervisory role, with very little opportunity directly to influence the actual running of the enterprise. This, however, would contradict the intentions of the GDR leaders to employ combines to carry out

(A)

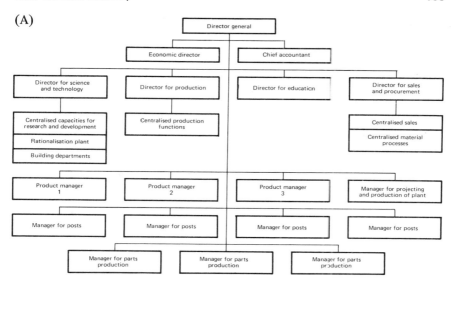

(B)

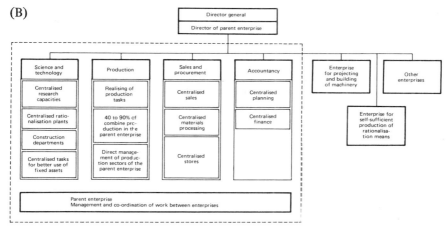

Figure 6.2 *(A) Basic management structure of a combine with central combine management. (B) Basic management structure of a combine directed by a parent enterprise. From Collective authors (1979c).*

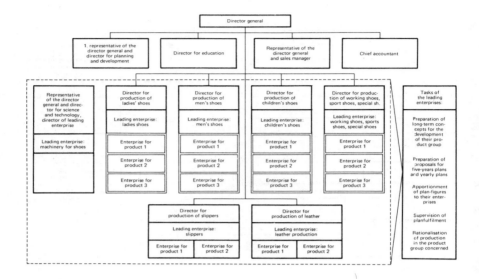

Figure 6.3 *Basic management structure of a combine with leading enterprises. From Collective authors (1979d).*

State aims. Category 3, which is roughly equivalent to the taking over of competitors by the market leader in the British economic system, has the advantages of product amalgamation and of being able to turn over job lots to smaller enterprises. However, there are three main disadvantages: it is extremely difficult to select the most suitable parent enterprise and director-general from the enterprises to be merged; the selected parent enterprise is not necessarily the most efficient and could, therefore, simply by virtue of its supremacy, set incorrect standards for the other enterprises; the parent enterprise could take over certain parts of the programme which are of benefit to it or get rid of those which are not profitable, in order to increase its own efficiency. Combines in the consumer-good sector may also have disadvantages as far as the consumer is concerned, especially category 4. It could easily happen that well-developed microstructures are destroyed, products are dropped, product lines are limited even more and the individual distribution channels of the formerly separate enterprises are abandoned. In addition, this form of combine particularly facilitates the multiple subordination of enterprises.

Together with improvements in internal organization, better-quality management is necessary. This is the only sure way of carrying out intensification tasks, such as economizing on raw materials and the introduction of new production methods (Ina Ladig, 1980, points out that at least a quarter of the energy and raw-material economies in the fields of science and technology, planned for

1981–5, should be achieved by means of the increased use of micro-electronics). An East German survey, based on a questionnaire given to executive personnel, suggests that there are great possibilities for improved management, partly because the existing organization is rather poor and partly because too many short-term directives are still necessary (Ladensack, 1980).

INTENSIFICATION TASKS OF THE COMBINE

The intensification tasks of the combine concern the more efficient use of capital, materials and labour. With respect to capital, cne of the most important combine tasks is to increase production by means of a more efficient utilization of existing machinery. In this regard combines are more flexible than individual enterprises. Enterprises have limited plant flexibility, concerning, for example, the manufacture of new products, but combines have the ability to bring about considerable alterations and production improvements by means of the reallocation of production and the restructuring of complete enterprises or parts of enterprises. This is due to the fact that rationalization has been neglected for many years in the GDR, while old machinery is still used for far too long, in spite of high maintenance costs. The combines have access to a far greater reservoir of machinery than the individual enterprise and thus can ensure a higher degree of self-sufficiency. With the limited allocation of new machinery, improvisation with available plant acquires great significance. This explains why it is intended that departments within enterprises should be given the special role of producing complete or modified plant necessary for the rationalization process, including multi-purpose machinery (Mielsch, 1979). Combines are thus able to carry out quicker and more effective rationalization. The high cost of this type of self-sufficient production is often criticised, however, resulting in attempts being made to discover and employ better criteria for the evaluation of such production (for example, cost reduction due to labour saving). Investment planning has expanded to include scrapping, repair, modernization and capacity use (Strauss and Rentzsch, 1979). For this purpose a complicated model has been prepared (Brossmann, 1977), which could bring only very limited improvements because of its inability to balance the relations of scrapping, repair, modernizing and investment needed in the enterprises or combines with the given investment and repair capacities in the economy as a whole (Melzer, 1977). It is hoped to decrease the use of building materials and the share of investment allocated to construction by concentrating on modernizing existing buildings rather than constructing new ones (Wolf, 1979). Construction times should be considerably shortened and investment made more effective as a result of better planning and project preparation and improved project sequences and performance evaluation. It is hoped that combine director-generals will make improved investment decisions as a result of their branch knowledge and proximity to production. Although investment decisions are highly centralized, directors have been given greater responsibility for carrying out the programmes.

During the frequent discussions about increasing productivity, it is commonly stressed that '. . . the modernization of existing machinery and plants often produces an equivalent or even better result than new investments' (Zschau and Hempel, 1978). The enterprises are often entreated to adopt new methods which increase productivity and economize on funds and materials. If it is considered that, for example, 70 per cent of industrial production costs are accounted for by expenditure on materials and that more than half of the manpower involved in the productive sectors is used for the production and distribution of energy and materials (Heinrichs, 1978), it becomes clear why economies in the use of materials are so important in the drive to increase productivity. This process has been hindered up to now by the leading role played by the 'gross value' indicator. In March 1980 two additional indicators, for 'net production' and 'material costs per 100 marks commodity production', were introduced (Beyer and Schmidt, 1980). Although these exist alongside the gross value target, the idea behind the new indicators is to encourage economies in energy and raw materials, the rising world prices of which are a burden for the economy of the GDR. In particular, it is hoped in the chemical industry to use gas and oil more efficiently by means of better refining; in the iron and steel industry to economize on precious metals usage by galvanizing, painting or applying a synthetic coating to tin, in order to make it less prone to corrosion; and to make similar economies in the non-ferrous metallurgy industry by better prefabrication of parts for electrical engineering. Generally speaking, economies in material use are also hoped for in the metal processing industry, through more efficient prefabrication in the earlier stages of production (Koziolek, 1980). Future growth is to be realized with no or little increase in energy and materials, which is why targets are posited for energy, oil and petrol consumption (and measures taken like new speed limits for lorries). In construction, for example, it is planned that during the period 1981 to 1985 materials use is to decrease by 15 per cent (by encouraging reconstruction rather than new construction), and energy consumption to fall by 30 per cent, mainly by better building insulation (Junker, 1980). These targets can be attained only if combines and enterprises play a more active part in technological progress (Friedrich, 1980).

As far as labour is concerned, the following problems are discernible: the labour shortage is aggravated by the use of out-of-date extremely labour-intensive plants: labour is wasted in inefficiently-organized ancillary services (such as storage, repairs and transport); the often extreme discontinuity of production runs in a single month (10 per cent, 20 per cent and 70 per cent of production accounted for in the consecutive three ten-day periods of the month); alternating amounts of work stoppage and overtime; and the extensive manpower requirements of the control mechanisms. Due to the existence of some obsolete plants, the GDR spends approximately 20 billion marks per annum on maintenance.

Although 670 000 people are employed in maintenance — that is, about 9 per cent of all available manpower (Schulz, 1978) — this workforce is still not large enough to carry out the necessary repairs (conference report in *Wirtschaftswissenschaft*, 10, 1978, p. 1243). This is due to the threefold increase in the stock of fixed assets, relative to the number of maintenance workers, since the beginning of the 1960s and the increasing complexity of plant. Losses per year, due to work stoppages caused by maintenance work, are estimated to be approximately equal to the gains from increased productivity (*Wirtschaftswissenschaft*, 7, 1978, p. 852).

There are hardly any remaining labour reserves to be tapped since more than 90 per cent of all employable people work in the GDR. It is hoped, therefore, that combines will employ manpower more efficiently. In the parent enterprise of the petro-chemical Schwedt Combine, for which it is planned to double capital assets during the period 1978—81, it is expected that the 24 000 employees (a quarter of total personnel) needed for the new plant will be taken from other parts of the enterprise as a result of manpower economies (Beyer and Packebusch, 1980; Martens, 1980). This case is known as the 'Schwedt initiative' and has been widely publicized and recommended. Targets for 'labour productivity' and 'science and technology', better related to each other in future five year planning, are also aimed at saving manpower in combines and enterprises (Rahmel and Völkel, 1980).

THE ENTERPRISE (see Figure 6.4)

Specific aims lie behind the almost completed reform of the entire economic administration and management system, as well as the improved structure and organization of combines: the better realization of State goals; aid expansion and reduce existing obstacles (Melzer and Erdmann, 1979). But concentration on the combine has probably had negative effects on the autonomy and incentives of enterprises.

The new combine regulations state that the enterprise is, within the framework of its adaptation into the process of reproduction and management of the combine, an economic and legally independent unit. This, in fact, is not at all clear, but there are certain important aspects: in contrast to the Soviet Union, where the *obyedineniye* (roughly comparable to the combine) forms the lowest level in the economic structure, this position is still held by the enterprise in the GDR; the independence of the individual enterprise is limited (the 'intensification effect' means that combine decision rights have been increased at the expense of the enterprise); enterprise incentives are adversely affected by the uncertainty arising from the power of combine heads to alter functions and tasks of enterprises and to transfer functions, tasks, machinery and production from one enterprise to another; the degree of autonomy depends on how inte-

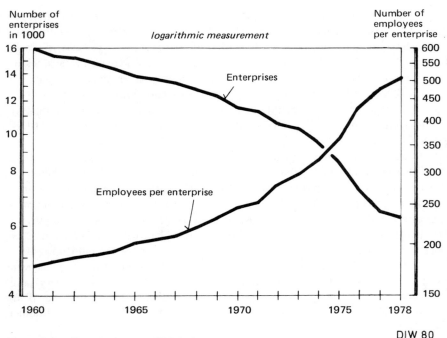

Figure 6.4   *Concentration in GDR industry.*

grated the enterprise is within the combine — some enterprises may be very dependent while others are relatively free.

The enterprise is given tasks and plan figures from the combine and is fully
responsible for realization and plan fulfilment (Friedrich and Krömke, 1979).
The enterprise is part of the combine, but, in relation to the assigned tasks, has
all the rights of an economic and legally independent unit (Buck and Schramm,
1980). The enterprise has its own funds and accounting system and basically is
required to follow the principle of self-financing. The enterprise director is fully
responsible for following both the enterprise and the combine plan, but takes
part in all important discussions concerning the combine.

In the 1960s the enterprise was the most important social and legally independent production unit, but by the end of the 1970s the combine is now the
basic economic unit of production. The considerable rights given to the enterprise during the period of the New Economic System were greatly reduced by
the re-centralization at the beginning of the 1970s. In the regulations in force at
the time enterprises, combines and VVBs were equal partners, but at present
the independence of the enterprise has been decreased in favour of the combine.
The old regulations of 1973 still apply to remaining VVBs, while for enterprises
not directed by a combine new regulations have been devised. These are adjusted
to those for the enterprise within a combine, but, even so, the enterprise directed

by a ministry or other central authority seems to have a little more independence.

Subsections of enterprises (such as works, plants, workshops, branch offices and chain stores) are economic and legally dependent units and have the duty to fulfil those parts of the plan under their responsibility and have work concerning the internal accounting system of enterprises. They can receive funds and rights and duties can be transferred to them. Although the 'independence' of subsections is generally very limited, some (like research institutions, data processing offices, rationalization plants, sales and service organizations) are somewhat more independent (Hesse and Schüsseler, 1977).

Foreign trade enterprises (AHBs) have been subordinated to combines with the aim of increasing exports and overcoming the separation of production and sales on the world market. Even before 1978 the Carl Zeiss-Jena Combine, the Petro-chemical Combine in Schwedt and the Timepiece Manufacturing Combine in Ruhla had AHBs, whilst other examples followed (Luft, 1980a), such as the Robotron, Agricultural Machinery, Ship-building, Micro-electronics and Rail Vehicles Combines. (Note that some AHBs have been directly subordinated to ministries, such as Ministry for Tools and Processing Machinery, the Ministry for Agriculture, Forestry and Foodstuffs and the Ministry for Mining, Metallurgy and Potash.)

Altogether there are in fact three types of AHB. Apart from those directed by combines and ministries, some are still directly subordinate to the Ministry of Foreign Trade. Altogether there are now about 45 AHBs compared with about 27 in 1960 (Luft, 1980b). Basically, the AHBs not directed by combines are supposed to sign long-term cooperation treaties with combines (Hildebrandt, 1979).

The new relations between AHBs and producers are supposed to improve product mix and increase export efficiency. An encouraging sign is that the leading person of the AHB is a member of combine management in 73 cases (*Neues Deutschland*, 28/29 April 1979, p. 5). The AHB directed by a combine has the legal position of an enterprise, but, at the same time, the AHB is still subject to the tasks, rights and duties assigned by the Ministry of Foreign Trade.

Thus the AHBs play a dual role. On the one hand, their activities and incentives are very limited as the State foreign trade monopoly is unchanged and they have to follow foreign trade plans as well as government price and credit policy. On the other hand, they are supposed to help combines and enterprises make better offers to foreign purchasers, to encourage contacts with the world market, to advertise East German products, to sign better treaties and allow the combine to participate more in export tasks. Thus the important problem of allowing future export demands more influence on production can hardly be solved. Nevertheless, a small step has been taken in allowing combines producing special export products to participate far more in exports, in so far as they have obtained permission to sign export treaties by themselves (*Eigengeschäftstätigkeit*) for certain finished goods (Engler and Maskow, 1979). But the incentives for combines to increase exports are very limited as long as they do not share in foreign currency earned.

There exists a three-stage system of accounting in the combine: for the combine as a whole, aimed at maximizing the efficiency of the entire unit; for the enterprise, which, apart from the aspects discussed earlier, is influenced by combine funds and redistributions of financial resources by the combine head; for the subsections. The solution of problems important to the combine as a whole (such as investment projects, important rationalization projects, science and technology tasks, the transfer of machinery or production) requires the centralization of financial means from enterprise funds. (The director-general is thus allowed to centralize parts of enterprise net profits and funds for amortization, science and technology, risk and performance.) The director-general can redistribute these resources for special purposes as well as make payments to the State budget.

Enterprises have to fulfil assigned tasks, but, since they also receive financial means from the combine, there exists the danger that enterprises will not be interested in reducing costs (Girlich and Neuhäuser, 1979). The intensification rights of the director-general, as well as the ability to redistribute centralized financial resources, can have a powerful effect on the profit situation of the individual enterprise. If a parent enterprise takes over certain beneficial parts of the production programme and gets rid of the non-profitable elements, then the other enterprises may show only a very low level of efficiency. These examples make it clear that not only is the degree of enterprise independence determined by the combine management, as pointed out by Jewstignejew (1980), but so is the basic profit situation of the enterprise.

Measurement of Performance

The use of the gross value measurement of performance is still a great problem: it not only encourages an increase in the amount of materials used but also combines to reach a higher level of plan fulfilment simply by increasing the number of production stages in the combine, thereby counting material inputs more than once (Büchner et al, 1978). To overcome both effects, the combines have had to use the key figure *Endprodukt* ('commodity production' of the combine minus deliveries of materials between the enterprises of a combine) since January 1979 (Hoss, 1979). This key figure, used in addition to 'commodity production' has, however, been criticized in the GDR because it can be inflated by increasing ineffective revenue between different combines (Lange, 1980a). It has also been pointed out that enterprises which are saving materials are disadvantaged with respect to plan fulfilment, because their 'commodity production' is decreasing while the *Endprodukt* of the combine is increasing (Lange, 1980b). As already mentioned, the introduction in 1980 of the new key figures for 'net production' (commodity production minus deliveries of materials, including those from outside) and 'material costs per 100 mark commodity production' will surely lead to an improvement. The positive effects would be greater if the system of plan fulfilment would change to a principal 'net calculation' basis and if the 'premium fund' and 'performance funds' were to become related to 'net production', instead of 'commodity production'. But, as far as can be seen, net output and gross output values will in future stand side by side.

PROSPECTS

Although it is still premature to draw up a balance sheet of positive and negative economic and administrative effects, it seems that, in spite of initial friction, the completed alterations in the entire economic administration and management system have improved planning; within the combines the more direct information channels encourage more constructive decision-making. Whether or not it will actually be possible to solve the various economic problems within the combine is a debatable question (problems such as the building up of an effective organization structure; raising the quality of management; harmonizing the interests of enterprise and combine; integrating plant and equipment to reach higher capacity use; developing a better measurement of performance; reduction of costs; and using resources in optimal fashion).

Enterprises have been allowed some very limited degree of independence within the combine because the economic leaders of the GDR need them as a buffer against the powerful position of the director-generals and to improve enterprise performance. In the opinion of the East German writer Gerd Friedrich '. . . economists of other socialist countries partly came to the opinion that the building of large production units causes the enterprise not only to lose its economic and legal independence, but also to lose its independent accounting position, which then becomes only an imperfect system of internal accounting. The experience up to date shows clearly that such action brings the danger of taking away responsibility from the enterprise for the duties it still has to perform under its guidance concerning the plan. As a rule, this will prevent enterprise initiative, hinder possible economies and cause commodity-money relations to inadequately stimulate work in the enterprise' (Gerd Friedrich, 1980a).

In general it must be pointed out that combine formation cannot solve all the main problems of the planning mechanism in the GDR (as the economic leaders might have expected). Therefore improvements would seem to be necessary. The motivation of director-generals should be improved to enable them to overcome bureaucratic obstacles, while at the same time following State directives, and persuade the relevant minister to agree to numerous compromises about aims; director-generals have to show imagination in seeking ways to improve efficiency, in the face of the distorted prices and the inadequate performance evaluation system, which results in inadequate profitability calculations; to achieve this they will have to think beyond the planning and incentive system which concentrates solely on productivity growth. The independence of the enterprise should be enlarged; and enterprises should be given a greater say in combine decision-making and their incentives improved. Prices should be improved in order to make decision-making more efficient. Enterprises should be allowed a more independent financial and profit situation and measurement of performance improved. Planning itself should be improved, not only as regards the coordination of enterprise and combine, but also to take better account of consumer and foreign demand (Gerd Friedrich, 1980b).

REFERENCES

Arnold, K.H. (1980) In *Berliner Zeitung*, 19 May.
Beyer, H.J. & Packebusch, W. (1980) In *Die Wirtschaft*, 2. p. 15.
Beyer, H.J. & Schmidt, H. (1980) In *Die Wirtschaft*, 3. p. 22.
Brossman, K.U. (1977) *Komplexe Grundfondsplanung*. East Berlin.
Büchner, H. et al (1978) In *Wirtschaftswissenschaft*, 10. pp. 1168ff.
Buck, H. & Schramm, L. (1980) In *Wirtschaftsrecht*. 1. p. 6.
Burian, W. (1978) In *Wissenschaftliche Zeitschrift der Hochschule für Ökonomie*, 3. p. 105.
Collective authors (1976) *Leitungsorganisation in den Betrieben und Kombinaten*. East Berlin. p. 368.
Collective authors (1979) *Grundfragen der sozialistischen Wirtschaftsführung*. East Berlin.
    (a) pp. 167ff; (b) pp. 344ff; (c) pp. 349 and 353; (d) p. 355.
Engler, H. & Maskow, D. (1979) In *Wirtschaftsrecht*, 1. pp. 21ff.
Erdmann, K. (1979) In *FS – Analysen*, 5. pp. 17ff.
Friedrich, G. (1980) In *Einheit*, 6. pp. 576ff.
Friedrich, G. (1980) In *Wirtschaftswissenschaft*, 7. (a) pp. 772–773; (b) pp. 780–782.
Friedrich, G. & Krömke, C. (1979) In *Einheit*, 12. p. 1269.
Friedrich, G. et al (1979) *Grundfragen der Sozialistischen Wirtschaftsführung*. East Berlin. (a) pp. 167ff; (b) pp. 344ff.
Gabler, U. & Wichler, E. (1979) In *Wirtschaftswissenschaft*, 5. pp. 562–563.
Gerisch, R. & Hofmann, W. (1979) In *Wirtschaftswissenschaft*, 2. pp. 129–130.
Girlich, E. & Neuhäuser, C. (1979) In *Wirtschaftsrecht*, 1. p. 29.
Hartmann, K. (1978) In *Die Wirtschaft*, 9. p. 5.
Heinrichs, W. (1978) In *Wirtschaftswissenschaft*, 8. p. 904.
Hesse, K. & Schüsseler, R. (1977) In *Wirtschaftsrecht*, 2. pp. 95ff.
Hildebrandt, K. (1979) In *Wirtschaftsrecht*, 3. pp. 127–128.
Hochbaum, H.U. & Siefarth, G. (1978) In *Wirtschaftsrecht*, 4. pp. 216ff.
Hofmann, W. (1979) In *Die Wirtschaft*, 10. p. 16.
Honecker, E. (1978) In *Neues Deutschland*, 25 May. p. 4.
Honecker, E. (1979) In *Neues Deutschland*, 12 February. p. 2.
Honecker, E. (1979) In *Neues Deutschland*, 14 December. p. 5.
Hoss, P. (1979) In *Die Wirtschaft*, 1. p. 18.
Huber, B. (1980) In *Rias Monitor*, 20 March.
Jewstignejew, R. (1980) In *Sowjetwissenschaft, Gesellschaftswissenschaftliche Beiträge*, 3. p. 267.
Junker, W. (1980) In *Neues Deutschland*, 20 June. pp. 3–5.
Klinger, G. (1980) In *Staat und Recht*, 3. p. 199.
Koziolek, H. (1980) In *Einheit*, 6. pp. 589–590.
Kühnau, K.H. (1979) In *Staat und Recht*, 1. p. 13.

Ladensack, K. (1980) In *Sozialistische Arbeitwissenschaft*, 3. pp. 164–165.
Ladig, I. (1980) In *Die Wirtschaft*, 6. p. 5.
Lange, U. (1980) In *Wirtschaftswissenschaft*, 3. (a) p. 339; (b) pp. 338–339.
Leptin, G. & Melzer, M. (1978) *Economic Reform in East German Industry*. Oxford, London and New York: Oxford University Press. pp. 182ff.
Luft, K. (1980) In *Voprosy Ekonomiki*, 6. (a) p. 133; (b) p. 132.
Martens, H. (1980) In *Einheit*, 7/8. p. 724.
Matterne, K. & Tannhäuser, S. (1978) *Die Grundmittelwirtschaft in der Sozialistischen Industrie der DDR*. East Berlin p. 220.
Mätzig, K. & Neumann, C. (1975) In *Wirtschaftswissenschaft*, 8. pp. 1238–1239.
Melzer, M. (1977) In *Vierteljahrshefte zur Wirtschaftsforschung des DIW*, 4. p. 245.
Melzer, M. & Erdmann, K. (1979) In *FS – Analysen*, 8. pp. 25ff.
Melzer, M. & Scherzinger, A. (1978) In *Vierteljahrshefte zur Wirtschaftsforschung des DIW*, 4. pp. 379ff.
Melzer, M., Scherzinger, A. & Schwartau, C. (1979) In *Vierteljahrshefte zur Wirtschaftsforschung des DIW*, 4. p. 369.
Mielsch, W. (1979) In *Presse – Informationen der DDR*, 16 October pp. 2–3.
Mittag, G. (1978) In *Neues Deutschland*, 27/28 May. p. 3.
Mittag, G. (1978) In *Neues Deutschland*, 26/27 August. p. 3.
Mittag, G. (1979) In *Einheit*, 9/10. p. 938.
Penig, L. et al (1978) *Wirtschaftsrecht für das Staatswissenschaftliche Studium – Grundriss*. East Berlin. p. 70.
Rahmel, G. & Völkel, B. (1980) In *Sozialistische Arbeitswissenschaft*, 4. pp. 270ff.
Ritzschke, G. & Steeger, H. (1975) In *Einheit*, 3. pp. 283ff.
Scholl, G. (1978) In *Wirtschaftswissenschaft*, 11. pp. 1324–1325.
Schulz, E. (1978) In *Die Wirtschaft*, 15. p. 5.
Strauss, W. & Rentzsch, G. (1979) *Handbuch Grundfondsökonomie*. East Berlin.
Wilhelm, K.H. (1980) In *Die Wirtschaft*, 6. p. 16.
Wolf, I. (1979) In *Wirtschaftswissenschaft*, 10. pp. 1191ff.
Zschau, U. & Hempel, W. (1978) In *Die Wirtschaft*, 5. p. 3.

7
The Industrial Enterprise in Czechoslovakia
Luděk Rychetník

THE SITUATION BEFORE 1970

By 1953 the Czechoslovak industrial enterprise worked on similar principles to the Soviet one at that time (as described in the introductory paper). This situation had been reached in several stages of nationalization and other institutional changes, starting from a post-war market economy with shortages, widespread rationing of consumer goods and raw materials and indicative central planning.

From 1955 onwards many drawbacks of the system were acknowledged. A set of measures was outlined during the 1956 Communist Party conference and elaborated on and carried out in the 1957–8 reform. This involved: increased emphasis on perspective and medium-term planning, leaving annual planning to the responsibility of enterprises and larger units; the amalgamation of enterprises into associations (which made it possible to abolish the '*glavki*', State branch management bodies); a greater role for financial planning and the financial system in general; enterprise funds dependent on profit, labour productivity and other indicators, the relationship being given by normatives set beforehand for a period of several (preferably five) years and managers given greater freedom in the use of the funds, financial assets being transferable from one year to another; planning indicators understood as forming an interconnected system affecting the behaviour of the enterprises.

After successful development in the years 1959 and 1960, economic problems started to accumulate and led to a breakdown of the 1961–5 five year plan during its second year. Among the reasons were inconsistencies in the reform and an older and permanently increasing technological gap (especially in machinery production), which was causing heavy foreign trade losses. The investment targets of the five year plan turned out to be over-optimistic and met with rapidly increasing prices of capital goods and construction costs. The reform was abandoned in 1963 and economic management re-centralized to the ministries.

Two cures for economic ills were considered at that time: (1) a return to medium-term central planning and a gradual improvement of the planning and management system, hand in hand with a restructuring of the economy under central control; (2) a basic change of the planning and management system towards full use of the market and the elimination of excessive State control of the economy, but retaining medium- (and long-term) central planning in an indicative form. The first line prevailed in earlier years and the second became more influential after 1966.

In January 1965 the Central Committee of the Communist Party issued a document called 'Principles of Improvement of the Management System' which envisaged a combination of central planning and a regulated market ('socialist commodity-money relations'). The fourth five year plan was prepared for the period 1966–70. But annual plans diverted from the five year plan from the beginning, and enterprises were not required to follow central plan targets but rather to satisfy market demand in mutual competition. The system of enterprise taxation was restructured and unified: the enterprise paid a capital charge (6 per cent of the depreciated value of fixed assets); payment from stocks (2 per cent); payment from 'gross income' (sales minus material costs) of 18 per cent; and, later, a payroll surtax on 'excess' wages. This and the price reform of 1967 were to equalize economic conditions, eliminate price distortions and prepare conditions for rational behaviour of economic agents and relaxation of central price control. The trend towards an independent enterprise run by a workers' council (with a manager responsible to it) and operating in a regulated market milieu was halted only after the 1968 events.

THE SITUATION DURING THE 1970s

Directive planning and central control of the economy began to be re-established in the Spring of 1969 (starting with prices and investment), but there was no return to the pre-1966 system. The financial system retained a great deal of its importance, enterprises having to finance their needs primarily from sales. After covering prime costs, including wages and other personal and non-personal outlays, the remaining profit and depreciation allowances were distributed in the following way: payments to the State budget (taxes) had first call, followed by those to the branch directorate and other obligatory payments; then payments could be made to enterprise funds, each designed to serve a special purpose (stock, construction, cultural and social needs, rewards, and possibly other funds).

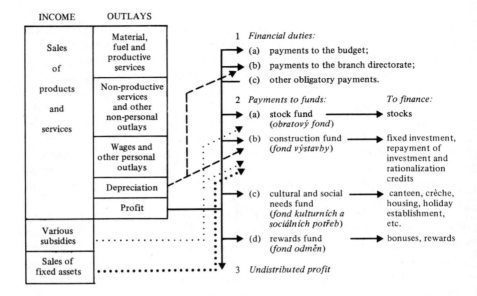

Figure 7.1   *Scheme of income distribution and enterprise funds during the 1970s.*

Undistributed profit could be retained for future use, while end-of-year remainders of funds could be transferred to the next year. Figure 7.1 shows a simplified distribution of incomes and profit to the funds.

There was also no return to the old 'gross output' indicator (*hrubá produkce, valovaya produktsiya*) as a measure of performance. Instead, the enterprise had to fulfil targets for deliveries of goods to the domestic market, export by territorial classification and fixed investment and was set financial indicators, namely profit, 'rentability' (profit/fixed assets ratio) and cost/output ratio. The wage bill limit was related to the volume of sales plus (or minus) the change in the stock of finished and unfinished products (*výkony*). Labour productivity was calculated from the same indicator ('*výkony*' per worker). But the financial identity of the enterprise was somewhat marred by redistributions of depreciation allowances and profit among enterprises.

In 1977, a reform of wholesale prices was carried out. Its purpose was to 'bring prices nearer to actual social costs'. The type of price used in calculations was the 'production price': the profit margin being a mark-up on capital.

THE 1978–80 'EXPERIMENT' AND ECONOMIC SYSTEM AFTER 1980

Under the pressure of shortages and rising world prices of fuels and materials and growing ecological dangers during the 1970s, the old problems of inefficient use of resources and insufficient technical progress emerged with even stronger urgency. This time, the answer is being sought in gradual adjustments of the existing system. Some changes had already been made in 1975 in connection with the commencement of the sixth five year plan.

Between 1978 and 1980 12 associations of 150 industrial enterprises, nine foreign trade corporations and 21 research institutes were involved in a 'complex experiment in efficiency and quality management'. The aim was to test a set of new planning and management rules and some organizational changes, which took up ideas associated with the 1958 reform and made use of recent experience and theoretical discussion in Czechoslovakia and other socialist countries. The results of the first two years of the experiment were encouraging and most of the tested elements were incorporated into the planning and management system to be made operational during the 1981–5 planning period.

An official document setting out the new rules was published in March 1980, entitled 'Set of Measures to Improve the System of Planned Management of the National Economy after 1980'. It indicates continuity with the past and future and it is then said explicitly in the text that the measures are to be looked upon as a step in a gradual process of improving the economic mechanism. At the same time, however, the measures are intended to form a complex whose elements are linked together and support each other in their final effect.

In the division of managerial responsibilities, the industrial ministries (odvětvová ministerstva) and the branch directorates (generální ředitelství, obory) are to pay more attention to the elaboration of long-run prospects and the lines of international division of labour and socialist economic integration, structural changes and innovations in their respective industries and branches. But they are also expected to use their authority and 'secure the efficient and first-rate fulfilment of the plan targets' by the enterprises in their charge.

The 'economic unit' (výrobní hospodářská jednotka, VHJ) operating on a khozraschyot basis, is considered to be the basic business unit, however. The VHJ is a collective term denoting several different types of large production organizations: it can be a large 'branch' enterprise to which a smaller enterprise may be attached (koncern); an association of enterprises of a comparable size and production programmes (trust); or a vertical integration of enterprises (kombinát). It is: the subject of taxation and payments to the State budget; the bearer of the central plan targets; responsible for technical and economic development within its scope of production; responsible for a 'differentiated application' of the khozraschyot principle to all its intra-organizational levels. In particular, the constituent enterprises are to have all the necessary power and responsibility for their technical, economic and social functions.

Planning

National economic planning is to become a two-directional process. The five year plan targets will be developed, in a stepwise process, by the central bodies from prospective macro-economic considerations, projections of technological development and from background material provided by the economic units. The annual plans will be designed by the economic units through a 'counter-planning' procedure and will specify the ways of implementing the five year plan targets. As a part of macro-economic prospective considerations, the State Planning Commission, together with industrial ministries and other central bodies of economic management, elaborate 'long-run complex programmes' (*dlouhodobé komplexní programy*) of structural and qualitative changes. They should include the whole innovation cycle from research to utilization. The specific tasks which arise out of these programmes are incorporated into the five year plan in the form of 'State target programmes' (*státní cílové programy*), which are subject to the Government's approval and have a binding character. They are also tied to the 'long-run target programmes of Comecon countries' (*dlouhodobé cílové programy zemí RVHP*).

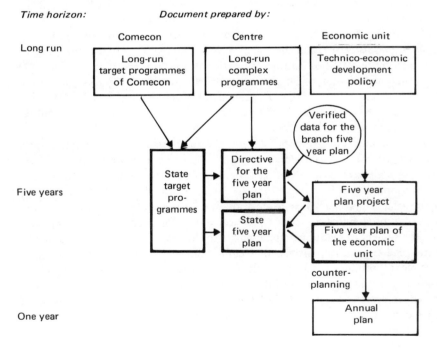

Figure 7.2 *Simplified scheme of planning procedure after 1980. Arrows indicate the sequence of the documents. Heavy frame indicates a binding State plan.*

The economic units, being guided and coordinated by branch directorates, continuously elaborate their 'documents of technico-economic policy' (*technicko-ekonomické koncepce rozvoje*), including programmes of modernization and concentration of production. The economic units also provide branch directorates with 'verified data' for the branch five year plan. The development policy document of the economic unit, together with a 'central directive' (*směrnice pro sestavení pětiletého plánu*), serves as a basis for the unit's five year plan project, elaborated by the economic unit. These projects are then collected from all economic units, summarized and consolidated by the central bodies. An extensive use of material and monetary balances should secure, 'proportionality', rough equality of quantities demanded and supplied, in the plans. The resulting five year plan, with its annual specifications, is considered to be the main document of economic life. Finally, its targets are broken down and assigned to the economic units which, in turn, elaborate and specify implementation in their annual plans. There will be no annual State plans to be passed by the National Assembly, as has been the case until now. Figure 7.2 shows a simplified scheme of the planning procedure.

Plan indicators are stated in terms of nominal tasks and their time limits, values in constant prices, input norms and various efficiency and cost ratios. The set of binding indicators should be gradually narrowed down to concentrate on decisive technico-economic processes. Six areas are listed as the most important: technical development, production and sales; reproduction of fixed assets; production inputs; labour and wages; and financial plan. A new indicator with an important role in wage planning is 'value added' (*vlastní výkony*), defined as sales plus (or minus) the change in the stock of finished and unfinished products *minus* the cost of fuel, materials, and services purchased from other organizations and non-productive cost. It is a 'net'-type indicator whose use in the experiment seems to contribute to material economies. Value added, corrected by profits (plus) and losses (minus) from foreign trade operations, is called 'adjusted' (*upravené vlastní výkony*).

Wages

The wage bill limit (*použitelný objem mzdových prostředků*) consists of two components, the 'basic wage bill' and the 'incentive component'. The 'basic wage bill' (*základní složka, závazný limit*) is specified as a share in the planned volume of 'adjusted value added': coefficients are individualized by enterprises, but fixed beforehand for each year of the five year period; if the plan is over-fulfilled, a reduced coefficient (by half, on average) will be used to obtain the wage bill increment. Basic wages amount to about 80 per cent of the total wage bill. The 'incentive component' (*pobídková složka*) makes up the remaining 20 per cent. It is related to the planned level of the indicator for 'productive fixed assets rentability' (*rentabilita výrobních fondů*), defined as the profit/productive fixed assets ratio. If the economic unit accepts a higher level (lower, but by no more than by 3 per cent) in its annual plan, the incentive component limit is increased (reduced) proportionally. A reduced coefficient is applied if the plan is over-fulfilled. A progressive reduction of the limit would ensue if the unit's annual plan shows rentability being less by 3 to 15 per cent than the State five year plan target. The minus-15 per cent point corresponds to zero incentive component.

Finances of the Economic Unit

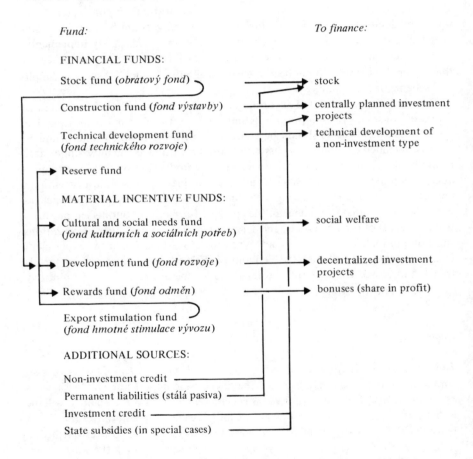

Figure 7.3   *Funds established for the economic unit after 1980. The stock fund is formed at the economic unit only if the fund's operation is centralized to the unit. Arrows indicate financial flows explained in the text.*

In principle, all planned (and unplanned) outlays of the economic unit should be covered by its sales and credits. Non-investment subsidies from the State budget will be used in accordance with special government-approved rules, and investment subsidies will be granted in exceptional cases only, subject to government decision. Financial resources can be reallocated among the economic units only up to the level of depreciation allowances; a part of profit can be transferred from one economic unit to another only in 'quite exceptional cases'. An economic unit (and an enterprise, if it is managed directly by the branch directorate) forms eight specialized funds. The funds and the purpose they are designed to serve are shown in Figure 7.3.

An enterprise within an economic unit forms the cultural and social needs fund and, usually, the stock fund (unless its management has been centralized to the economic unit). Other funds can be formed if the degree of centralization within the economic unit requires it. The reserve fund, construction fund and technical development fund are also formed at the level of the branch directorate (*resortní fondy*). Note that the branch directorate has finances at its disposal, but it is not subject to the financial discipline of *khozraschyot*.

Rules of Fund Formation

With the exception of the technical development fund, the funds are fed from profit (after payments to the State budget and branch directorate have been made) and depreciation allowances according to special rules. The material incentive funds (see Figure 7.3) receive their allocation only after the financial funds have been satisfied. Consequently, some funds may not get their due allocation if the economic unit has not made sufficient profit to draw on. This occurred in some economic units during the experiment (Lér, 1980).

The Financial Funds are as follows:

The stock fund is fed from profit and is used to cover stock;
The construction fund is fed from depreciation allowances, profit, sales of fixed assets and other sources: it is used to finance centrally-planned investment projects and to repay investment and rationalization credits;
The technical development fund of the economic unit is formed from contributions by constituent enterprises, where they represent a part of production costs, and from incomes earned from past projects financed from the fund: it is used to finance the branch or enterprise targets for technical development and to cover innovations in their implementation stage;
The reserve fund of the economic unit receives undistributed profit and allocations from the export stimulation fund: it can be used in the years when insufficient profit has been made and to cover foreign trade losses: if the amount in the

reserve fund exceeds a certain limit the excess will be remitted to the branch reserve fund (*resortní reservní fond*).

The Material Incentive Funds are as follows:

The cultural and social needs fund is fed from profit: it receives a basic quota at
the level of 0.8 per cent of the annual wage bill *plus* some additional allocations,
but no more than 2.8 per cent altogether: an additional allocation of 0.4 per
cent is rewarded for fulfilment of each of the following indicators (*podmiňující
ukazatele*): profit or the ratio of total costs to value added; labour productivity
measured as value added per employee; production assortment; fixed assets utilization; additional allocations of 0.4 per cent can be made from the export stimulation fund and price increases for technically progressive, fashionable or first-
quality products (but *minus* deductions for low-quality and technically-backward
production);
The development fund is intended to finance small investment projects, costing
no more than two million Koruna, which must be planned by the economic unit
and approved by a higher management body subject to various efficiency criteria:
renewal and modernization projects are preferred (see below): the fund is fed
from depreciation allowances, profit and other sources according to normatives
set in such a way that depreciation provide no more than 40 per cent of the resources needed for the approved projects and profit provides no less than 30 per
cent (half of that amount being dependent on the fulfilment of 'rentability' and
half on the production assortment targets): additional allocation can be obtained
from price increases for technically advanced, fashionable and first-quality products (*minus* the corresponding deductions), from the export stimulation fund,
and from a permanent reduction of the stock fund ensuing from a faster stock
turnover (note that the latter rule has introduced a direct channel between current assets and investment);
The rewards fund: rewards, premiums and bonuses paid out of this fund are not
considered as a part of wages, but as a share in profit and are related to good
individual performance contributing to product quality, high technical level or
labour economies: the fund is fed from profit up to the level of wage economies
against the wage limit *plus* additional allocations (also from profit) or reductions
according to the technical level and quality of production, and from the export
stimulation fund;
The export stimulation fund is fed from foreign trade profits, subject to the
level of foreign trade efficiency and fulfilment of the foreign trade volume target,
foreign trade efficiency being measured by a 'difference indicator' (*rozdílový
ukazatel*), a ratio of the attained price (Czechoslovak border carriage free) to the
domestic wholesale price: incentives begin after a minimal threshold level of the
difference indicator has been reached: the stimulation is progressively increased
(reduced) if a higher annual plan is accepted (if a lower plan is accepted or the

plan has not been fulfilled): annual plan over-fulfilment brings a lower increase: the export stimulation fund is formed at the level of the economic unit, which allocates the fund's assets to various enterprise stimulation funds, according to their contribution to foreign trade results, and to the reserve fund.

Payments to the State Budget and Branch Directorates

Under the new rules, the economic unit makes payments for all its constituent enterprises, namely a payment out of profit (*odvod ze zisku*), a capital charge (*odvod ze jmění*), and a contribution to social security (*příspěvek na sociální zabezpečení*), paid as a percentage of wages. Reduced rates or a fixed-sum reduction allow for the new needs of self-financing. In 1983, the existing law on payments will be amended.

Investment

From the point of view of their financing, two categories of investment projects are recognized: 'binding and centralized constructions' (*závazné a centralizované stavby*), financed from the construction fund; 'limit investment' (*limitní investice*), including projects costing more than two million Koruna, projects costing less than or equal to two million Koruna, and machines and installation not included in construction projects; these are financed from the development fund. The overall volume of the latter category of investment is controlled by two types of limit: projects costing more than two million Koruna are regulated by the limit on their commencements; those below that and machines and installations are limited indirectly, by setting the normatives of the development fund creation at a suitable level: this will be done by the branch directorates, which must fit into a global limit.

All investment projects must be planned ahead, however, and approved by the higher management bodies. Construction projects, arising from the State target programme, costing more than ten million Koruna are assessed centrally and implemented through the State plan. Other investment projects will usually be initiated by an economic organization, which asks for their approval and inclusion in the plan. These projects are assessed by the branch directorate and the State Bank according to given criteria. Preference will be given to projects implementing an approved plan of technical development of the economic unit, or utilizing a foreign licence, modernizing or reconstructing existing production fixed assets, saving labour, fuel or material, or contributing to an improvement in the balance of payments.

Prices

A wholesale price reform will be carried out in 1981—2. It will raise the prices of fuels and some raw materials and the ensuing end products. This will be realized in addition to the earlier announced regular increases of fuel prices by 2 per cent every year during the period 1980 to 1985. These latter increases must only be partially reflected in the prices of the end products. Other price changes will adjust the profitability in the wholesale prices to the price attained in foreign markets. Similarly, the effect of higher input prices will not be allowed to be passed on to the product price if the foreign market price is low. There will be also some scope for more flexible price adjustments if the situation requires it. Advanced foreign markets will be also used as a criterion in setting the price limits for new products. Price is to be used as a tool for stimulating high technical levels of products. Special wholesale price increases and reductions will be applied according to the export efficiency or, alternatively, according to evaluation by State testing bodies. Under certain conditions (to be announced) it will be possible for the purchaser and supplier of capital goods to negotiate the price.

CONCLUSION

The Czechoslovak experience can be described as a search for a suitable solution within given geopolitical constraints. The most recent stage in this search has been the set of new rules establishing the economic mechanism for 1981—5, as has been described above. If looked upon as a development stage, it can be evaluated as a step towards economic realism. Financial discipline should be tighter and a more meaningful use of categories of prices, costs and profits could be introduced, providing that the complexity of the rules and their exacting administrative procedures will not check implementation. If, however, they are looked upon as an answer to new conditions on world markets, shortage of labour and resources and growing ecological dangers at home, they are hardly adequate. At the same time, some problems already present in the previous system are likely to become more urgent.

Balance of Power and Responsibility

Firstly, there is the problem of a proper balance between the degree and scope of power to control the economy and financial responsibility for the consequences of the decisions taken at each level of the organizational hierarchy. A great deal of effective decision-making about investment, structural development and technological advance has been centralized to bodies positioned above the economic unit in the hierarchy. The *khozraschyot* sphere does not extend above the economic unit, however: hence more important decisions with long-term consequences for the economic unit and the enterprises, and sometimes for the whole economy, are being made without the financial discipline and responsibility of *khozraschyot*. This problem has been partly recognized: 'losses and extra costs' of enterprises 'caused by the decisions of the branch directorate' can be covered from the branch reserve fund (*New Rules*, 1972, paragraph 25). However, this provision cannot save lost opportunities or prevent wider national economic losses. This is a systemic flaw of most contemporary 'mixed' economies, but the high degree of centralization in Czechoslovakia makes the situation more costly and dangerous. In the future a solution will be perhaps looked for along the lines of the discussion about 'full' or 'complete' *khozraschyot* (*úplný chozrasčot*), under which all bodies of economic management, including the centre, would work on a self-financing basis, keeping a profit and loss account (Dvořák, 1979; Rusmich, 1979).

Limits of Directive Planning

The methodology of directive planning suffers from a logical inconsistency, which has serious practical consequences: it checks the rate of technical progress and limits the level of efficiency that an economy can reach. The indicators of a directive plan serve as targets by which enterprise performance is evaluated and rewarded. This role requires indicators to be an objective and accurate picture of the enterprise's future production possibilities. But this requirement is inconsistent with the tendency of enterprise to hide reserves (Nove, 1977). Moreover, the 'true' possibilities of technological advance and their time-schedule can never be known precisely in advance, since they depend on the essentially elemental and unpredictable power of human creativity and many other mostly random factors. Furthermore, the idea that economic reality can be satisfactorily described by a set of abstract indicators, which could then serve as 'fund-creating', is dubious. It is labour, whose results satisfy human needs, and efficient organization and management earning high income at low costs, which create funds, not the fulfilment of a plan target. This inconsistency cannot be avoided by leaving annual planning to the responsibility of economic units. The bargaining about reserves is then limited to the period of preparation of the five year plan only, but there arises the need to fix key indicators and normatives for five years (the 'tolerance' limits within which the normatives can be adjusted every year only bring the whole affair back to a shorter period).

Khozraschyot and Objective Efficiency Standards

Khozraschyot may help to establish an objective efficiency norm in the economy, valid for all producers, in the form of socially necessary costs. For the reasons discussed above, plan targets cannot serve as such a general norm. Similarly, theoretical calculations can only approximate it; they cannot substitute its objective existence and function in the economy. But macro-economic efficiency depends on its very existence. Only a generally valid efficiency norm distinguishes backward enterprise from the advanced ones and makes it possible to discover reserves and identify progressive elements in technology and management. The efficiency level of an enterprise depends only partly on its staff and, therefore, the wage fund cannot be determined by efficiency (profitability) only. A suitable wage structure should incorporate a national wage policy standard and reflect the difference between the real contribution of the enterprise employees and other factors. Under the new rules, the three components of personal income, the basic wage, the incentive component and a share in profit (the rewards fund) would be allowed to express this difference.

Socially necessary costs are an inherently dynamic phenomenon. Their level would decline and rise even if all monetary factors were excluded. They depend on technical development, changing availability of natural resources and, also, on changing consumer preferences. They represent a vehicle which brings uncontrollable elemental forces of human ingenuity and creativity into the economy. Similarly, as for technical progress, their development can be predicted only approximately and controlled only partly. Any attempts to control them fully close the door on human spontaneity and creativity which, consequently, find their outlet outside the institutionalized economic life. This results in innovatory lethargy. An efficient economic mechanism must be based on recognition of the role of uncontrolled elemental forces in economic life. If they are given sufficient room in the institutional arrangement, they can be channelled into desirable directions and useful activities and become a source of progress. But unpredictability and a component of risk cannot be fully excluded; they will be always present (the inseparability of risk from innovations has already been recognized; Valenta, 1969; Ježek, 1976).

Price Flexibility

Under the new rules, prices should play an important informational role in economic decision-making, both at the centre and at the economic unit. However, the directive aspects of planning did not permit introduction of real flexibility into the price system, which is needed for such role. Domestic prices cannot reflect consumers' satisfaction with the product, they cannot immediately signal the relationship between quantity demanded and supplied; the important link between use value (quality, technical level), price, and material stimulation must go through a lengthy route via price-setting bodies and quality-testing institutions, which can be often less objective than a demanding market. The rules try to substitute the price-controlling function of the domestic market by foreign markets, but that can be only a partial help. However, existing tensions and shortages in the economy do not permit the relaxation of strict price (and production) controls. The new rules cannot be more than a step in a gradual move towards an economic system more suited to an age of scientific technological revolution and, also, of fuel and materials scarcity and highly competitive world markets. Nevertheless, the question of 'how much time is available' still remains.

Balance of Professional Decision-making and Democratic Control

With the newly-acquired responsibility for annual counter-planning and the possibility of considering and proposing development strategies, initiating modernization projects or of adjusting production programmes and technology according to the development of prices and costs, the management of an economic unit has sufficient power to affect the life of its workers. This power should be counterbalanced by adequate democratic control; otherwise there is a danger of various social conflicts developing into disruptive forms. The rules contain a section on workers' participation, which has been given only a very narrow role, limited to technical, economic and some legal aspects of the spheres of production and labour.

The Socialist Manager

Which features of a socialist manager would fit well into the economic system outlined in the new rules? Does he (or she) belong to the Schumpeterian or Walrasian type of enterpreneur (see Radice in this volume)? Two characteristics would distinguish the manager from these types. S/he must have an ability to share divided responsibility in accordance with the division of decision-making power along the organizational hierarchy. The manager of an economic unit must be able to take a decision in coordination with a colleague in the enterprise 'below' and the branch directorate 'above' him. There is no place for the individualistic entrepreneur of classical capitalism in the present hierarchical structure of management. S/he must be also able to cooperate with the particular form of social control to which s/he is subject and to harmonize socio-political preferences with technical—economic considerations.

As regards the motivation to work and take the risk of success or failure, the rules emphasize 'coordination of moral, political and economic factors'. No doubt this is more realistic than an appeal to political and moral motives alone or an exclusive appeal to high material rewards, which might even become counter-productive in the egalitarian milieu of the Czechoslovak society. Recent sociological research has indicated that the 'feeling of a well-done job' is a generally recognized and shared value among industrial workers (Rak, 1980). Some of that ethos is also likely to be present among white-collar workers and managers. The manager would make good use of the art of equilibrating disparate efficiency levels by bringing the backward plan or enterprise to the level of a progressive one. But at the same time, s/he should be able to initiate and carry through a far-reaching innovation. It would involve various planning exercises and dealing with the participating sections of the managerial hierarchy. The disequilibrating effect of the innovation may be spread and damped in the planning stage.

REFERENCES

Dvořák, J. (1979) In *Politická Ekonomie*, 27. pp. 897–907.
Ježek, T. (1976) In *Politická Ekonomie*, 24. pp. 327–338.
Lér, L. (1980) In *Hospodářské Noviny*, 33. p. 1.
Nová Úprava Finančního Hospodaření Podniku (New Rules of Financial Management of Enterprises) In *Hospodářské Noviny*, 1972, 4, Appendix.
Nove, A. (1977) *The Soviet Economic System*. Ch. 4, London: Allen & Unwin.
Rak, V. (1980) In *Sociologický Časopis*, 16. pp. 316–323.
Rusmich, L. (1979) In *Politická Ekonomie*, 27. pp. 257–268.
Soubor Opatření ke Zdokonalení Soustavy Plánovitého Řízení Národního Hospodářství po Roce 1980 (Set of Measures to Improve the System of Planned Management of the National Economy after 1980) In *Hospodářské Noviny*, 1980, 11 and 12, Appendix.
Usnesení ÚV KSČ o Hlavních Směrech Zdokonalování Plánovitého Řízení Národního Hospodářství a o Práci Strany (Resolution of the Central Committee of CP on the Main Lines of Improvement of Planned Management of the National Economy and on the Work of the Party) In *Rudé Právo*, 30 January 1965.
Valenta, F. (1969) *Tvůrčí Aktivita – Inovace – Efekty* (Creative Activity – Innovations – Effects). Prague: Svoboda. 262 pp.

FURTHER READING

Feiwel, C.R. (1968) *New Economic Patterns in Czechoslovakia*. White Plains, New York: IASP.
Selucky, R. (1972) *Economic Reforms in Eastern Europe*. New York: Praeger.

8
The State Enterprise in Hungary: Economic Reform and Socialist Entrepreneurship

Hugo Radice

INTRODUCTION: THE NEW ECONOMIC MECHANISM OF 1968

The purpose of this chapter is to describe the economic role and behaviour of the State enterprise in Hungary since the 1968 reforms. From the perspective of the nature of the enterprise in the socialist countries as a whole, the main issue is the extent to which these reforms have fundamentally altered the behaviour of Hungarian enterprises. Accordingly, the chapter does not attempt to chart the empirical detail of enterprise regulation and control, but rather to analyse the main structural and behavioural features of the enterprise system. I begin by summarizing the formal characteristics of that system under the 1968 reforms, and the more significant modifications since then, culminating in the 1980 round of further reforms. I then look in turn at relations between enterprises and the centre, other enterprises, workers, and the world markets. Lastly, I discuss the concept of socialist entrepreneurship, which seems to me to be at the heart of the problems surveyed.

Immediately before the 1968 reforms, the enterprise system in Hungary differed little from that of other Comecon countries: there had been elements of reform, such as reductions in the number of plan indicators and the introduction of a charge on assets, but the elaboration of central plans into obligatory enterprise plans, and the central allocation of supplies, remained untouched. The main specific difference in the Hungarian case arose from the 1963 regrouping of enterprises, which created levels of enterprise concentration of an unparalleled height (Economic Research Institute, 1974).

The central feature of the 1968 reforms lay precisely in the abandonment of obligatory enterprise plan targets and supply allocations. The objectives of promoting productivity, innovation and flexible response were to be met by freeing enterprises to form horizontal relations with each other and with markets of final demand. The dominant criterion of success became profitability, which, given more rational prices, would both reflect enterprise performance and form the sources of enterprise investments and for increases in personal incomes. The social interest embodied in the national plan was to be expressed indirectly in the form of economic regulators, including fiscal instruments, wage and price controls, credit policy, foreign exchange multipliers, etc. The intention was that these regulators would mould the initiatives of profit-oriented enterprises into patterns corresponding at the aggregate level to central preferences: as a consequence, the regulators had to form a coherent whole, and to be reasonably constant both through time and across enterprises. In essence, the aim was to create a 'guided market economy' (Csapó, 1966; for details of the reform see Friss, 1971).

It is important to note that in a number of significant respects features of the traditional system were retained. The form of ownership of enterprises, including the right to create and dissolve them, was unaltered, as was the specification of the enterprise's sphere of productive activities. The rights of the enterprise to transfer assets were not extended significantly, and the appointment of the enterprise director remained the prerogative of the supervising sectoral ministry. Nor was any change in the internal management system of enterprises envisaged, such as new forms of worker representation. The reforms in addition had only limited application to sectors of the economy such as energy, transport and communications, education and health.

Three further limitations are important for our subsequent analysis. First, in order to ease the transition to the new system a complex structure of so-called 'bridges' was announced as a temporary measure: in particular, special taxes and subsidies to mitigate the differential effect of enterprise profit potential caused by the price reforms which were part of the package, or by the changes in effective foreign exchange rates. Secondly, it was accepted that in the investment sphere major projects designed to alter significantly the industrial or product structure of industry would be a matter for central decision-making; current market conditions would in such cases give inadequate guidance to enterprises. Thirdly, although the flows of information between the enterprises and supervisory bodies were to be expressed predominantly in money (value) terms rather than in physical terms, the financial relations envisaged, for example in credit policy, related to the performance of specific tasks rather than to the overall performance of enterprises.

Since 1968 there have been a considerable number of changes in the various elements of the New Economic Mechanism (see Portes, 1977, and Hare, Radice and Swain, 1981). In the early years, excessive income-differentiation both between enterprises and between workers and managers led to a considerable elaboration of the wage regulation system (Marrese, 1981). The re-emergence in 1970–71 of overinvestment, and an associated balance of payments deficit, forced the authorities to cut back by halting new credits. Eventually, at the November 1972 session of the Party's Central Committee a series of decisions were taken which, to many outside observers, indicated a significant degree of 're-centralization'. Workers' wages were increased by 8 to 12 per cent across the board, regardless of enterprise circumstances, and in future wage levels were to be tied more closely to a centrally-determined 'table'; and 50 large enterprises were placed under special ministerial supervision, while a number of ailing giants (eventually six) were to be entirely reconstructed. Nevertheless, the leadership reiterated its faith in the basic principles of the reform.

The period 1973–80 was dominated by the impact of the OPEC oil price rises and the subsequent Western recession and inflation (see Tardos, 1975 and 1978, and Marer, 1981). Between 1972 and 1975 Hungary's dollar terms of trade fell by some 23 per cent, and the resultant loss of national income has been estimated at 6 per cent (Portes, 1977a). This struck a heavy blow at the attempt to move towards unified domestic and world market prices, given the requirement of domestic price stability. Although new rounds of price changes were enacted in 1975 and 1976, and the forint was steadily (if only partially) re-valued, stability of both prices and enterprise incomes was maintained by a proliferation of subsidies and taxes. The realization that, in monopolistic markets and with prices detached from costs, profits were not always attributable to good performance led to the introduction of a differentiated profits tax to cream off 'unfair profits'. As a consequence of all this, the regulatory system lost what Hungarian economists call its 'normative character': the fiscal system became an ever-shifting jungle of regulations, instead of providing a stable environment, and the financial condition of enterprises increasingly lost any connection with efficiency.

Nevertheless, the principles of 1968 have never been disavowed, and indeed even in the most difficult years one can find some measures which go against the general trend, such as the more competitive allocation of hard-currency credits for export promotion from 1976. The round of reforms introduced in January 1980 undoubtedly signals a renewed determination to follow the re-form path (for details see Horváth, 1980). The new reforms centre on changes both in the relative structure of prices and in the methods of price adjustment (Varga, 1980). As regards relative prices, those of materials and energy sources were increased by an average of 30 per cent and those of food industry products by 11 per cent, while prices of finished manufactures have declined by 11 per cent. Consumer prices have gone up, with accompanying (but not fully compensating) wage rises, and considerable progress has thus been made towards the aim of relating consumer prices also to costs through a uniform turnover tax. The considerable reduction in price subsidies has been roughly matched by cuts in the taxation of wages levied on enterprises, and the abolition of the assets charge. The overall result is that all prices should reflect costs more closely, and enterprises should be stimulated in particular to economize on energy, materials and labour.

More remarkably, domestic prices of all goods are to be adjusted to capitalist world market levels, at least over some 70 per cent of total industrial output. Officially fixed or limited prices have been reduced in number, with many materials and semi-finished goods becoming 'uncontrolled'. The key basic rule is that the producer price is to be set in the first instance by applying to costs the profit margin earned on hard currency exports, and although purchasing enterprises may bargain with the producer around this price, it cannot exceed the domestic price of the imported equivalent. The purpose is clear: failure to keep up with world productivity standards will hit domestic as well as export profits, from both the input and output ends. Special reserve funds within the enterprise will allow for the smoothing of temporary fluctuations in world market prices, but the fiscal regulators will no longer be differentiated in order to protect individual enterprises.

The evident objective of these and associated measures is to reinstate the aims of the 1968 reforms. It has been emphasized that the regulators will now be both more uniform and more stable, that inefficient enterprises will no longer be propped up, and that the tendency towards excessive growth in both investment and personal consumption will be restrained in the coming years in order to bring supply and demand into balance (on current indications, the targets in the new five year plan will be modest indeed).

Whether these intentions will be fulfilled must depend on how far the loss of reform momentum in 1968—80 was due to external factors or to inexperience, and how far to inadequacies intrinsic to the reforms. Our analysis of the position of the State enterprise during this period ought to shed some light on this question.

One further introductory point may be useful. The analysis below concerns, unless otherwise stated, the large industrial enterprises under the ultimate authority of sectoral ministries. I have already noted that the regrouping of enterprises in 1963 created extremely high levels of enterprise concentration in Hungary. In terms of the overall concentration of employment, the study by the Economic Research Institute (1974) found that 73 per cent of workers were employed in enterprises with over 1000 employees in 1971; only Czechoslovakia and Romania show higher percentages, and among Western countries only The Netherlands had a figure of over 40 per cent. The same study examined the 1920 enterprises (including local enterprises and cooperatives) in manufacturing and construction in 1972. Of these, 74 large State enterprises were found to be in the 'top 50' by either production value, assets or employment: they accounted for 53 per cent of total assets, 46 per cent of profits and 34 per cent of employment. These are essentially the enterprises whose behaviour is examined in the remainder of this chapter.

RELATIONS BETWEEN STATE ENTERPRISES AND THE 'CENTRE'

It is by now rather well established that since 1968, under the reformed system described above, the vertical relations of dependence which characterized the earlier system of directive planning have not been broken (Bauer 1976; Tardos, 1976; Nyers and Tardos, 1978). Why have relations between enterprises and the centre proved so resistant to change? Their most pervasive feature is the persistence of *vertical mutual dependence* in the setting of economic objectives, the financing of their realization, and the allocation of responsibility for success or failure. It is characteristic of large State enterprises that they do not construct their own plans mainly on the basis of (guided) market opportunities. Instead,

'we have enterprises which, owing to the established organizational setup and the regulations in force, interpret themselves the expectations of the leading social organs and try to conform to them' (Nyers and Tardos, 1978a).

There are no clear dividing lines between centre and enterprise, as regards decision-making powers or financial resources, *especially* in relation to investments (Berend, 1975, Deák, 1975). In principle, investments in the 'enterprise sphere' are both determined and financed by the enterprise (with the possibility of obtaining competitively-allocated credits), while those in the 'State sphere' are determined and financed by the centre. But enterprises know that they can obtain 'State' funds if their own investment plans can become established as 'State' objectives; while central organs know that they can demand enterprise financial participation as a condition for being chosen to carry out a 'State' project.

This would be of no great concern if common investment decision criteria could be utilized in both spheres and over all types of financing, with due allowance for preferential treatment of certain sectors. But despite the application of a formal common criterion of the net present value type for large projects (the D-index), and the repayment of budget funds on a par with bank credits, the actual behaviour of both enterprises and the centre remains basically the same (Hare, 1981). The 'clean' information required to operate such criteria is unavailable, because persistent direct intervention in enterprise affairs has qualitatively undermined the functioning of the economic regulators. In response to short-term pressures, regulators have been altered more frequently than was intended. More significantly, and in part consequentially, they have been differentiated by sector, subsector and even enterprise. The existence of so many possibilities of variation in the regulators, and the multiplicity of central organs each in negotiation with the enterprise, allows the latter to engage in multi-channel vertical bargaining. The centre's only available response is to allow the de facto reassertion of single-channel bargaining through the sectoral ministry. The consequence for the enterprise, however, is that profitability has little if any connection with efficiency. As a result, high profitability leads to the loss of State financial support (always in short supply), while low profitability leads to its return (since low profitability can be put down to the imposition of central objectives on the enterprise).

The re-emergence of the sectoral ministry manifested itself in the success with which in the 1971–5 plan period they succeeded in determining a pre-allocation of bank credits; and in the *'tervzsüri'* (plan jury) process used in the preparation of the 1976–80 plans of the largest enterprises (Balassa, 1977). Nevertheless, the functional ministries, and the reform economists and politicians, have continually opposed any formal return to the old system in this respect: the working-out of the recent price reform took place in inter-ministerial com-mittees, with the participation of representatives from the sectoral ministries, not the other way round. But tensions between sectoral and functional direct intervention, while certainly of interest, cannot explain why direct intervention of any kind is so persistent.

In the previous section, a distinction was drawn between the 1968–73 period, in which it could be argued that the reform 'got out of hand' in various respects, and the post-1973 period, in which Western inflation and recession and the ad-verse movement in the terms of trade seriously disrupted the Hungarian economy. An account of these factors certainly gives the immediate reasons for changes in economic policy, but what interests us is why the changes tended to take the form of increased direct intervention at the enterprise level, rather than – as the reform economists wanted – changes in the levels of the various regulators. If this was because of 'conservative forces' in sector ministries, the Party and trade unions, and indeed among enterprise managers, why were such forces not increasingly undermined by the reform process?

Granick (1975) has put the main emphasis of his explanation on the 'full employment constraint', interpreted as essentially political. The system can tolerate neither significant aggregate unemployment, nor excessive non-volun-tary relocation of labour at the enterprise level. This has certainly been much debated in Hungary, and, as we have seen, in introducing the 1980 measures the leadership has insisted that inefficient enterprises will be closed down or taken over, and labour reallocated. I return to this point below.

A second necessary element in our explanation concerns the persistence of widespread and general conditions of shortage. The evidence for this is not so much queues in the shops (which hardly exist), but the continuing phenomenon of 'rush-work' at the end of years, quarters and months (Laki, 1980a). The persistence of rush-work is seen as arising ultimately from the way in which the system remains geared to quantitative expansion. If enterprises are under no pressure to compete actively and respond to market signals, then corrective intervention by the authorities can have an effect only if it cuts through the market signals and influences the physical allocation of effort within the enter-prise. While this provides a valuable insight into the processes at work, it leads only to a reformulation of our question: we now have to ask why the obsession with the growth of physical output remains so strong. This could be answered by an extension of Granick's argument: perhaps the political constraint is not the negative one of avoiding unemployment, but the positive one of ensuring increases in living standards as well.

To this I would add the equally political constraint imposed by the requirement of maintaining the unity and hierarchy of the administrative system as a
whole. If the centre were really to withdraw from the visible tutelage of enterprises, it would lose a necessary foundation stone of the structure of political
power, namely its monopoly right to form and interpret the social interest.
Genuine enterprise autonomy − the ability to *reproduce* both materially and
socially the enterprise with its own resources − would undermine the centri-
petal nature of power. Enterprise directors are bound to fear this too, for they
would have to take real responsibility for the performance of their enterprises.
It is this constraint that confronts all proposals which postulate 'a separation of
the administrative functions of the State from its economic ones', for example
by setting up institutions which can play the role of a capital market while
renouncing any claim to represent the State interest (Nyers and Tardos, 1978b).
It may well be that Marrese (1978) is right in suggesting that the system can
only oscillate between a stronger and a weaker 'visible hand' (Marrese's term for
this is 'cyclical centralism'), perhaps in accordance with the rhythm of the
investment cycle (on which see Sóos, 1976; Bauer, 1978).

INTER-ENTERPRISE RELATIONS

The patterns of inter-enterprise relations are not surprisingly closely related to
those of relations between enterprises and the centre: given the dominance of
these vertical relations, horizontal links are unable to develop on the basis of the
autonomously-perceived interests of enterprises. Despite the ending of compulsory inter-enterprise supplies, there are persistent complaints about the
difficulty of establishing new supply sources for components and other intermediate goods. Undoubtedly this has much to do with the persistence of sellers'
markets, a combination of excess demand and the monopoly position of many
suppliers. The latter are not interested in adapting their production to the
requirements of new customers, which in many industries are increasingly
complex and differentiated.

How do enterprises respond to this as would-be purchasers? Firstly, by
'borrowing' or other ad hoc exchanges with other enterprises; secondly, by
taking every opportunity to build up stocks; thirdly, by paying over the odds;
fourthly, by using spare hard currency to import from the West; and lastly, by
producing the required inputs themselves (Laki, 1980b). The result is an unjusti-
fiably high degree of vertical integration, and the duplication of production on
a small scale of the shortage goods.

Smaller enterprises provide one obvious answer to this problem, but their
number has continued to decline since 1968. In the early reform years, agricultural cooperatives extended their activities into industrial production, often as

subcontractors to State enterprises, but these activities were met with restrictions by the authorities during the 're-centralizing' period of 1971–3. The rate of formation of new companies is negligible. The larger and more successful industrial cooperatives are more concerned with establishing relations with the centre similar to those enjoyed by State enterprises than with exploiting the profitable but fragmented markets in intermediate goods. Large State enterprises are often unwilling to subcontract to small enterprises or cooperatives, partly because they do not trust them to maintain continuity of production, and partly because they cannot exert leverage on them via the economic hierarchy in the way they can on other large State enterprises.

Cooperation on a large scale between large State enterprises often takes place within the context of permanent involvement by higher authorities. In some cases, this is present from the outset, as with the central development programme for buses, which brings together RÁBA (engines, rear axles), Csepel (chassis) and Ikarus (bodywork and final assembly). Conflicts among these enterprises can be resolved only by the supervising authorities, who as initiators (entrepreneurs?) have final responsibility. Relations of mutual dependence can of course be self-sustaining in an autonomous way, where central interests are not directly involved, and where both or all parties have a strong enough interest: but the desire to obtain financial support from the centre undermines the first condition, and product diversity (itself often the result of taking on new 'central' tasks) undermines the second.

Such problems are most acute when significant product or process innovation is involved (Abonyi, 1981, section II.3). While major investments in innovation may be initiated by the centre, or promoted by enterprises into centre objectives, it is quite another matter to ensure necessary parallel innovations and investments by supplier or customer enterprises. Although these can in principle be financed by National Bank credits on a commercial basis, the risk involved in such projects means that credit applications require a helping hand from superior authorities: hence, when the preferred solution of innovational self-sufficiency is impossible, a 'package' is put together by the visible hand of the relevant ministries.

Relations among large State enterprises are, then, part and parcel of the more basic problem of enterprise–centre relations. With regard to the role of smaller enterprises, it is now argued that legal and institutional changes which would promote their growth and formation rate would not only improve the supply situation, but would also help to bridge the divide between the socialist economy and the 'second' economy (Gábor, 1979). Those involved in the latter would be encouraged to move into more socially useful areas of production.

ENTERPRISES AND THE LABOUR MARKET

I do not intend here to discuss the methods of wage regulation under NEM (see, e.g., Marrese, 1981), but rather to look at the general features of the labour market and enterprise behaviour in it. The labour market in Hungary, as elsewhere in Comecon, is characterized by a general shortage of labour, coupled with evidence of low labour productivity ('unemployment within the factory'). The immediate cause of the shortage may be seen as due to the drying-up of the agricultural labour surplus. 'Extensive' industrialization was pre-dicated on a steady flow of labour from agriculture. This permitted a certain pattern of labour utilization in industry, in which the low cost of labour to the enterprise was complemented by the lack of industrial skills and experience of the new industrial workers. Both the technical and the social organization of labour was adapted to a low productivity and intensity of the mass of unskilled and semi-skilled workers, while experienced skilled workers enjoyed a very different social and economic position as shop-floor leaders and 'fixers'. The emergence of labour shortage has led the authorities to increase the effective cost of labour by taxes on wages (especially on wage increases) imposed on enterprises, and to increase their administrative interference in labour markets (e.g., in attempting to discourage high labour mobility). Inevitably, however, it must take considerable time for the labour shortage to have a real effect on the patterns of labour utilization *within the enterprise*. Thus low productivity may persist because of the resistance of both management and workers to changes in the social organization of industrial labour.

There are, however, other more permanent and 'system-specific' factors at work. First, there is the question of incentives and income differentiation. The conflict between effective incentives and the danger of excessive income differen-tiation has been met by on the one hand differentiating wage norms by sector and subsector, and on the other hand by guaranteeing wage increases regardless of enterprise performance. The former response serves, of course, to reinforce the vertical bargaining system described above.

Secondly, since from the standpoint of the worker as individual (i.e., abstract-ing from his or her views on income differentiation in general) incentives in State industry are too small, the 'second economy' provides a significant safety valve, but one that is not without contradictions (for a general review see Gábor, 1979). While this safety valve function must account in part for the rather permissive attitude of the authorities (who are also well aware that the second economy satisfies important consumer needs), if participation in the second economy extends too far it has adverse effects on productivity in the 'first' economy. This applies directly to the individual worker in terms of the number of hours spent in secondary activity. But it also applies socially, if the second economy becomes too extensive, and especially if its *reproduction* becomes detached from the first economy (e.g., if inputs can be sourced in their entirety from the second economy itself): for this means that, for significant sections of the workforce, their employment in the socialist economy may end up as the secondary employment, with seriously disruptive consequences for the organization of production in state enterprises.

Thirdly, levels of productivity below that which is technically and socially possible are reproduced because of the lack of effective discipline over workers, especially the 'external' discipline of the threat of unemployment. This may be seen as an unbreachable constraint, part of the Hungarian 'social contract' (cf. p. 134 above). Workers simply do not believe threats of closure or redundancy, and rightly so.

Fourthly, and related to this, it is in the interests of both management and workers to retain labour reserves, both in the form of an excessive labour force and of a 'low productivity cushion', *regardless* of the financial disincentives. If the director is to improve his long-term bargaining position with the centre, he should be in a position to respond to *short-term* demands from the centre, since these will often be the product of acute difficulties felt by the centre, and 'credit' can be built up by a director able to offer solutions. To do so involves costs of many kinds (and resources, regardless of costs), but in the circumstances described such costs can be shifted on to the centre. Thus, in so far as this is a general phenomenon, the financial disincentives against labour hoarding simply become part of the general structure of costs, and lose their effectiveness. If the centre responds by differentiating the disincentives, they become another element in the enterprise—centre bargain.

Lastly, in a more sociological vein, enterprise directors play the role of universal uncle/aunt within the enterprise. They occupy a vital position at the borderline between the enterprise as a social organization and the world outside. Their rights and responsibilities are ill-defined: they move in a world of bargains, contacts and favours — for the most part legal, legitimate, necessary, but emphatically *not* either market-place relations, or ones deriving from a Weberian bureaucrat's rule-book. While this is widely recognized with regard to enterprise relations with the outside world, it is also true *within* the enterprise. The director must protect and champion his/her workforce, both collectively and individually, in order to secure their cooperation (and to avoid their leaving for another enterprise). For similar reasons, the role of the Party secretary cannot simply be one of watchdog over the enterprise director and the workforce, as Andrle (1976) has noted.

ENTERPRISES AND THE WORLD MARKET(S)

Given the importance of foreign trade to the Hungarian economy, a complete picture of the State enterprise requires discussion of its relations with both Western and Comecon 'world markets'. From a policy standpoint, the over-riding problem is the recurrence of deficits, particularly in hard currency trade. This deficit, it has been suggested, is closely related to the investment cycle, in which imports are the 'safety valve' when the economy overheats during an investment boom (Bauer, 1978). From 1973, the dramatic deterioration in Hungary's terms of trade (amounting in its effects to the loss of 6 per cent of GNP by 1975) shifted the norm around which these fluctuations took place from one of slight deficit to one of severe deficit. The Hungarian strategy had to be one of adapting the structure of foreign trade to world market price relativities, and this now implied a shift towards exports which were less raw-material intensive and reflected the country's comparative advantages. It was no longer sufficient to aim simply at increasing the proportion of more advanced industrial products in exports to the West.

The 'guided market' approach has emphasized the need to link domestic prices directly with world prices, to follow an active exchange-rate policy, and to eliminate the insulation of enterprises from world market pressures by sub-sidies, quotas and other direct controls. Although these principles were set aside in the post-1973 period, they are now firmly reinstated in the January 1980 measures: import subsidies are to be phased out, and forint convertibility of a sort is again an objective.

Considerable debate has taken place on the effectiveness of different policy measures in maintaining foreign trade balance and in stimulating exports, for example, the relative efficacy of average and marginal exchange rates (Kozma, 1981). The proliferation of subsidies clearly makes enterprises more interested in increasing revenues by bargaining over subsidies than by improving produc-tivity, quality or product range. It is also agreed that the removal of subsidies to imports and exports must be complemented by a refusal to bail out enter-prises through *other* forms of support if their foreign transactions are unprofit-able.

The institutional structure of foreign trade, and the methods of control, are certainly more flexible and variegated in Hungary than in other Comecon countries. Many large enterprises have foreign trade rights, and others are in-creasingly free to devise appropriate forms of association or contract with foreign trade enterprises, or among themselves. Import licences are increasingly general rather than product-specific, and hard currency earnings may de facto rest with the enterprise to finance needed imports. Formal cooperation agree-ments with Western firms have flourished chiefly among smaller enterprises, but some large enterprises too have engaged in relations of real cooperation (such as long-term contract supply) in an imaginative way. Joint ventures in production in Hungary have, however, hardly developed at all (Radice, 1981). Since 1975, an increasing share of National Bank credits has been confined to export-promotion projects offering rapid increases in export earnings: this allows the effective linking of hard-currency and domestic credits in a single package. There is, however, evidence that these credits tend to go predominantly to large enterprises.

Much of the difficulty experienced in creating an environment which will compel enterprises to compete effectively on Western markets clearly arises from the general circumstances of enterprise—centre relations discussed above. There are, however, a number of features specific to the foreign trade of enter-prises. In particular, the economic environment presented by Western markets is very different from the familiar domestic and Comecon one. This is partly just a question of the greater risk-propensity, flexibility and marketing skills required. In principle, the cost of developing these attributes can be offset by the centre, whether through generally lower (but *not* enterprise-specific) effec-tive exchange rates, or through larger personal incentives. But it also has much deeper roots which are less amenable to such policy measures. Production and management systems are often geared to 'markets' where purchases are fixed in volume and product specification for many years: this focuses managerial attention on static scale economies and on learning curves, and militates against continuous innovation and the differentiation of products to meet changing customer needs. The result is that exporting to the West requires not merely the shouldering of extra costs, but the thorough restructuring of enterprise attitudes and practices, in production as well as marketing. Not surprisingly, it is often said that enterprises can be divided into those which export mainly to Comecon markets, and those which export mainly to the West: only the more dynamic and enterprising are able to develop both at once. The stimulus to export to the West is often not the attractiveness of Western markets, but either inability to break into Comecon markets (i.e., exclusion from the bilateral State trading agreements), or the desire to earn hard currency to finance imports of equipment or technology.

The Hungarian enterprise also feels the effects of the Comecon trade system as a customer, in a way comparable to the problem of domestic supply discussed above. The difficulties of maintaining any effective and regular contact as an end-user with Comecon suppliers are very well known (see e.g., Schweitzer, 1977). The result is to reinforce the tendency to look to the West, especially for machi-nery: in any case this may be unavoidable if the imports needed have not been allowed for in the foreign trade plans.

For some time after the 1973 price rises there were calls in Hungary for a return to closer ties with Comecon: energy supplies had to be secured, and dependence on Western markets was too threatening to domestic economic and political stability. But closer integration with their Comecon partners was bound to conflict seriously with the general aims of the reforms, in the absence of significant changes in Comecon practices of the sort which Hungary had openly advocated up to about 1972. If Comecon cannot meet Hungary's import requirements, hard currency must be earned, and Comecon practices cannot be allowed to reinforce the reluctance of enterprises to export to the West. The great dilemma is how to overcome this reluctance without resorting to direct central intervention.

ON SOCIALIST ENTREPRENEURSHIP

The need for socialist entrepreneurship is a persistent theme in pronouncements at the highest political level in Hungary, as well as in discussions of enterprise behaviour among economists. What meaning can we attach to the phrase, and what are the real chances of realizing it, if we are convinced that it is necessary?

One initial implication of the use of the phrase concerns the conception of 'market economy' in the reform debate. This is *not* the market economy of Walrasian (or Lange–Taylorian) general equilibrium theory: it is much more the 'market as process' of Schumpeter, or even perhaps of Mises or Hayek. It concerns grasping opportunities in the face of ignorance and uncertainty, creating as well as responding to (Mises would say 'discovering') the possibility of economic gain. As a consequence, debates about monopoly in the classic liberal tradition (the structure–conduct–performance paradigm) are as much off the mark in Hungary as they are in the West: atomistic competition is a meaningless comparator if static equilibrium is not the goal, and the world is inherently uncertain.

In view of the emphasis in Hungarian debates on structural change and innovation, and inevitably also on political and ideological grounds, Schumpeter is a more apt starting point in our quest than Mises. The question may be put: is it possible for the Schumpeterian economic dynamic to be divorced from private ownership of production? As far as I am aware, only Brus (1975) has examined this with specific reference to Schumpeter. As he points out, Schumpeter's model of the socialist economy is so constructed as to preclude an answer, since for Schumpeter the functioning of the socialist economy reduces at every turn to an *administrative* problem, because socialism is equated with public ownership (Brus, 1975, chapter 1). But how can the apostle of 'creative destruction' limit his considerations to the benign 'administration of things'? The answer lies not in his failure to understand Marx's method, but in the fact that despite appearances his model of socialism in *Capitalism, Socialism and Democracy* is not an abstract model, but one set in a very specific historical context. For Schumpeter, capitalism was giving way inevitably to socialism precisely because creative destruction was no longer required as the source of material progress: innovation had become a matter of routine. While he derided the Keynesian proposition of the vanishing of investment opportunity, he replaced the 'euthanasia of the rentier' with the euthanasia of the *entrepreneur*. Naturally, since capitalism had dispensed with the entrepreneur, the superior socialist system would hardly need or want to resuscitate him. History has been as unkind to Schumpeter as it has been to the stagnationists — indeed, more so in view of the renewed stagnation in the West since 1975.

Brus refers also to Hayek's views on the dilemmas of the socialist manager, which seem much more pertinent to our inquiry (Hayek, 1949). Dickinson (1939) had argued that unless the manager 'bears responsibility for losses as well as for profits he will be tempted to embark upon all sorts of risky experiments on the bare chance that one of them will turn out successful'. Arguing that 'either beforehand, or more likely retrospectively, all his calculations will have to be examined and approved by the [planning] authority', Hayek writes:

> . . . is not the real problem the opposite one — that managers will be afraid of taking risks if, when the venture does not come off, it will be somebody else who will afterward decide whether they have been justified in embarking on it? As Dickinson himself points out, the principle would be that 'although the making of profits is not necessarily a sign of success, the making of losses is a sign of failure' [Dickinson, 1939a]. Need one say more about the effects of such a system on all activities involving risk? It is difficult to conceive how under these circumstances any of the necessary speculative activities involving risk-bearing could be left to managerial initiative. But the alternative is to fall back for them on that system of strict central planning to avoid which the whole system [of Dickinson and Lange-Taylor] has been evolved. [Hayek, 1949]

Ironically, Dobb had made almost exactly the same point 15 years earlier in a work that seems to have escaped the attention of Hayek and later contributors:

> How far . . . either a collectivist or a communist society would be likely to be creative is still more difficult to decide. Both would certainly lack much of the easy fluidity of individualism. The administrators would run the bureaucratic danger of becoming hidebound and unimaginative. They might be shy of facing uncertainties through timidity of opposition to the results of change and of the contumely which they risked should the dice fall for them on the wrong side. Democratic requirements might fetter them to the 'average daring of the community', instead of permitting those above this average to experiment on their own. Whether in conquest of these difficulties a communist society might give birth to a creative will and a spirit of progress to match the adventures of the undertaker's [entrepreneur's] proudest hour is a secret as locked and barred against us as were the possibilities of capitalist enterprise to the mediaeval schoolmen. [Dobb, 1925a]

In the light of Hungarian experience thus far, the secret is still locked and barred. Entrepreneurship in this sense must be ruled out by the hierarchical decision structure which still dominates the world of the large State enterprises. It finds expression in the activities of smaller, less-favoured State enterprises and industrial cooperatives, and of course in the second economy. The measures in the Hungarian economic reforms, 1968 or 1980 version, attempt to tackle the problem through incentives and disincentives, but in their application these stimuli seem always to involve the hierarchical control and manipulation of the entrepreneurs-to-be, which contain an unresolvable contradiction. Mere profit-seeking (or loss-avoiding) is not the same as entrepreneurship, if profit can be increased or loss avoided by vertical bargaining. Perhaps that in itself should be treated as a form of entrepreneurship: it certainly characterizes aptly the more buccaneering Hungarian enterprise directors. But it implies that private interest *supplants* social interest rather than that the two are harmonized.

Brus' analysis would suggest that the nature and possibilities of entrepreneurship must depend on the prevailing relations of production in society — with which Dobb, but surely not Hayek, would concur. The obvious historical alternative in Eastern Europe is Yugoslav-style self-management, but this is rejected by Brus, and by Hungarian reformers, again because it promotes particularistic interests excessively, and generates unemployment and inflation to an unacceptable degree. For Brus, the only answer can lie with the attainment of a real socialization of production, and this requires political democracy: it may be noted that the latter requirement, together with 'no class divisions and little inequality of reward', forms the basis of Dobb's definition of communism in the work cited above (Dobb, 1925b). If this is the case, then the very same self-limitations which allowed the Hungarians to carry through their economic reforms — namely, the exclusion from discussion of their political implications — must now be seen as preventing the resolution of the fundamental problems of the State enterprise in the reformed system.

ACKNOWLEDGEMENT

I am grateful to participants in the Gregynog seminar, and to Dr Paul Hare (University of Stirling), for their comments on an earlier draft.

REFERENCES

Abonyi, A. (1981) Imported technology, Hungarian industrial development and factors impeding the emergence of innovative capacity. In Hare. Radice & Swain (see below).
Andrle, V. (1976) *Managerial Power in the Soviet Union*. Farnborough: Saxon House.
Balassa, A. (1977) Achievements of and lessons from the medium-term planning in the Hungarian enterprises. *Acta Oeconomica*, 18/1, p. 57.
Bauer, T. (1976) The contradictory position of the enterprise under the new Hungarian economic mechanism. *Eastern European Economics*, XV/I.
Bauer, T. (1978) Investment cycles in planned economies. *Acta Oeconomica*, 21/3.
Berend, I. (1975) The investment system (problems of planning and control). *Eastern European Economics*, XIV/2.
Brus, W. (1975) *Socialist Ownership and Political Systems*. London: Routledge & Kegan Paul.
Csapó, L. (1966) Central planning in guided market model. *Acta Oeconomica,* 1/3–4.
Deák, A. (1975) On the possibility of enterprise decisions on investment. In *Eastern European Economics*, XIV/2.
Dickinson, H.D. (1939) *The Economics of Socialism*. Oxford: Oxford University Press. (a) p. 219.
Dobb, M.H. (1925) *Capitalist Enterprise and Social Progress*. London: Routledge (a) pp. 376–377; (b) pp. 45–47.
Economic Research Institute (1974) On industrial big enterprises. *Acta Oeconomica*, 12/1.

Friss, I. (Ed.) (1971), *Reform of the Economic Mechanism in Hungary*. Budapest: Akadémiai Kiadó.

Gábor, I.R. (1979) The second (secondary) economy. *Acta Oeconomica*, 22/3–4.

Granick, D. (1975) *Enterprise Guidance in Eastern Europe*. Princeton: Princeton University Press.

Hare, P.G. (1981) The investment system in Hungary. In Hare, Radice & Swain (see below).

Hare, P.G., Radice, H.K. & Swain, N. (Ed.) (1981) *Hungary: a Decade of Economic Reform*. London: Allen & Unwin.

Hayek, F.A. (1949) 'Socialist Calculation III: the competitive solution', title of reprint as ch. 9 of *Individualism and Economic Order*. London: Routledge, p. 199; originally in *Economica* VII/26 (NS), May 1940.

Horváth, L. (Ed.) (1980) *Gazdasági Szabályozók (Economic Regulators)*. Budapest: Közgazdasági és Jogi Könyvkiadó.

Kozma, G. (1981) The role of the exchange rate in Hungary's adjustment to external economic disturbances. In Hare, Radice & Swain (see above)

Laki, M. (1980a) *Év Végi Hajrá az Iparban és a Külkereskedelem (Year-end Rush-work in Industry and Foreign Trade)*. Budapest: Magvető Kiadó (English shortened version forthcoming in *Acta Oeconomica*).

Laki, M. (1980b). The need for new activities and the possibilities of enterprise (Mimeo). Budapest: Institute for Market and Economic Research. p. 4.

Marer, P. (1981) The mechanism and performance of Hungary's foreign trade. In Hare, Radice & Swain (see above).

Marrese, M. (1978) Cyclical centralism: Hungary's gift to the understanding of bureaucracies. Discussion Paper No. 78–51, Dept of Economics, University of British Columbia.

Marrese, M. (1981) The evolution of wage regulation in Hungary. In Hare, Radice & Swain (see above).

Nyers, R. & Tardos, M. (1978) Enterprises in Hungary before and after the economic reform. *Acta Oeconomica*, 20/1–2. (a) p. 37; (b) p. 41.

Portes, R. (1977) Hungary: economic performance, policy and prospects. In *East European Economies Post-Helsinki*. Washington: Joint Economic Committee of the US Congress. (a) p. 780.

Radice, H.K. (1981) Industrial cooperation between Hungary and the West. In Hare, Radice & Swain (see above).

Schumpeter, J.A. (1943) *Capitalism, Socialism and Democracy*. London: Allen & Unwin

Schweitzer, I. (1977) Some peculiarities of Hungarian machine imports from the Soviet Union. *Acta Oeconomica*, 18/3–4.

Sóos, K.A. (1976) Causes of investment fluctuations in the Hungarian economy. *Eastern European Economics*, XIV/2.

Tardos, M. (1975) Impacts of world economic changes on the Hungarian economy. *Acta Oeconomica*, 15/3–4.

Tardos, M. (1976) Enterprise independence and central control. *Eastern European Economics*, XV/1.

Tardos, M. (1978) Adaptation to the changes on the world market in Hungary (Mimeo). Colloque Franco-Hongrois, Université de Paris X-Nanterre.

Varga, Gy. (1980) *Price System and Price Mechanism – 1980*. Budapest: Institute for Economic and Market Research (Mimeo).

9
The Industrial Enterprise in Yugoslavia

Ljubo Sirc

THE ECONOMIC – LEGAL INDIVIDUALITY OF ENTERPRISES IN THE LAUNCHING PERIOD

The original criticism of Tito by Stalin was political and may have been largely due to a clash of personalities. None the less, it gave the Yugoslav leaders an opportunity to revise their economic views. In his speech of 26 June 1950, introducing workers' councils, Tito explained that until the Resolution of Cominform in 1948, which attacked the Yugoslav leadership, the Yugoslav Party had excessive illusions about the Soviet Union so that the Party uncritically transplanted everthing that was being done there, including things out of line with the particular Yugoslav conditions and even things which were not in the spirit of the science of Marxism–Leninism. The Soviet-trained head of Yugoslav planning, Boris Kidric, added that the Yugoslav leadership started with its own application of Marxism–Leninism under the Yugoslav conditions some time ago and had been gradually reducing the acceptance of sometimes entirely wrong, obsolete and essentially reactionary Soviet prescriptions. According to Kidric, an important move was to restore the economic–legal individuality of enterprises in order to rid the economy of the all-powerful parasitical bureaucracy of a capitalist character. This was not a step backward, but the liquidation of elements of capitalist 'monopolism' hidden in the system of bureacratic socialism (Kidric, 1950a).

Kidric was worried that his reforms could be considered reactionary, since in his own view commodity production and commodity exchange were remnants of capitalism; however, he said that, on the one hand, enterprises would not be run by workers as owners but by workers as administrators, and, on the other, that there would be planning of basic proportions. Under these conditions 'socialist commodity exchange' would give birth to opposed interests, but not to class antagonism. Neither had the reforms anything in common with the NEP (New Economic Policy). In fact, planning-operative guidance would not be liquidated, while the planning of basic proportions would make the anarchy inherited from capitalism impossible, and would eliminate capitalist disproportions.

Kidric spoke about higher associations of producers and of general directorates as supervisory-planning bodies, but these were soon scrapped. The plans themselves should from then on harmonize with objective economic laws which had been throttled under the old system. The plan had prescribed the production of one kind of goods while the market demanded another. Further, Kidric thought that planning on the basis of socialist ownership would in principle liquidate the contradictions between use value and exchange value. This would be achieved by a planned determination of basic wages to which a rate of accumulation would be added, a proportion analogous to the rate of surplus labour. If the enterprise succeeded in producing more than that prescribed by the plan of minimum utilization of capacities, it would earn a variable part of the wages fund, on which the same rates of accumulation would be calculated, while the rest could be paid to the workers. Thus, Kidric thought, the spontaneity of the capitalist law of the average profit rate would be abolished. In fact, the rates of accumulation were to provide funds for investment and public expenditure. The enterprises would be in charge of expanded reproduction only to a *minimum* extent; the bulk would be determined by a plan of major investment projects.

The current decisions − direct operational decisions − were to be left to the workers' councils in enterprises. They were to include the control of the enterprise labour force in order to correct the previous unreasonable extensive rise in employment which had led to 'a problem of labour force' (Kidric, 1950b). As Kidric pointed out, until 1950 people were being hired (sometimes pressed into factories by force) without an analysis having been made of the economic and political consequences of such actions. This admission shed a strange light on Tito's accusation that, in the Soviet Union, the role of the workers was not much different from what it was under capitalism, except that there was no unemployment.

From then on, neither the Yugoslav government nor the population looked back. The general feeling is that central planning worked so badly that the decentralized decision-making is much superior, despite the many shortcomings of market self-management. It is also thought that life in Yugoslavia is much better than life in the other East-European countries. Of course, one has to compare equal with equal − before the War only the northern regions could even approximately be compared with Hungary or Czechoslovakia. It must not be forgotten either that, during the centralized planning, personal consumption per head fell by almost one-third compared with 1939, although not exclusively because of the irrationalities of the system: manual workers were to some extent protected, but the rest of the population suffered badly.

THE PLANNING OF PROPORTIONS AND INVESTMENT

In 1952, the Yugoslav enterprises could operate according to their own lights except that the planning authorities at different levels, primarily federal and republican, ordered: the minimum utilization of capacities; and the basic wages fund and the rates of accumulation. In addition, all important investment projects were determined by central and other authorities and financed out of investment funds at different levels, but the execution of projects was normally left to the lowest level. Another feature was that the director of an enterprise was appointed by the people's committee of the commune, was ex officio a member of the workers' council and was responsible for the carrying out of planning and legal provisions.

In spite of these limitations, there was an overnight improvement in the economic climate. Goods which had been difficult to come by appeared again in the shops, albeit at a high price. The elimination of the restriction caused by detailed planning and interference by authoriies in the day-to-day business of enterprises was a great success, whether it shows in statistical figures or not. It also helped to relax the political pressure on the population.

It was soon apparent, none the less, that the arrangements did not make any sense. The enterprises were keen to produce as much as they could sell, and more (unsaleable stocks continued to accumulate), so that there was no need to provide for a minimum utilization of capacities. It occurred to nobody that the workers would try to maximize variable wages per worker instead of per enterprise (as some Western theoreticians postulated), and, if they did, it would soon be realized that they had no idea about how to dose the output with such precision. Furthermore, nobody, including Kidric, knew how to calculate the rates of accumulation for goods or group of goods. since nobody knew how to calculate surplus labour. All that could be done was to 'photograph' relationships as they were and elevate them into 'planned proportions'. The results were distressing.

The original Act on planning was abandoned, although it remained legally valid until the late 1960s; the minimum utilization of capacities was dropped; the prescribed wages were chopped and changed; and the rate of accumulation was replaced by an interest rate. The attempt at introducing more or less uniform interest rates soon proved that, far from abolishing capitalist anarchy, the central planning of investment, under both the old and the new system, had produced complete chaos. Some capacities were under-utilized by more than

50 per cent whatever the enterprises tried to do; the rises of stock reached 13 per cent of the GNP per year, at least nominally. The leaders themselves concluded that there was an investment mania, and that investment was 'political' rather than economic. The professional economists added that this was hardly surprising, since there was no known investment criterion applied in Yugoslavia. But what was to be done? Nobody knew how to redirect investment and any slow-down in investment would lead to even more unemployment and to even more under-utilized capacities, which could create social tensions. A solution was to hand over investment (expanded reproduction) to the 'associated producers' themselves.

DISTRIBUTION BY 'ASSOCIATED PRODUCERS'

After an attempt by a head of the Planning Institute to use the 1961—5 plan to turn the wheel back towards more centralized decision-making, this plan was abandoned and all short- and long-term competences were transferred to the workers' organs. Even the appointment of a director was now within the jurisdiction of the workers' council, although they had to select him from a list prepared by a commission, half of whose members were nominated by political authorities, Later, the yearly plans were replaced by policy resolutions, so that nobody is certain what role is played by plans in the Yugoslav economy.

Reform, again directed by a Slovene, Boris Kraigher, was made in two parts: the first, in 1961, almost immediately required an antidote: the second, in 1965, went through, but not without causing untold complications. The problem is that workers and their bodies see only one purpose in their jurisdiction over enterprises, and that purpose is to distribute as much money amongst themselves as is available — and more. From 1961, the nominal increase in workers' wages, or personal incomes as they are officially called, rose to 20 per cent per year, although the annual growth of industrial labour productivity was just 5.5 per cent in the 1960s and fell to 3.5 per cent in the period 1971—5. It should be stressed that these figures refer to gross or total labour productivity (i.e., leaving out the other factors of production, especially capital). In real terms the average annual increase in wages was 6.8 per cent in the 1960s, but collapsed to 1.6 per cent in the period 1971—5. These rises were brought about after real wages had stagnated in the 1950s at the 1939 level. This happened at the expense of the rest of the population, particularly the peasants. The fall in average real consumption per capita from the 1939 level, caused by central planning and the Stalinist blockade, reached about one-third in 1952 and recovered to the pre-war level only in 1960.

The rate of growth of real wages below that of industrial productivity in the 1970s occurred because the rest of the active population caught up; because almost 10 per cent of consumption came to be paid out of moneys transferred to their families by guest-workers in the West; and because the high social wages, particularly pensions, accounted for at least 20 per cent of consumption. Another consequence of the high social wages and social services available is that some part of enterprises' revenue has to be collected to pay for these items. In 1979 (*Ekonomska Politika*, 10 December 1979, p. 19), on average 7.3 per cent of gross enterprise revenue (value added) was taken away in taxes and contributions, 8.7 per cent went on interest payments and insurance premia, 8.4 per cent was paid in contributions to labour communities (solidarity funds, etc.), and 3.5 per cent was used for depreciation over the legal minimum and other unspecified items. This left 72.2 per cent of gross revenue as net revenue, of which 37.2 per cent was paid out as personal incomes, 6.8 per cent spent on collective consumption, 10.1 per cent allocated for expanded reproduction and 2.0 per cent added to reserves. The remaining 16.1 per cent represents the taxes and contributions collected out of personal incomes. Hence total taxes, both out of gross revenue and out of incomes, amount to 23.4 per cent of gross revenue, of which a considerable part has to be used for transfer payments. Enterprise savings of 10.1 per cent of gross revenue, however, are cancelled by the fact that they correspond almost exactly to insufficient depreciation and nominal rises in the value of inventories (Gligorov, 1980). Thus the upward pressure on wages by self-managing 'associated producers' is so strong that the internal accumulation by enterprises has by now fallen to zero, which means that on average the enterprises are left with just enough (and often not even that) to pay for the replacement of the wear and tear of capital. Any new investment is by now mostly paid out of bank credits fed out of monetary issue, private savings of the population and, of late, also out of foreign loans.

In spite of this situation, the 'investment mania' begun in the initial planning era continues so that, in the late 1970s, the share of fixed investment in the GDP reached 35 per cent, and in the GSP even 40 per cent. Whilst the 'associated producers' are so keen on higher wages that the managers, now called either 'individual management organs' or, if there is more than one at the top, 'collective management organs', have to comply with them lest workers strike or become otherwise uncooperative, they do not show much interest in investment decisions. They leave these to the managers; they know that they have neither the knowledge nor the information required to take them, nor the time to acquire the knowledge or information since they have another job to do.

Therefore, investment is in the hands of managers and banks, but everybody admits that there is still no clear-cut investment criterion, that there is no capital market and that there is not even much investment project assessment. On the other hand, the workers do not object to more and more investment if it is financed out of external resources because there is always hope that it would raise their productivity and thus enable them to press for higher wages. Their willingness to countenance investment has the consequence, bad from a general point of view, that investment goes to existing enterprises and complements the already-employed workers, as opposed to going where capital productivity is highest or where it may even create new employment. Local authorities are, of course, also interested in investment in their own area, regardless of what the result of investment elsewhere could be, and push enterprises in that direction. In view of all this, it is still said that investment in Yugoslavia is 'political' (*Ekonomska Politika*, 30 June 1980, p. 5). One of the difficulties is, of course, that any economic calculation is difficult because workers' wages are supposed to be a residual so that there is no labour market and no price for labour, while payments for capital are unrealistic, as we shall see.

The consequence is that investment in Yugoslavia is rather inefficient, compared with that in similar 'capitalist' countries. The gross incremental capital—output ratio in Yugoslavia has by now climbed to over 5.5:1, while it is approximately 3.5:1 for Greece and Spain (same or higher growth with investment of just over 20 per cent of the GDP instead of over 30 per cent). The net incremental capital—output ratio even seems to be over 3.5:1 in Yugoslavia, compared with about 2:1 for Greece and Spain and as low as just over 1:1 for Portugal (at least until 1975).

Interest rates in Yugoslavia are ridiculously low (6 per cent approximately), while the rate of inflation is over 20 per cent per year. None the less, they are becoming quite a burden for Yugoslav enterprises since the enterprises borrow so much. At present, they seem to pay as much in interest rates as they nominally accumulate. This state of affairs has triggered off a tremendous resentment of banks, as if the banks were in the first place responsible for the low accumulation in enterprises, combined with high investments and investment's low efficiency. Nationalizing banks a second time has been mentioned, although nobody knows what that should mean. It is a demagogical slogan which in fact means that enterprises should break out of economic reality and workers could consume more than the production of consumer goods. Some commentators believe that it should be possible to deal with the vagaries of distribution by raising the interest rates instead of abolishing them altogether as some politicans suggest. The latter course would lead to a chaos worse compounded, while the former would condemn some producer-good enterprises to close down and thereby raise unemployment. The reason is that the production structure is hopelessly distorted, geared to wasteful investment, and is becoming more so year after year.

ATTEMPTS AT COPING WITH THE FREE DISTRIBUTION OF ENTERPRISE INCOME

The Yugoslav leaders realized that full autonomy of enterprise was not feasible in the Yugoslav environment. They introduced wages and prices control, continuously protesting that this was only a temporary measure until the system is completed. Simultaneously an effort was made to work out a theoretical solution, primarily by the leading ideologist, Edvard Kardelj, who, however, unfortunately died in the spring of 1979. The original reformer Kraigher died in a car accident in 1967.

Self-management would have received a bitter blow had the autonomy of enterprises been curtailed by government decree. Therefore, the idea of self-management agreements and social contracts was given currency. By such agreements and contracts the 'associated producers' were to limit themselves, primarily their own wages. In the background was the threat that legal sanctions would be introduced if self-restraint failed. That was the beginning of a wide-spread activity in which everybody concludes agreements with everybody else on everything under the sun, spending much time on this purposeless occupation because, as a rule, the agreements and contracts are completed too late, when all the harm has been done. The provisions are usually vague, so that there is much opportunity for avoidance and, if the worst comes to the worst, for evasion. The most important example is wages. In this respect, provisions are often simply disregarded or, finally, waived. Not only do the workers have no intention of abiding by them; they could not even if they wanted to. The results of the enterprise become known only after the auditing of its accounts some time after the end of the year to which they apply, while the wages have to be paid on account from the beginning of the year. It is easy to be over-optimistic about the results, particularly as, due to inflation, neither the non-labour costs nor the prices are known in advance. Nor is it known to what extent the products can be sold and how much of them is simply to fill the stocks. The excess payments cannot be rescinded because this may lead to strikes or, at least, to so much dissatisfaction among the workers that they refuse to co-operate with management or even with workers' councils.

At the end of 1979, wages were frozen at the level of November 1979, with a further proviso that wages will not be allowed to rise at the same rate as prices in 1980. It was also decided that wages in the best-paying enterprises would be allowed to rise only at a pace lower than in the worst-paying, with the effect that the efforts of the staff in the best enterprises will slacken because they serve no useful purpose from the workers' point of view, while in the worst there will be no incentive to improve the performance since the relative pay is increasing anyway. All this is happening because two principles, payment according to the result of enterprise and equal pay for equal work, have become inextricably entangled. The reason is that the workers refuse to be made responsible for the working of enterprises, because they will not and cannot have anything to do with it, and the consequent demand for parity of wages or for agreed differentials. Of course a market self-management system cannot function under these conditions, because nobody is responsible for anything.

THE 'IMPROVED' SYSTEM OF SELF-MANAGEMENT

Although the dark picture outlined above was quite clearly discernible at the end
of the 1960s, Edvard Kardelj constructed an intricate structure on the basis of
elements which must themselves have contributed to the confusion. The results
of his endeavours were embodied in the constitution of 1974 and in the Act of
Associated Labour in 1976. Further, he produced two books on the subject,
one in 1972 and another in 1978. In his first book, *The Contradictions of Social
Property in the Contemporary Socialist Practice*, Kardelj described the difficulties as they appeared to him and tried to work out solutions compatible with
Marxism. Although his way of thinking is very involved, I shall try to reproduce
the main ideas because they have determined the present state of the game in
Yugoslavia (Kardelj, 1972a).

The original idea was to 'equalize' the incomes of enterprises so as to achieve
an acceptable system of distribution. In fact workers receive comparable wages,
but business conditions cannot be equalized, so that the development was
spontaneous, under the influence of subjective individual decisions, without any
responsibility. The workers behaved in a voluntaristic way; in other words, they
paid themselves excessive wages. Bad tendencies were spontaneously reproduced
in the attitudes of workers who were not interested in the administration of
capital under the system. Self-management does not automatically eliminate
bad phenomena and tendencies; in the end it is always people who prevail, not
the system. Contradictions, similar to capitalist contractions, appeared, but
without class character. There are elements of exploitation. In fact, market
distribution is not distribution according to work; it is influenced by various
factors. Thus, for instance, product per worker is normally higher in an enterprise with a higher composition of capital. In principle, personal incomes should
be proportional to work, but there are no objective measures by which to
distribute these according to work. The distribution according to work is only a
social convention. This sounds very imprecise, and Kardelj himself says that there
could not be any 'democratic decision-making' where there is no precise system
of economic rights and responsibilities of working people and organizations of
associated labour to each other. This need for precision obviously cannot be met
if, as Kardelj stresses, an enterprise's income is not the result only of its own
work, because surplus work flows from one organization to another; neither are
there any absolute rights of an individual to income on the basis of the measure
of his work. The income of any working organization belongs to all workers.
This is a marvellous sentiment, but makes life rather difficult for those who are
supposed to cope with distribution. But even the income of a workers' collective is not their group property, but social property — that is, common property
of all workers. Therefore, the worker is the freer in his administration of income,
the less he behaves in a group-owner or monopolistic way and the more he
takes equal rights of other workers into account.

How is this to be achieved? Kardelj first decried the possibility that one part of society manipulates the working class and said that excessive State intervention inevitably became voluntaristic, then regretted that the de-centralization carried through in Yugoslavia had caused hesitation with respect to the role of the State and planning. The three inseparable component parts of the Yugoslav system were the market, social planning and economic and social solidarity of workers, though they are in a contradictory relationship with each other. It is hoped that through scientific planning the market will become a simple 'technical device' and will even wither away. Society has not only the right but the duty of planned direction of the market. Kardelj's prescription was that workers could not be allowed 'to allocate as personal income more than belonged to them according to standards for the quantity and quality of work, which will be determined — sometimes among conflicts — by workers in associated labour, in the form of self-management agreements and social contracts, possibly with additional social regulative measures, however, on the basis of cbjective economic necessities and of solidarity amongst working people' (Kardelj, 1972b).

To summarize: Kardelj came to the conclusion that there was no way for the workers to pay each other according to work, which in fact should have made them self-manage the enterprises responsibly. Therefore, he fell back on the argument that all work and all income were social, to justify a new form of planning limiting the freedom of workers' self-management in individual enterprises. And he warned that, in practice, no system can prevent inequality and non-socialist relations. He has travelled a long way from the original belief that the abolition of private ownership of the means of production would also abolish all difficulties. Although his own arguments were under an indelible influence of Marxist doctrine only slightly tinged by practical consideration, he himself complained that the Yugoslav practice was excessively burdened by ideology.

INTERPENETRATION OF ENTERPRISES

Kardelj established that spontaneity and the market did not lead to distribution according to work (he implied that nothing could), and therefore suggested that planning in the form of self-management contracts should come to the rescue. There was much talk about how this had to conform with objective economic laws, but it was never made clear what these were or in what criteria they express themselves. Article 69 of the 1974 Constitution says that workers (of course on the basis of scientific perceptions and economic laws) 'independently adopt plans and programmes for the work and development of their organizations and communities, they align these plans and programmes with each other and with the social plans of the social-political communities and on this basis assure the alignment of relationships of the whole material and social reproduction in accordance with their common interests and aims, determined on a self-management basis.' The Act on Planning of 1976 did not clarify matters any better.

In reality, it seems that nobody quite knows what to do in spite of a tremendous planning activity. The mechanism of agreements and contracts suffers from slowness, imprecision, difficulty in application, etc. (*Ekonomska Politika*, 12 November 1979, p. 20). Furthermore, there is the basic criticism that deficiencies in the conception of the system itself make it without a logical and clear structure (*Ekonomska Politika*, 3 March 1980, p. 18). In his second book, *Free Associated Labour – Brioni Discussions*, Kardelj has not provided any solution in his discussion of self-management plans (Kardelj, 1978a). In *Ekonomska Politika* of 3 March 1980 (p. 5) there is the complaint that Yugoslavia has neither a market nor a plan. Agreements and contracts are also used to provide guidelines for prices and wages. As a result, it is said that the primary distribution has been left to numerous virtually uncoordinated agreements (*Ekonomska Politika*, 12 November 1979, p. 19). At any rate, many enterprises do not abide by proportions they themselves have accepted (*Ekonomska Politika*, 8 October 1979, p. 3).

Kardelj and legal provisions are being quoted at length; in fact, the whole argument is being developed to show that Yugoslav enterprises are *de iure* autonomous, but that they are autonomous in a vacuum. The market is eroded and distorted and it is thought that this is right and proper because in its purer form it does not lead to results wanted by ideologists. However, nothing has replaced it since in Yugoslavia central planning is still considered to have been a dismal failure, not only for practical but for theoretical reasons. The enterprises themselves certainly cannot produce coherent plans out of the blue.

According to Article 93 of the Constitution, with respect to enterprises, State organs have only those rights that the Constitution gives them and these are very limited, although they can step in as *ultima ratio*. But from where can State organs gather what is economically the best course to follow? Perhaps, by way of solution, Kardelj started claiming as early as in his 1972 book, that it was abstract-liberalist to expect that workers on their own could solve everything. He did not specify what this meant, but the Constitution stresses, in the introductory Article VIII, the role of the Yugoslav League of Communists in public life. In his speech at the 30th session of the Yugoslav Presidency of the Central Committee on 13 June 1977, Kardelj decided against spontaneous decisions by workers. They needed support of the organized forces of socialist conscience and action – in other words, of communists. This implies some kind of omniscience for Party members. How can they know what kind of investment is optimal if the market is suppressed and planning confused?

Another attempt at a solution is perhaps the insistence that labour and resources should be associated. In spite of Kardelj's, insistence that basic organizations of associated labour, any economically viable unit, should be the starting point of the organizational structure, it is claimed that the concentration of means of production and centralization of social capital are inevitable. Moreover, according to Kardelj, there is no way of telling how much concentration and integration is desirable (Kardelj, 1978b). The Act on Associated Labour provides for several basic organizations to be linked into a 'working organization' which can again participate in one or more 'combined organizations' and even other forms of organizations. Vertical, horizontal and conglomerate integration is allowed. The legal provisions are vague so that all depends on the appropriate agreements among the composing units.

From the very beginning — even before the adoption of the Act on Associated Labour — this vagueness opened the door for the establishment of mammoth enterprises, sometimes for no better reason, as Kardelj says (1972c), than that political authorities had put 'informal' pressure on enterprises because they were told by higher authorities that integration was a good thing. In this context, one should not forget that, in spite of all legal provisions and speeches, organizations of associated labour do depend on what is called 'social-political communities' (*Ekonomska Politika*, 21 July 1980, p. 5) and they tend to drive all units in their territory into large enterprises, sometimes one large enterprise.

The further, somewhat better, reason, is that neither the commodity market nor the capital market work. Because of the lack of the latter, the placement of capital, except ploughing back, is difficult so that, as Kardelj says (1978c), 'reproduction entities' became necessary within which capital could circulate on an administrative basis. The lack of a functioning commodity market also fosters the move away from purely commercial relations to relations based on 'common income', that is, a purely administrative relationship (*Ekonomska Politika*, 24 March 1980, p. 5). As a result, there is an endless redistribution of income within administrative units (*Ekonomska Politika*, 24 March 1980, p. 5; 24 December 1979, p. 18) as well, as Kardelj points out (1972d), as a flow of capital from unit to unit. Nobody is responsible for his decisions (*Ekonomska Politika*, 24 March 1980, p. 5).

Economic giants are the worst. The 200 largest business organizations possessed, in 1978, 58 per cent of all business resources and produced 49 per cent of the GSP (*Delo*, Ljubljana, 28 November 1979, p. 33). To put it in a different way: the 200 had 33 per cent more fixed and working capital per employee than the Yugoslav average, but produced only 12 per cent more per employee than the average. Almost all on the list of the biggest had losses. The mine and metallurgy combine of Zenica, for instance, had sales which were two billion dinars short of costs. The excessively large and insufficiently flexible factories were the main source of bad financial results. The losses of the giants and of others are covered out of bank loans and all sorts of solidarity funds. No wonder an economist said there was an excessive stress on 'solidarity' (*Ekonomska Politika*, 16 June 1980, p. 20).

RESULTS

Yugoslav enterprises are formally autonomous, but the frustration of the market, the lack of responsibility, and the tendency to integration deprive them of both motivation and criteria for economic rationality. In particular, investment decisions are arbitrary, which is fatal in view of the investment of more than one-third of the GSP at present. The present level of consumption is excessive because it is not supported either by the present level, or quality, or structure of production (*Ekonomska Politika*, 28 July 1980, p. 5), but it is pitifully low in comparison with the resources used, if compared with some other countries. Although such comparisons are difficult, it can be said that between 1960 and 1976 the economies of Greece and Spain grew faster than the Yugoslav economy and the economy of Portugal about as fast. To achieve that, Greece and Spain required just over half the Yugoslav net investment as a percentage of the GDP, and Portugal less than one-third. As a consequence, the Portuguese GDP per head is about the same as the Yugoslav (although in Yugoslavia internal differences are enormous), but the Portuguese private consumption is about 40 per cent higher than in Yugoslavia and its collective consumption about 13.8 per cent of GDP as opposed to the Yugoslav 17.9 per cent. Greece's and Spain's personal consumption is about 30 per cent higher than the Yugoslav per unit of output. The worst is that the Yugoslav component parts of the economy seem to move on divergent paths, which means that the situation is deteriorating, while economic forces push other countries to align the various sectors with each other.

AUTHOR'S NOTE

The chapter also contains some findings (regarding comparative growth rates) of a research paper by the author, which is to be published in *Revue d'Etudes Comparatives Est-Ouest*.

REFERENCES

Broz-Tito, J. (1950) In *Komunist*, 4–5. p. 1.
Gligorov, K. (1980) In *Ekonomska Politika*, 9.6. p. 18.
Kardelj, E. (1972) *Protislovja Druzbene Lastnine v Sodobni Socialistnicni Druzbi*. Ljubljana: Drzavna Zalozba Slovenije. (a) see pp. 5–87; (b) p. 77; (c) p. 99; (d) p. 86.
Kardelj, F. (1978) *Svobodno Zdruzeno Delo-Brionske Diskusije*: Ljubljana: Drzavna Zalozba Slovenije (a) pp. 122–124; (b) pp. 239–40; (c) p. 270.
Kidric, B. (1950a) In *Komunist*, 6. p. 6.
Kidric, B. (1950b) In *Komunist*, 1. p. 46.
Kraigher, B. (1967) *O Reformi*. Celje: CZP Komunist.

Postcript on Poland

Domenico Mario Nuti

During the five months that have passed since the Gregynog Conference Poland has undergone further significant economic and political changes. The analysis contained in the Polish section of this volume does not require changes but I am grateful to the publishers for the opportunity to provide supplementary data and comments on current trends and economic reforms.

THE ECONOMY

The Polish economic situation has deteriorated dramatically since the summer of 1980. In the second half of 1980 industrial output fell by over 10 per cent with respect to the first half, declining by about 3 per cent over the year; gross agricultural production fell by 17 per cent with respect to the (poor) 1979 level (*Życie Gospodarcze*, 11 January 1981). National income produced in 1980 can be estimated to have fallen by 4 to 5 per cent. Shortages of consumption goods (especially foodstuffs such as meat, sugar and fats) have become acute and endemic; rationing is unavoidable. Shortages of intermediate goods, especially imported or import intensive, have reduced the level of utilization of productive capacity. In November 1980 drastic cuts in investment were introduced, involving the suspension of work on over 200 unfinished projects; as a result the amount of unused new machinery — currently of the order of over $1.5 billion — is expected to rise by 40 per cent during 1981; in order to stop Ministries and enterprises from continuing work on the suspended projects the government at the end of January instructed the Central Bank to stop financing 49 investment projects accounting for 10 per cent of the total investment in progress (*Financial Times*, 7 and 27 January 1981). In the last quarter of 1980 the total wage bill rose at a rate of 18 per cent. In 1981 monetary incomes of the population are expected to rise by an unprecedented yearly rate of 17 per cent. In view of the

157

fall in consumption pro capite — inescapable given a 15 to 20 per cent fall in investment, productivity and utilization rates, fall in exports, and the burden of debt — it is impossible to achieve price stability and market equilibrium. Either inflation, running at about 15 per cent at the end of the year, will continue and accelerate further in 1981, or shortages will become even more acute. Gross external debt totalled $21 billion at the end of 1979 and rose to around $24.5 billion in 1980 (see R. Portes, *The Polish Crisis: Western Economic Policy Options*, RIIA, London, February 1981). Given the weight of short-term debt, interest and current repayments exceed the value of exports, and fresh finance of the order of $4 billion a year is needed for the next five years if further drastic cuts in capacity utilization are to be avoided; a concerted effort on the part of Polish and Soviet authorities and Western government and bankers is required to avoid default and economic disaster (see Portes, op. cit., pp. 40–45).

A fundamental ingredient of any plan for economic recovery is a Social Pact between the Polish government and the new trade union Solidarność, now fully recognized and allegedly comprising over ten million members (i.e., 70 per cent of the workforce), including 60 per cent of the total Party membership. The new union, however, appears totally reluctant to enter such a pact and pursues some of the militant economic demands which had been accepted in the Gdańsk agreement between strikers and government on 31 August 1980. (The agreement included a five-day 40-hour working week, retirement at 50 for women and 55 for men, three years' maternity leave, full pay to strikers, and substantial improvements in public services and housing). The new union's advisers take the view — illogical but politically expedient and effective — that if the union put forward proposals for policy remedies it would implicitly accept responsibility for the economic problems of the country. In these circumstances, the net result of economic arithmetic and the balance of political forces is a possible Soviet intervention and an even more likely internal militarization of the whole economy and society (which might be widely accepted as the lesser evil), although the new Premier General Jaruzelski's appeal for '90 days of calm' still has a slender chance of success.

REFORM PROPOSALS

Against this background, the shape that the reform of the planning system, and in particular the industrial enterprise, might take is the object of wide debate. Last November the Polish Economics Association (PTE) published a set of comprehensive and far-reaching reform proposals, aimed at strengthening central planning of investment, growth and economic equilibrium, at the same time promoting 'a fundamental increase of independence and responsibility of enterprises and voivodships' and 'of real and not purely formal workers' and territorial self-management and other forms of social participation and activization' (*PTE o reformie, propozycje zasadniczych rozwiązcń reformy gospodarczej w Polsce*, November 1980, section II). A particularly important role is given, in this proposal, to international prices and the rate of exchange; in particular, it is suggested that both internal prices and prices for trade within Comecon should be linked, eventually, to international prices in trade with the West, through a 'commercial' rate of exchange, implying at least partial convertibility and trade liberalization, but retaining trade controls in the short run. Similar proposals have been put forward by academic economists at a regional level (see, for instance, the Wrocław Economic Academy's reform proposals in *Życie Gospodarcze*, no. 2, 11 January 1981). The most authoritative set of proposals to date is that of the Party–Government Commission for Economic Reform (Komisja do spraw Reformy Gospodarczej, *Podstawowe założenia reformy gospodarczej (projekt)*, Warsaw, January 1981).

This proposal, which still has the status of a pure project for further discussion and possible subsequent implementation, is the product of four months' work on the part of the Commission and a 500-strong body of experts and political representatives. The difficult economic situation is fully acknowledged, and is attributed to 'the increasing deformation in the functioning of the socio-political system and the economy'. For the first time in Polish official documents, it is acknowledged that the restoration of equilibrium is an essential precondition of any attempt at decentralization (section II, on 'Economic conditioning of reform'). Some actual measures are suggested, such as the sale of government debt and the pre-payment for durable goods. Trade liberalization is endorsed, but tight controls are envisaged on investment planning, with credit discipline even for centrally decided investments, in order to avoid 'the negative experience of the 'seventies, when an inflation of projects exceeding several times over the investing capacity of the national economy led to the excessive broadening of the investment front and the sharp worsening of effectiveness of development programmes' (p. 8). The most interesting organizational aspects of the reform proposals are: (1) the right of enterprises to form voluntary associations (i.e., mergers); (2) the stipulation, for the first time in East European reform proposals outside Yugoslavia, that 'The enterprise should have the right to diversification of its activity, by either deciding a new production profile or establishing links with enterprises in other branches' (§ 67); (3) the strong emphasis on parametric planning (i.e., prices, taxes and subsidies), leaving open the question of whether enterprise funds (including the wage fund) should be linked to value added or profit (§ 82). Reform implementation is envisaged in three stages: a price reform and minor organizational improvements by mid 1981; new enterprise legislation and a shift to a 'parametric' system by the end of 1981; full implementation in 1982.

REFORM IMPLEMENTATION

Actual changes in the organizational regime of industrial enterprises to date have been scant and contradictory. A new decree of 17 November 1980 (*Uchwała nr 118/80 Rady Ministrów w sprawie zmian w systemie kierowania przedsiębiorstwami państwowymi w 1981 r.*) envisages only two yearly directives for enterprises — (1) the value of export deliveries to the two main currency areas and (2) real investment, leaving everything else to contracts between enterprises — only to undermine these provisions immediately by adding compulsory physical targets for the deliveries of goods and services to armaments and security, the production and distribution of 46 production goods (e.g., energy, metals, plastics, cement, paper, wool, motor cars, computers), according to a priority system, and the supply of 52 consumption goods, namely 19 foodstuffs (meat, fish, dairy products, rice, sugar, fats, tea, coffee and lemons) and 33 manufacturing products (from shoes to cars, from soap to shirts). The enterprise wage fund is linked to 'the value of net output' (not clearly defined in the decree) through a very low elasticity coefficient of 0.3, indicating an attempt to contain the total wage bill of enterprises but implying, if literally implemented, drastic redundancies in view of the higher pay rates. A recent decree of the Ministry of Finance (10 January 1981) establishes bank control over the formation of the enterprise wage fund and wage payments, with unspecified sanctions for excess wage payments, suggesting that wage pressure is still mounting. In these circumstances it is unlikely and undesirable that the pace of economic reform should be as rapid as envisaged in the project formulated by the Party—Government Commission for Economic Reform.

13 February 1981   Domenico Mario Nuti

Index

Page numbers in *italics* refer to Tables and Figures.